The CHEW

WHAT'S FOR DINNER?

100 EASY RECIPES for EVERY NIGHT of the Week

The
CHEW
WHAT'S FOR DINNER?

Edited by PETER KAMINSKY and ASHLEY ARCHER

KINGSWELL

LOS ANGELES • NEW YORK

Content coordinator: Kerry McConnell

Food
Photographer: Andrew Scrivani
Food stylists: Martha Tinkler, Jackie Rothong, Ian McNulty, Lauren Palmeri
Prop stylist: Francine Matalon-Degni
Crafter: Tom Tamborello

Crafts
Photographer: James Ogle
Crafters: Tracy Kleeman, Adrienne Henry, Michael Buckholtz, Jamie Smith
Hand Model: Ai Takami

The Chew: What's for Dinner? — Photographer Credits:
Donna Svennevik/ABC: 15, 50, 69, 108, 111, 127, 129, 151, 189, 205, 206, 208, 209; Fred Lee/ABC: 97, 139; Heidi
Gutman/ABC: 117, 123; Ida Mae Astute/ABC: 107, 135; James Ogle/The Chew: 1, 9, 25, 30, 38, 39, 43, 77, 79, 93,
95, 163, 177, 215, crafts on 130, 131, 146, 147, 148, 149, 226, 227; Lorenzo Bevilaqua/ABC: 84, 99; Lou Rocco/ABC:
vii, 10, 19, 27, 29, 33, 41, 53, 63, 71, 115, 121, 133, 143, 173, 221, 223, 233

Cover photographer: Bob D'Amico © American Broadcasting Companies, Inc.

All photography unless otherwise noted © American Broadcasting Companies, Inc.

For information address Kingswell, 1101 Flower Street, Glendale, California 91201.

The Chew: What's for Dinner?
Book design by Vertigo Design NYC
Library of Congress Cataloging-in-Publication Data
The Chew, what's for dinner?: food, life, fun / edited by Peter Kaminsky and Ashley Archer. — First edition.
pages cm
Includes bibliographical references and index.
ISBN 978-1-4013-1281-7
1. Cooking, American. 2. Dinners and dining — United States. 3. Chew (Television Program)
I. Kaminsky, Peter. II. Archer, Ashley. III. Chew (Television Program). IV. Title: Chew.
TX715.C529 2013
641.5973—dc23
2013010164

The Chew: Back 2 Back
Editorial Director: Wendy Lefkon
Executive Editor: Laura Hopper
Design by H. Clark Wakabayashi

ISBN 978-1-4847-5864-9
FAC-008598-15233

First Bind-up edition October 2015
1 3 5 7 9 10 8 6 4 2

This book is dedicated to all of the talented, hard-working people who make up the creative, production, and technical staff of *The Chew*. They give their best every day and we love them for it.

CONTENTS

The CHEW

INTRODUCTION

If *The Chew* has done nothing else, I hope it's shown that home cooking shouldn't feel like math, it should feel like finger painting. A splash of wine into this, a little extra butter into that, a squeeze of lemon over these…yeah, baby!

Every day I stand in front of the studio monitors and watch *The Chew* as an excited fan. I groove on the beautiful food and the laughs as these easy friends pull a meal together in a few minutes. They inspire me by making it look fun. And useful.

As a below-average cook with above-average ambition, I imagine myself making whatever delicious dish they're making that weekend or, if it's stunningly easy, that night.

It's a seduction of sorts, like this book. Ever since we started the show we have wanted people to swap the stressful idea of "making dinner" for the fun of creating something new for themselves and their family.

If we did it right, this book should have something for every possible kind of home cook, every day of the week.

We also built this book around the rhythm of people's lives. Weekdays are often rushed, but weekends shouldn't be. And if we are cooking for special occasions, we want to show love through care and time spent.

So we put a little fancy weekend stuff like Lobster Thermidor (see page 191), some simple midweek yummies like Chicken Marsala (page 48), the perfect dish for date night, and a recipe for Sunday dinner that will stand the test of time.

As we say on the show, we hope our recipes are just the start. Don't be afraid to get finger painting and make them your own work of delicious art.

—Gordon Elliott

IT'S MONDAY!
(OR TUESDAY, WEDNESDAY, OR THURSDAY)
WHAT'S FOR DINNER?

QUICK AND EASY MEALS TO MAKE ON BUSY WEEKNIGHTS

BREAKFAST + DINNER = "BRINNER!"

SWEET TREATS FOR THE MIDDLE OF THE WEEK

ON THE CHEW, we think everyone should cook, because everyone has it within them to do it well. The problem is weeknights. How do you find the time? The recipes that follow are proof positive that you can make simple and delicious meals any night of the week with just a few ingredients from your pantry and a little bit of shopping. **THE PAYOFF IS HUGE.** Homemade food is more nutritious; contains less fat, salt, and chemicals than most store-bought stuff; and tastes better. Sure you could order in a pizza or open up a can of soup and throw it over a chicken breast, but it is so much more fulfilling and healthful to cook a meal with the best-tasting natural ingredients. If there is another person who likes to cook or help in your family, it's that much easier and that much more quality family time. Who doesn't like to sit down to a home-cooked meal with the family? For many of us, it's the only time of the day we get to **DO SOMETHING TOGETHER** and that is very precious. And speaking of precious, did I mention that it's cheaper too?

"But I can't cook," you say. To which I say, yes, you can, and these recipes will prove it. Whether you start at the age of eight or twenty-eight or forty-eight, you've got to start somewhere. Don't worry if it's not perfect. **WHO NEEDS PERFECT?** You just need good, and our Chew Crew promises these easy meals are good. Just get in there and do it. Pretty soon you will be **FREAKIN' AWESOME** as a home cook. And speaking of awesome home cooks, here are some thoughts on Monday through Thursday home cooking from my partners on *The Chew*.

—Clinton

SALAMI AND EGG SANDWICH | CHORIZO MANCHEGO STRATA | CHILLED TOMATO AND BREAD SOUP | GRILLED SHRIMP WITH GRAPEFRUIT SALAD | ZUCCHINI CRUDO | GINGER ALE CARROTS | GRILLED APRICOT AND RADICCHIO SALAD | CHEESE RAVIOLI WITH GARLIC, MUSHROOM, AND ROSEMARY SAUCE | PASTA FAGIOLI | KIELBASA AND BEAN STEW | LOBSTER ROLL | SHOESTRING FRIES | CAPRESE SANDWICHES | PATTY MELT | ONION RINGS | SPICY SAUSAGE SLIDERS | ANGEL HAIR CAPRESE | SEARED SCALLOPS WITH RAISINS, PISTACHIO, AND SPINACH | SPAGHETTI WITH GREEN TOMATOES | CHILI SALMON WITH MANGO CUCUMBER SALSA | ANGEL HAIR WITH OLIVE OIL, GARLIC, AND CHILI FLAKES | LEFTOVER NOODLE PANCAKE WITH FALL FRUIT SLAW | GRILLED CHICKEN THIGHS WITH WATERMELON FETA SALAD | GRILLED CHICKEN CLUB | CHICKEN MARSALA | CHICKEN SALTIMBOCCA WITH CAPERS AND GRAPEFRUIT | HOT SAUCE FRIED CHICKEN | DORM ROOM CHICKEN CHILI | 60-SECOND GUACAMOLE | GRILLED SKIRT STEAK WITH CAULIFLOWER HASH | GRILLED SKIRT STEAK SANDWICH WITH CHARRED CORN MUSTARD | PAN-SEARED STRIP STEAK WITH MUSHROOMS AND CARAMELIZED ONIONS | PORK TENDERLOIN SCALLOPINI | OZ FAMILY FRIED RICE |

QUICK AND EASY MEALS TO MAKE ON BUSY WEEKNIGHTS

"I'M A LITTLE BIT of a creature of habit. Liz and I eat a lot of pasta during the week, always with a great salad. In summer I like a rib eye and a Greek salad. I think to cook well, quickly, and with low stress, there isn't enough that can be said about how important it is to build your pantry: good spices, vinegars, olive oils, canned tomatoes, anchovies, canned beans—things that aren't perishable. I shop from a rough list, but I never actually follow it—most of the time I see something in the store that really gets me excited and start building from there. That's kind of our Monday through Thursday plan.**"

—Michael

"GOOD DOESN'T MEAN A BIG PRODUCTION. On a weeknight, we're usually talking just a course or two. At the supermarket, I check out what's on special or if something looks particularly good. When it's farmers' market day, you can't beat that. Then there's my pantry. I keep good tomato sauce, beans, lentils, split peas, inexpensive balsamic (that I reduce by about half), extra virgin olive oil, spicy spices (like chipotle flakes, chili powder, or pimento), and homemade bread crumbs (dark golden brown).

What do I make out of all this? Many, many things, but I guess my go-to easy dishes are roasted chicken legs and thighs with paprika and balsamic glaze; spaghetti with garlic, oil, and chili flakes, sprinkled with toasted bread crumbs; a big green salad with white beans, eggplant Parmesan, and celery root; sweet potato hash with sunny-side up eggs; white bean, lentil, or split pea soup with (to jazz it up) arepas or johnny cakes with polenta, or quick whole grain drop biscuits. Nothing takes more than ten minutes or so of prep and very little standing over the stove.**"

—Mario

PEOPLE SAY THEY DON'T HAVE THE TIME, but take one day and log how you spend every single chunk of 10 minutes and you will quickly see how much time goes to checking your phone or Facebook or other nonessentials. If you can find a way to consolidate 15–20 minutes of that time, you can make a home-cooked meal. What I focus on is my pantry, fridge, and freezer, stocked with the things that I know my taste buds rely on for satisfaction. I'll always have canned beans and dry pasta. I eat a ton of quinoa. For breakfast I'll do a hot grain cereal with coconut milk and maple syrup. I keep lettuce on hand because I'm big on making the easy choice the healthy choice. If salad fixings are the first thing I see when I open the fridge, I'm probably going to go for it. But I like to spice up my salads, so I usually have hard fruits like apples and pears that won't go bad quickly. In my freezer, I have my glazes, sauces, stocks, and frozen herbs: ingredients that I can just add to a pot that instantly flavor it up.

—Daphne

FIRST THE SHOPPING—I will look in my cabinet and see what I have, and then go shopping with a loose list that I can adjust if something in the store catches my fancy. I always start with produce—that's what dictates the rest—then dairy, and then meat, and we do a lot of pasta. I'm one of those people who loves meatloaf and seeing what I can make work with the meat and vegetables I have on hand. A lot of times my husband and I will do what we call abundant salads: we chop a medley of veggies together on our big cutting board. If we have some leftover meat, that goes in too. And then there's grits—I'll throw anything into grits. I just did some this past weekend with butternut squash and herbs. But they have to be good grits. I'm lucky that way; I get great grits from Tennessee. Gotta be white grits too, no exceptions.

—Carla

Salami and Egg Sandwich

SERVES 4 | COOK TIME: 4 MINUTES | PREP TIME: 15 MINUTES | COST: $

Easy

Around my house my mom was the master cook, but my dad was "the Sandwich King." If I had to pick a favorite—and that's not easy—I'd probably have to say nothing beat his salami and eggs. Something fantastic happens to salami when you fry it—you get a crispy crust, almost like bacon. Then with some Hungarian ShaSha Sauce (basically hot mustard and hot pepper), compliments of Lizzie's mom, and sliced pickled onion, you have a full-frontal attack on your taste buds.

4 egg knot rolls or potato rolls

2 tablespoons unsalted butter

1 pound salami, thinly sliced

2 tablespoons extra virgin olive oil

4 eggs

1 cup spicy mustard or ShaSha Sauce (recipe follows)

1 cup thinly sliced or Pickled Red Onions (recipe follows)

1 bunch basil (leaves only)

Kosher salt

Freshly ground black pepper

1. Preheat a griddle or nonstick skillet to medium-high heat.

2. Split the rolls, and butter each half. Place on the griddle and toast until browned. Set aside.

3. Put the salami on the griddle in four separate mounds and warm through, allowing some pieces to crisp.

4. Using the olive oil to grease the griddle as needed, fry each of the eggs, about 1 minute per side for over easy. Assemble the sandwiches by spreading spicy mustard or ShaSha Sauce on each of the buns, adding the salami, topping with the sliced or Pickled Red Onions and basil leaves, and finishing with a fried egg. Season with salt and pepper and place the bun on top and enjoy.

IT'S MONDAY! WHAT'S FOR DINNER?

QUICK AND EASY MEALS TO MAKE ON BUSY WEEKNIGHTS

FOR THE SHASHA SAUCE

12 hot banana peppers
from a jar, tops removed
and chopped

4 cloves garlic

1 cup yellow mustard

1 cup white wine vinegar

½ cup sugar

2 tablespoons all-
purpose flour

TO MAKE THE SHASHA SAUCE

1. In a food processor, puree the peppers, garlic, mustard, and vinegar.

2. Pour the puree into a medium saucepan, then add the sugar and bring it to a boil over high heat. Lower the heat and simmer the mixture for 30 minutes.

3. In a small bowl or juice glass, mix the flour and ½ cup water to make a smooth paste. Whisk it into the pepper mixture and continue to simmer for 20 minutes, stirring regularly, until it becomes very thick. Let the sauce cool, and then pour it into a covered nonreactive container (such as a glass jar). The sauce can be refrigerated for up to 1 month. Makes 2 cups.

FOR THE PICKLED RED ONIONS

2 pounds red onions, sliced

White wine vinegar (amount will vary for each jar)

Sugar (amount will vary for each jar)

Kosher salt (amount will vary for each jar)

2 teaspoons mustard seeds

1 tablespoon crushed red pepper flakes

2 tablespoons coriander seeds

2 tablespoons black peppercorns

4 cloves garlic

2 bay leaves

TO MAKE THE PICKLED RED ONIONS

1. Pack the onions into two 1-quart jars and cover with water to come within ½ inch of the rim. Pour the water out into a measuring cup. Note the volume, pour off half the water, and replace with the vinegar. Add 2 tablespoons sugar and 2 tablespoons salt for every 3 cups of liquid.

2. Pour the vinegar mixture into a nonreactive saucepan. Add the mustard seeds, red pepper flakes, coriander seeds, black peppercorns, garlic, and bay leaves, and bring to a boil over high heat. Allow the liquid to boil for 2 minutes, and then remove it from the heat.

3. Pour the hot liquid into the jars to cover the onions and screw on the lids. Refrigerate for up to 1 month.

4. Makes: 2 quarts

Chorizo Manchego Strata

SERVES 8 | **COOK TIME: 40–50 MINUTES** | **PREP TIME: 15 MINUTES** | **COST: $**

Easy

I've yet to meet the person who doesn't like bread pudding. For breakfast—maybe with a splash of maple syrup and a bunch of raisins staring at you from its eggy, breadful depths—it's hard to beat. Now, if you make it savory you've got a quick dinner that comes together without much fuss. There are two kinds of chorizo that you are apt to find in America. The hard kind is from Spain and is already cooked. The softer kind is from Mexico and is more suited for a hash than this recipe. But fear not, admirers of things Mexicano, I top off my strata with a very Mexican tomatillo salsa. You can probably make this with any hard cheese that has good meltability, but if you can, go with the original from La Mancha in Spain: gotta go Manchego.

8 cups crusty sourdough bread, preferably day-old

2 tablespoons extra virgin olive oil

1 large onion, chopped

1 pound Spanish chorizo, medium dice

2 cloves garlic, peeled and sliced

12 eggs, whisked

1½ cups milk

1½ cups half-and-half

1 tablespoon red chili flakes

2 cups Manchego cheese, shredded

Kosher salt

Freshly ground black pepper

Store-bought tomatillo salsa, to serve

1. Preheat the oven to 375 °F.

2. Cut the bread into 1-inch cubes, and set aside.

3. In a large sauté pan, heat the olive oil over medium-high heat. Add the onion and sauté for 2–3 minutes until soft. Lower the heat to medium and add the chorizo. After 2 minutes add the garlic and cook just until fragrant, then set aside to cool.

4. Whisk together the eggs, milk, half-and-half, chili flakes, and 1½ cups of cheese, and season with salt and pepper. Add the bread and chorizo mixture to the eggs and toss to coat. Press down firmly to coat all of the bread in the egg mixture. Pour into a greased baking dish. (At this point you could cover and refrigerate overnight.)

5. Bake for 35–40 minutes uncovered, then let stand for 5–10 minutes. Grate the remaining cheese over the top, and serve with tomatillo salsa.

QUICK AND EASY MEALS TO MAKE ON BUSY WEEKNIGHTS

Chilled Tomato and Bread Soup

Easy

SERVES 8 | COOK TIME: 2 MINUTES | PREP TIME: 20 MINUTES

INACTIVE COOK TIME: 1 HOUR TO OVERNIGHT | COST: $

Opera fans in Italy have been known to throw rotten tomatoes on-stage when they are not pleased with the performance. Before you aim a tomato because of a poorly sung aria, make sure you are not heaving almost-rotten tomatoes, because super-ripe, over-the-hill tomatoes are the basis of one of the favorite quick summertime meals in my home. Toss them into a food processor with day-old bread, salt, herbs, and olive oil, and you have a real Tuscan bread soup. It's flavorful and healthful, so we always keep a big container of it in the part of the refrigerator where we store the stuff we call "Kids Can Eat as Much as They Want, Whenever They Want."

5 pounds very ripe heirloom tomatoes, cored and cut into chunks

3 cups torn-up day-old Italian or country bread

½ cup fresh basil leaves

2 tablespoons fresh thyme leaves

Kosher salt

Freshly ground pepper

¼ cup extra virgin olive oil

Zest and juice of 2 lemons

2 teaspoons red pepper flakes

4 scallions (whites and about 2 inches of greens), thinly sliced

8 ½-inch-thick baguette slices, toasted

1. In a food processor or blender, blend the tomatoes until smooth. Add the day-old bread, basil, and thyme, and season with salt and pepper. Blend. If too thick, thin with water. Refrigerate for at least 1 hour to chill, but it's even better the next day.

2. In a medium mixing bowl, gently mix the olive oil, lemon zest and juice, red pepper flakes, and scallions together. Season lightly with salt.

3. Divide the chilled tomato soup among eight bowls. Float 1 slice of toast in the center of each bowl. Sprinkle the scallion mixture on top of each toast, and serve.

IT'S MONDAY! WHAT'S FOR DINNER?

Grilled Shrimp with Grapefruit Salad

SERVES 4 | COOK TIME: 18–20 MINUTES | PREP TIME: 20 MINUTES | COST: $

Easy

For our Mother's Day show, I wanted to do something bright, light, and flavorful instead of a big ol' hunk of meat like you'd do for Father's Day, so I came up with this fresh and delicious salad. One of our audience members, Hakim Chandler, volunteered to help me whip it up and said that he would make this recipe for his "soon-to-be-pregnant wife." I thought that might be a little too much information about the Chandler household, but he quickly corrected himself: "My soon-to-be-a-mother wife." Whew!

This is a twist on a classic Middle Eastern tabbouleh salad of bulgur wheat and fresh herbs with my additions of grapefruit sections, lemon zest, and, of course, good olive oil. Hakim was a little challenged in the lemon-zesting department until Carla, revealing another one of her hidden talents, told him to "hold the lemon like you are throwing a knuckleball!"

He did fine in the lemon-holding department and behind the stove. We agreed that this would be a great recipe to whip up for Mom while she is busy with their new baby.

FOR THE SALAD

2 cups water

½ cup bulgur wheat, rinsed

½ teaspoon kosher salt

Zest and juice of 3 lemons

½ cup extra virgin olive oil

3 cups flat-leaf parsley, chopped

¼ cup scallions, chopped

½ cup mint leaves, chopped

3 grapefruits, segmented and cut into thirds

TO MAKE THE SALAD

1. Bring the water to a boil. Add the bulgur, reduce to a simmer, and cook until the bulgur has absorbed all the water and is slightly tender, about 12 minutes. Season with the salt, and set aside to cool.

2. In a small bowl, whisk together the lemon zest and juice and olive oil.

3. In a large salad bowl, combine the parsley, scallions, mint, and grapefruit. Add the bulgur, pour the dressing over the salad, and toss to combine. Taste and adjust for seasoning. You might need to add more salt or olive oil. If you need more olive oil, add it 1 tablespoon at a time. Set aside until ready to serve.

FOR THE SHRIMP

**12 jumbo shrimp,
peeled and deveined**

2 tablespoons olive oil

Kosher salt, to taste

**Freshly ground
pepper, to taste**

TO MAKE THE SHRIMP

4. In a medium bowl, toss the shrimp lightly with the olive oil, salt, and freshly ground pepper.

5. Preheat a grill pan to medium-high heat. Grill the shrimp for 3–4 minutes per side, until the shrimp are pink and cooked through.

6. Divide the tabbouleh into four servings, and place 3 shrimp on each of the salads to serve.

15

Zucchini Crudo

SERVES 4 | **PREP TIME: 10 MINUTES** | **INACTIVE PREP TIME: 10–15 MINUTES** | **COST: $**

Easy

If you have a garden, then you know that you can save time "shopping" because it doesn't require anything more than going out the back door and picking whatever is ripe. You also know that when you have zucchini, you really have lots of zucchini. No big deal, because this fresh summertime salad goes with just about anything you might make, from grilled salmon to pork chops, from steak to lobster. Remember to salt your zucchini slices ahead of time, so that you remove some of the water and any bitterness. A simple lemon shallot vinaigrette brightens the flavors beautifully.

2 medium zucchini, thinly sliced

2 medium yellow summer squashes, thinly sliced

1 tablespoon plus ¼ teaspoon kosher salt

1 teaspoon garlic, peeled and minced

1 shallot, peeled and finely sliced

Zest and juice of 3 lemons

½ cup extra virgin olive oil

⅓ cup slivered or sliced almonds, toasted

⅓ cup fresh dill, chopped

1. Combine the zucchini and yellow squash in a colander in the sink, and sprinkle 1 tablespoon of the salt over it. Toss to coat, and set aside for 10–15 minutes, no longer.

2. In a large bowl, combine the garlic and shallot, sprinkle with the remaining ¼ teaspoon salt, and whisk in the lemon zest and juice. Whisk in the olive oil in a steady stream, then the almonds and dill. Taste for seasoning and acidity (it should be nicely acidic). Add the zucchini and squash to the dressing, toss, and serve immediately.

Use your fingers

The ingredients in any vinaigrette vary a lot—one lemon is super sour, another not so much; olive oil can be soft and floral, or sharp and peppery. To make sure you have the right balance, dip the tip of your finger and taste. Your tongue won't lie.

Ginger Ale Carrots

SERVES 4 | COOK TIME: 15–20 MINUTES | PREP TIME: 10 MINUTES | COST: $

Easy

I like this longtime Christmas favorite so much, and it's so quick, easy, and flavorful, I decided, why not make it on a weeknight? It will add some amazing flavors and textures alongside your main course. It's spicy, sweet, fruity, and fresh-tasting.

Carla stood by my side when I was making this and said it could work for lots of different vegetables. I haven't tried it yet, but I bet she's right. Cauliflower for sure. Maybe delicata squash. I'm not sold on the idea of broccoli, but if it floats your boat, give it a try and let me know.

1½ pounds young carrots, peeled, with greens trimmed (leave about 1 inch of the green tops on)

4–5 tablespoons olive oil

Salt

Freshly cracked black pepper

Zest and juice of 2 oranges, divided

2 cloves garlic, smashed

½ cup ginger ale

1 tablespoon ginger, finely minced

¼ cup chopped hazelnuts, toasted

¼ cup chopped parsley, divided

1. Preheat the oven to 400 °F.

2. In a large bowl, toss the carrots with the olive oil and season generously with salt and pepper. Add the zest and juice of 1 orange and the garlic cloves, and toss to coat.

3. Heat a large ovenproof sauté pan over medium-high heat. Arrange the carrots in an even layer. Pour in the ginger ale and cook the carrots on the stovetop until they begin to color, and then transfer to the oven and cook for about 10–15 minutes, or until fork-tender.

4. Once the carrots are cooked and the glaze has reduced, remove from the oven and allow to cool slightly.

5. Meanwhile, in a small bowl, mix together the remaining orange zest and juice, ginger, hazelnuts, and parsley. Season with salt and pepper. Garnish the carrots with the hazelnut mixture.

QUICK AND EASY MEALS TO MAKE ON BUSY WEEKNIGHTS

Grilled Apricot and Radicchio Salad

SERVES 4 | COOK TIME: 8–10 MINUTES | PREP TIME: 15 MINUTES | COST: $

Moderate

Grilling season is also ripe fruit season. One of my favorite sides for grilled steak is apricots tossed in a marinade and then grilled. The savory aspects of the marinade help tie the fruitiness of the apricots to the meat. You can certainly do this over a gas grill, but wood charcoal gives a certain extra quality of smoky char that is indescribable. You don't need to do this with apricots only. Any stone fruit will do the trick: peaches, plums, nectarines. It really presents the jewels of summer orchards in a new and great-tasting way.

1 shallot, minced

3 tablespoons red wine vinegar

1 tablespoon honey (chestnut if you can find it)

1 bunch mint (leaves only)

3 tablespoons extra virgin olive oil

Kosher salt

½ pound apricots, halved and pitted

1 head radicchio, quartered, with core intact

1 cup feta, crumbled

1. Preheat a grill or grill pan to medium-high heat.

2. In a mixing bowl combine the shallot, red wine vinegar, honey, mint, and 2 tablespoons of the olive oil. Whisk together and season with salt. Add the apricots and radicchio to the bowl, and toss to coat in the dressing.

3. Place the apricots and radicchio, cut side down, on the grill. Cook for 3 minutes, until they are slightly charred and have caramelized. Flip the radicchio and cook for 3 more minutes. Remove the apricots and add them to the bowl with the mint dressing.

4. Remove the radicchio from the grill and thinly slice. Add the radicchio and the feta to the bowl with the apricots, and toss to combine. Adjust seasoning and serve warm.

Cheese Ravioli with Garlic, Mushroom, and Rosemary Sauce

| SERVES 6 | COOK TIME: 8–10 MINUTES | PREP TIME: 10 MINUTES | COST: $ |

Easy

Attention ravioli lovers! Did you know you can enjoy ravioli just as much without tomato sauce, especially if you make this quick and super savory garlic, mushroom, and rosemary sauce? Once you boil the ravioli, put them in the pan with the other ingredients and add a little of that starchy pasta water, and in about a minute, you will have a beautiful, clean-tasting, fresh pan sauce. I like to throw a little pat of butter in mine, which Mario says isn't truly Italian. But the way I look at it, although I'm Sicilian and Greek, which makes me an olive oil kind of guy, I was trained in a French kitchen where the motto was "It's better with butter!"

Kosher salt

4 tablespoons butter

2 tablespoons olive oil

2 sprigs rosemary

2 cups cremini mushrooms, cleaned and sliced

Freshly ground black pepper

1½ pounds store-bought cheese ravioli (fresh or dried)

4 cloves garlic, peeled and thinly sliced

1 large shallot, peeled and minced

⅓ cup Parmigiano-Reggiano, plus more for garnish

1. Heat a large pot of boiling water over high heat and season generously with salt.

2. Heat a sauté pan over medium-high heat. Add 2 tablespoons of the butter and the olive oil. Once hot, add the rosemary sprigs and mushrooms. Toss the mushrooms and season with salt and pepper. Cook until the mushrooms have browned on all sides, about 5–6 minutes.

3. Meanwhile, drop the ravioli in the boiling water and stir with a wooden spoon, cooking 1–2 minutes less than the package instructions suggest.

4. Add the garlic and shallot to the mushrooms, and toss to coat. Cook 2–3 minutes, or until the garlic and shallot are soft.

5. Drain the ravioli, reserving some of the pasta water, and add the pasta to the sauté pan and toss to coat. Add about ⅓ cup of the pasta water, along with the remaining 2 tablespoons of butter. Add the Parmigiano-Reggiano, and toss the pasta until the sauce is creamy and emulsified. Serve immediately, garnished with more Parmigiano-Reggiano if you want.

Pasta Fagioli

SERVES 6 TO 8 | **COOK TIME: 30–35 MINUTES** | **PREP TIME: 15 MINUTES** | **COST: $**

Easy

Pasta fagioli! Say it with me: pasta *fah-joe-lee*. Damn, that's a fun word. The trick to making it quickly—and even though I'm a big shot Italian TV chef, I use this trick—is to buy canned beans. Molto fast, molto easy. Take note that it calls for tomato paste, not crushed tomatoes. When you add tomato paste to the onions and the hot oil, the flavor deepens and intensifies. I make it with pancetta, but chicken works as well; or, for you vegetarians, seitan or tofu. When I have leftover pasta dough, I always toss it into soups like this, but dried pasta is just as good. In fact, this is one of those recipes where almost anything you think to add is fine.

3 tablespoons pancetta, diced

6 tablespoons extra virgin olive oil

¼ cup Italian parsley, finely chopped, plus more for garnish

1 medium Spanish onion, finely chopped

2 tablespoons tomato paste

8 cups chicken stock

3 cups cooked borlotti beans or kidney beans (rinsed and drained if canned)

2 cups fresh pasta scraps or broken dried fettuccine

Kosher salt

Freshly ground black pepper

Grated Parmigiano-Reggiano, for garnish

1. In a Dutch oven, heat the pancetta and 2 tablespoons of the olive oil over high heat until almost smoking. Add the parsley and onion, and cook, stirring, until the onion is browned and soft, about 5 minutes.

2. Stir in the tomato paste, reduce the heat to medium, and cook for 5 more minutes. Add the chicken stock and beans, and bring to a boil. Lower the heat and simmer for 10–15 minutes.

3. Add the pasta, and simmer for 6–8 more minutes if using fresh, and according to package instructions if using dried. Remove from the heat, and season with salt and pepper.

4. Divide the soup among six serving bowls. Drizzle with the remaining olive oil, and garnish with the parsley and grated Parmigiano-Reggiano to serve.

Herbed up

When I cook a recipe like this with herbs, I like to put some in at the beginning so that it infuses the dish with a muted low-end flavor. Then I add some fresh herbs at the end to bring out those high notes.

Kielbasa and Bean Stew

SERVES 6 TO 8 | COOK TIME: 35–40 MINUTES | PREP TIME: 10 MINUTES | COST: $

Easy

When winter hangs in the heartland like an uninvited guest who won't go away, you want something hearty on your plate. That's when I turn to the undisputed king of sausages, the pride of Poland, the smoky, salty kielbasa. Stewed with sauerkraut, braised in beer, and cut with some sharp mustard greens, this is just the thing to whip up after an overtime shift at the auto plant or on any cold night when the walk from the car to the front door makes you pray for spring. This won't set the dogwoods blooming, but it'll surely warm you up.

2 tablespoons butter

1 yellow onion, sliced

Salt

2 tablespoons olive oil

1 pound kielbasa sausage, chopped

2 carrots, peeled and sliced into coins

1 tablespoon mustard seed

1 12-ounce stout beer

½ pound Yukon Gold potatoes, halved

1 bunch mustard greens or kale, stems removed and thinly sliced

2 cups sauerkraut, drained

2 cups chicken stock

3 tablespoons fresh parsley, chopped

1. In a large Dutch oven, add the butter, onion, and a pinch of salt. Cook on low until the onions have caramelized, about 10 minutes. Transfer the caramelized onions to a bowl and set aside.

2. In the same pan, add the olive oil and turn the heat to medium-high. Add the sausage and brown for 1–2 minutes. Add the carrots and mustard seed and cook for 5 more minutes. Deglaze the pot with the beer. Add the potatoes, mustard greens or kale, and sauerkraut to the Dutch oven, along with the caramelized onions.

3. Add the chicken stock and parsley to the pot, and season with salt. Cook for 20 minutes until the potatoes are cooked through.

Lobster Roll

| SERVES 4 | COOK TIME: 2 MINUTES | PREP TIME: 20 MINUTES | COST: $$ |

Easy

One of the unbreakable commandments of the Batali homestead is "Thou shalt never throw out any lobster." So if there's any leftover from Clinton's *magnifique* thermidor, my advice is to make this lobster roll. My other advice is to make your own mayonnaise. Lobster is such a noble ingredient, it wants something more than store-bought mayo. Whip up your own, preferably with the very best olive oil you can find. As for the buns, store-bought are fine; in fact, they are the only way to go, toasted, buttered, and heaped high with lobster.

1 lobster (steamed or boiled, with the meat picked out) or leftover lobster meat

1 stalk celery, small dice

½ teaspoon celery salt

¼ cup Fresh Mayo (recipe follows)

Salt, to taste

Freshly ground pepper, to taste

Butter, to brush the griddle

4 split-top hot dog rolls

1. Roughly chop the lobster meat and add to a bowl with the celery, celery salt, and Fresh Mayo. Season to taste with salt and pepper. Mix gently with a rubber spatula to combine.

2. Preheat the griddle to medium-high. Brush the griddle with butter. Toast each roll on both sides and fill with the lobster salad.

FOR THE FRESH MAYO

2 egg yolks

1 teaspoon lemon juice and zest

1 cup vegetable oil

Salt, to taste

Pepper, to taste

1 teaspoon Dijon mustard

Dashes of hot sauce, to taste

TO MAKE THE FRESH MAYO

1. In a bowl, mix the egg yolks and lemon juice and zest. Then drizzle in the oil slowly while whisking vigorously to emulsify the oil into the egg. Season with salt and pepper to taste. Add the mustard and hot sauce, and combine thoroughly. Makes 1½ to 2 cups mayo and can be stored in the fridge for up to 10 days.

NOTE: If the mayo doesn't come together or the emulsification is broken, it can be saved by putting a teaspoon of water in a fresh clean bowl and slowly whisking in the broken mayo until it recombines.

IT'S MONDAY! WHAT'S FOR DINNER?

Shoestring Fries

SERVES 4	COOK TIME: 5–10 MINUTES	PREP TIME: 15 MINUTES	COST: $

Easy

It's a shame that the only way most of us eat French fries is at a fast-food place or a restaurant. Think of all the meals you make at home that would be even more super with some hot, salty, crispy fries. Aside from a thermometer to make sure your oil is at the right temperature, there are no special chef secrets: just three ingredients and some paper towels to drain them. No recipe could be easier, or tastier.

Vegetable oil, for deep-frying

3 russet potatoes, peeled

Salt

1. Fill a Dutch oven two-thirds of the way with the vegetable oil. Heat to 360 °F.

2. Using the julienne attachment on a mandolin, cut the potatoes into strips and fry in batches until golden brown.

3. Drain the fries on a paper towel–lined plate and season with salt while they are still hot.

Caprese Sandwiches

SERVES 4 | **PREP TIME: 5 MINUTES** | **COST: $**

Easy

The English have their strawberries and cream; the French have their croissants and coffee; and we Italians have our wonderful caprese. Caprese is shorthand for the combination of fresh tomatoes, fragrant basil, and rich, creamy mozzarella, named in honor of the beautiful and idyllic isle of Capri. It really is the essence of summer, which is why I love to have caprese sandwiches when we go to the beach. One piece of advice: wait until you actually get to the beach before you assemble them, otherwise you will have soggy caprese, which is a major no-no. These sandwiches are also a Batali household go-to meal any night of the week.

1 baguette

2 pounds heirloom tomatoes

1 pound fresh mozzarella

Olive oil, to drizzle

Red wine vinegar, to drizzle

Coarse salt, to taste

Freshly ground pepper, to taste

1 bunch basil

1. Slice the baguette lengthwise.

2. Slice the heirloom tomatoes and the mozzarella into ½-inch-thick pieces.

3. Drizzle the baguette with olive oil and red wine vinegar. Layer the tomatoes and mozzarella on the bread, and season with salt and freshly ground pepper. Garnish with basil leaves, and sandwich the slices of bread together. Cut the baguette into 4 sandwiches and serve immediately.

Patty Melt

SERVES 4 | COOK TIME: 10–12 MINUTES | PREP TIME: 10 MINUTES | COST: $

Easy

A patty melt is not a burger, as any patty melt lover can tell you. The meat patty in a patty melt is all one thickness, instead of a lump that's thicker in the middle. It's also not served on a bun: you put it on rye bread with a piece of Swiss. It's important, as the juices from the meat seep into the bread, making it all gooey and delicious on the inside. When we made it on the show, Carla reminded the audience that you don't want any patty (or burger) to be much smaller than the bread (or bun) it's going on. That means you start with a patty that's just a little bit bigger than the bread, because the meat will shrink when you cook it.

1 pound 80/20 ground beef

Salt

Freshly ground pepper

4 slices Swiss cheese

2 tablespoons butter, plus more to brush the griddle

2 tablespoons olive oil

1 onion, sliced

⅓ cup ketchup

⅓ cup mayonnaise

3 tablespoons pickle relish

8 slices rye bread

1. Preheat a griddle to medium-high heat.

2. Shape the ground beef into 4 patties. The patties should be the shape of the bread. Season generously with salt and pepper. Brush the griddle with a little butter and cook the patties on the griddle for 3–4 minutes per side, for medium rare. Top the patties with the cheese after flipping. Remove when the cheese has melted and set aside.

3. Add 2 tablespoons of the butter and the olive oil to the griddle, and add the onion. Cook until the onion has softened, about 5 minutes. Remove from the griddle and set aside.

IT'S MONDAY! WHAT'S FOR DINNER?

Full steam ahead

A little trick that every short-order melt-maker (and burger-maker) knows is that you can melt a slice of cheese quickly if you put it on the patty, cover it with a lid, and give the griddle or skillet a spritz of water that instantly turns to cheese-melting-hot steam.

4. Mix together the ketchup, mayonnaise, and pickle relish.

5. Place the burger patties onto a slice of the bread. Top with some of the onions and a smear of the ketchup mixture. Top with another piece of bread.

6. Brush the griddle with more butter, and place each sandwich onto the griddle. Once the first side is golden brown and crisp, brush butter onto the top slice of bread and then flip the sandwich over. Cook for an additional 2–3 minutes until golden brown and crisp and the cheese has melted.

Onion Rings

SERVES 4 TO 6 | COOK TIME: 5–10 MINUTES | PREP TIME: 10 MINUTES | COST: $

Easy

Kids are often amazed when they find out that the onion rings they get at the burger stand can be just as good—even *better*—when you make your own batter and fry them up at home. The hardest part to this recipe is crowd control: they smell so good and look so tempting, it's hard to keep the family from snatching them just as fast as they come out of the fryer.

Vegetable oil

2 large onions, cut into ½-inch slices

1½ cups all-purpose flour

1½ teaspoons cayenne

2 teaspoons paprika

1 teaspoon kosher salt

2 eggs

1¼ cups milk, plus more if needed

2 cups panko bread crumbs

Additional salt, for seasoning

1. Fill a Dutch oven two-thirds of the way full with vegetable oil, and bring the temperature to 365 °F.

2. Separate the onion slices into rings.

3. In a medium-sized bowl, whisk together the flour, cayenne, paprika, and salt.

4. Dredge the onion rings in the flour mixture, shake off excess, and set aside.

5. Make a well in the flour mixture, add the eggs, and slowly pour in milk. Whisk until the batter has a smooth, thick consistency. Add more milk if needed. Dip floured onion rings into batter and let excess drip off. Then place rings in panko bread crumbs and thoroughly coat on both sides.

6. Working in batches, deep fry a few of the rings at a time for 1–2 minutes, or until golden brown.

7. Remove to a paper towel to drain. Season with salt immediately and serve while still hot.

Spicy Sausage Sliders

| MAKES 8 SLIDERS | COOK TIME: 5 MINUTES | PREP TIME: 5 MINUTES | COST: $ |

Easy

Once you say the word *sausage*, you've got my attention. As a true son of the Midwest, I love sausages, whether it's brats, chorizo, merguez, or Italian sausage. One of the things I don't love about sausages is that they take a long time to cook, so for this sandwich, I take the sausage meat out of its casings and make patties. They cook a lot quicker and develop a nice crunchy crust. I love grilled onions on regular (burger) sliders, so I figured, why not here too? And then, because I'm a Greek and we love to use yogurt and mint to fill out the flavor of grilled lamb, I thought it wouldn't hurt here. As you finish one slider and reach for the next (most people do), I think you'll agree I was right.

1 tablespoon extra virgin olive oil, plus more for grilling

1½ pounds spicy sausage, removed from casing

2 red onions, sliced into ¼-inch rounds

8 mini potato rolls, split

¾ cup Greek yogurt

2 tablespoons mint, chopped

Salt

Pepper

Handful of arugula leaves

1. Preheat a grill over high heat. Brush the grill with olive oil.

2. Form the sausage into 3-ounce patties, slightly larger than the rolls. Place on the grill and cook for 2 minutes on each side. Grill the onions alongside the sausage until charred and soft, about 2 minutes per side. Toast the bread on the grill.

3. While the patties are cooking, mix together the yogurt, mint, and olive oil, and season with salt and pepper.

4. Build the sliders with sausage patties, a smear of yogurt, arugula, and grilled onions.

Angel Hair Caprese

SERVES 5 | COOK TIME: 5 MINUTES | PREP TIME: 5 MINUTES | COST: $

Easy

Lizzie and I keep a good-sized garden in the summertime, so around mid-July, there are always a lot of tomatoes on hand. If we are ever stumped as to what we should have for dinner, our garden speaks to us, often in Italian. If you listen to your garden, it might also tell you that you have some zucchini that wants to jump in the pasta bowl. Lizzie and I are all for that, but mostly we go for the basic caprese combo of tomatoes, mozzarella, and basil with some pan-roasted garlic, crunchy bread crumbs, and hot olive oil. A great thing about using angel hair pasta is that it is so thin that it cooks up quickly.

Kosher salt

1 pound angel hair pasta

¼ cup plus 2 tablespoons extra virgin olive oil

4 cloves garlic, sliced

1 pound cherry or grape tomatoes, halved

1 bunch basil, torn, plus more for garnish

1 cup bocconcini, or fresh mozzarella, cut into cubes

Freshly ground pepper

¼ cup fresh bread crumbs

2 tablespoons parsley, chopped

1 tablespoon grated Parmesan

1. Bring a large pot of water to a boil and season generously with salt.

2. Drop the angel hair into the water and cook for 1 minute less than package instructions.

3. In a large sauté pan over medium heat, add ¼ cup of the olive oil and the garlic. Sauté over low heat until the garlic becomes fragrant (being careful not to let it brown), about 3 minutes.

4. Add the cooked pasta to the olive oil and garlic with a little pasta water.

5. Combine the tomato, basil, and mozzarella in a large bowl. Season generously with salt and freshly ground pepper. Add the pasta mixture and toss.

6. In a small sauté pan, toast the bread crumbs with the remaining olive oil, parsley, and Parmesan.

7. Divide the pasta among 5 bowls, and garnish with the bread crumbs and basil.

Add taste, subtract time

I always cook pasta for 1 minute less than it advises on the package and finish it in the pan. For this recipe, I toss it in the pan with hot olive oil, garlic, and a little bit of the pasta water. That way, the pasta finishes cooking by absorbing the flavor of the oil and garlic.

Seared Scallops with Raisins, Pistachio, and Spinach

SERVES 4 | COOK TIME: 5 MINUTES | PREP TIME: 5 MINUTES | COST: $

Moderate

The single most important thing in cooking scallops is *don't overcook them*! You want 'em with a crust on one side and very rare and moist in the middle. The second piece of advice I have is once you put them in the pan *don't move them*. If you start flipping them in the pan like an overcaffeinated chef, you'll never get a crust and you'll suck all the juice out and they'll be tough and rubbery. The third thing to remember is to dry them before sautéing by putting them on a paper towel in the fridge. If you don't, they will weep a lot of liquid in the pan and you'll never get a pretty golden-brown crust. If you follow those rules, you will turn out scallops just like the ones you get in a restaurant.

Scallops are a lot like chicken: you can pretty much cook them with anything. They like sweet ingredients, tangy ingredients, savory ingredients, spicy ingredients, and don't let me forget salt. I tried all of the above in this recipe. It came together in 5 minutes, and Carla tried to eat the whole thing before she let me grab a bite. I guess that was her way of telling me it was good.

½ cup white wine

⅓ cup golden raisins

6 tablespoons olive oil

10 large scallops, patted dry, foot removed

Kosher salt

Freshly ground black pepper

⅓ cup pistachios, toasted and roughly chopped

Zest and juice of 1 orange

3 tablespoons butter

¼ cup parsley, leaves picked and chopped

10 ounces baby spinach, cleaned

1. Heat two large sauté pans over medium-high heat.

2. Heat a small sauté pan over medium-high heat, and add the wine and raisins. Bring up to a simmer and cook for 3 minutes, just to plump the raisins.

3. Add 3 tablespoons of the olive oil to one pan. Season the scallops on both sides with salt and pepper, and then place the scallops in the hot pan. Let sit for 2–3 minutes before flipping, ensuring that the scallops develop a dark golden sear. Add the pistachios and the orange juice and zest. Remove the pan from the heat and stir in the butter and parsley.

4. In another pan, add the remaining olive oil and the spinach. Season with a pinch of salt and pepper, and toss to coat a few times. Once the spinach just starts to wilt, take off the heat, about 45 seconds.

5. To serve, place the spinach on a platter and top with the scallops and sauce.

QUICK AND EASY MEALS TO MAKE ON BUSY WEEKNIGHTS

Spaghetti with Green Tomatoes

| SERVES 4 TO 6 | COOK TIME: 9 MINUTES | PREP TIME: 5 MINUTES | COST: $ |

Easy

Clinton once asked us, "How do you satisfy a craving in your soul?" I'm pretty easy: maybe some golf on TV or Marvin Gaye on the stereo, definitely a little nap, and then a bowl of spaghetti, like this one, made with a pesto of parsley, mint, arugula, and basil stirred into fried green tomatoes. It's a perfect color for a St. Patrick's Day pasta feast, except where are you gonna find green tomatoes in March? One thing to remember is, when you quickly cook the tomatoes, don't be tossing everything around maniacally—let the tomatoes develop a little bit of a crust, then toss in your pesto for 1 or 2 minutes.

Salt

¼ cup fresh mint leaves

¼ cup fresh basil leaves

¼ cup Italian parsley leaves

¼ cup arugula, washed and spun dry

2 cloves garlic, chopped

¼ cup freshly grated Parmigiano-Reggiano, plus more for garnish

¼ cup plus 2 tablespoons extra virgin olive oil

Freshly ground black pepper

5 green tomatoes, cored and chopped

1 pound spaghetti

1. Bring 6 quarts of water to a boil in a large pot, and add 2 tablespoons of salt.

2. Meanwhile, in a food processor, combine the mint, basil, parsley, arugula, 1 clove of garlic, Parmigiano-Reggiano, and ¼ cup of olive oil, and pulse to form a chunky puree. Season aggressively with salt and pepper, and set aside.

3. In a sauté pan over medium heat, add the remaining olive oil. Add the tomatoes and the remaining garlic, cooking for 2–3 minutes, until they just start to caramelize, then remove from the heat. Add a full ladle of pesto into the pan.

4. Cook the pasta in the boiling water until just al dente. Drain the pasta, reserving the water. Add the pasta to the pan with the tomatoes and pesto. Add some of the starchy pasta water, and toss to coat. Top with a sprinkle of the Parmigiano-Reggiano, and serve immediately.

Puttin' up pesto

You can refrigerate or freeze the pesto part of this recipe and use it for a quick pasta sauce all on its own.

SOME PEOPLE SEE LEFTOVERS AS 'BEEN THERE, DONE THAT,' but time and time again on *The Chew*, we show that the leftovers from a good meal can be a stepping-stone to a better meal, or one that is just as good. In crafts we don't talk about recycling, we talk about upcycling: taking simple things and using them to make something that looks smart and elegant and is useful. It's the same with food. Look at it this way: if you put a lot of TLC into the food you made last night, or that roast you made during the weekend, you have already created flavor and texture. Now **ALL THAT DELICIOUSNESS** you created the first time is already there, and you just need a little imagination to reinvent it into something that is even more fun because it's front-loaded with flavor. Let the following recipes be a guide to the kind of creative thinking that makes yesterday into a better today. Apologies if that sounds like something that comes out of the mouth of a political candidate, but this is one campaign promise I guarantee, and the proof is on your plate.

Look for this icon **2 FER** for some delicious ways to breathe new life into yesterday's dinner. Once you start making new and **WONDERFUL MEALS OUT OF LEFTOVERS,** you will see that almost any recipe can be the basis for a two-fer, or even a 'three-fer.'

—*Clinton*

"AT SOME POINT DURING THE WEEK, we'll roast two to four chickens, and then we'll work other dishes off that chicken throughout the week too. Next night we'll do a risotto, or pasta, or maybe we'll repurpose the chicken for tacos, or chili, or that kind of stuff too. Remember, you can toss almost any vegetable, fresh or leftover, into a risotto: radicchio, kale, chard, fennel, etc. Lizzie always makes some kind of chicken salad for a sandwich that you can eat on the fly. **"**

—Michael

"INSPIRATION FOR HOW TO USE LEFTOVERS happens to me the way someone else can instantly imagine decorating a room or composing a song. Show me a bag of groceries or a half-full fridge, I can think of thirty meals. I just start thinking that way. I love leftovers, although my kids are a little trickier because they don't want the same dish the next day. So all you've got to do is think that today's steak or pot roast is tomorrow's tacos or enchiladas or ravioli filling. I always think about a transformation that isn't recognizable as yesterday's meal, although still has all that flavor that I spent time putting into it. Anything can become a ragù for pasta; leftover protein or produce chopped up a little bit more and cooked just a little bit, and tossed with good noodles, is delicious. It's a free meal almost. **"**

—Mario

The CHEW

WHAT I LIKE TO START FROM is a simple preparation, like grilled or roasted meat. My goal is to keep my taste buds excited, so I build a more complex dish the second night that totally changes flavors. For example, if you take a basic tomato soup, the next night you can reduce it down and use it to flavor a different soup or a chili. It's just about seeing the ways that dishes that you plan on making can be versatile in new dishes. Pasta is terrific for leftovers—I never eat a big portion; I like three, four bites and then that's enough for me, because at the end of the day I'm not going to get filled up on pasta in the right way. I need vegetables, I need protein and other stuff in my diet, but I'm also not going to make a quarter cup of pasta. I'll make a decent-sized batch and I'll look for ways to include it and really sauce it up in the days to come."

—Daphne

THE BIG IDEA WITH LEFTOVERS is *cook once and use twice*. While I like leftovers, I don't necessarily need to make my leftovers into something else. I cook with the intention of having that meal again. That doesn't mean it doesn't change. By the second day flavors marry and come together to make new flavors. Now if it's a chicken where I purposefully do two chickens, then I know that chicken's gonna be repurposed for something else, or we'll have a roast and I'll buy a bigger roast than we're going to eat, and it's tomorrow's meatloaf or enchilada or barbecue sandwich. If it was good to begin with, it's going to stay good as long as you are nice to it."

—Carla

Chili Salmon with Mango Cucumber Salsa

SERVES 4 | COOK TIME: 5–7 MINUTES | PREP TIME: 10 MINUTES | COST: $

Easy

The mark of a great salsa is how many things you can serve it with. If that's the way you rate your salsas, this one is near the top. It's great with meats, chips, and fish. I make it for parties and make enough of it to keep in the fridge to liven up leftovers. It starts with the cucumbers, which are great all through summer: cool, refreshing, crunchy, and loaded with filling fiber. Then the centerpiece—fresh mangoes—is great with grilled salmon, skin side down, nice and crispy. One of the cool things we have in New York in June is down on the Lower East Side, where this big trac-tor trailer full of mangoes arrives and they peel some right there for you, served with some sea salt . . . heaven! And, of course, there's the big daddy of antioxidants: fresh blueberries. Who says healthy food can't be fun food? You won't after you whip up a batch of this fresh salsa.

FOR THE MANGO CUCUMBER SALSA

2 cups mango, peeled and cubed

1 cucumber, peeled and diced

2 avocados, pitted and cubed

½ cup blueberries, rinsed

1 jalapeño, seeded and minced

Zest and juice of 2 limes

½ teaspoon kosher salt

2 tablespoons parsley, chopped

FOR THE SALMON

4 5- to 6-ounce skin-on salmon fillets

3 teaspoons olive oil

2 teaspoons chili powder

Salt

Freshly ground pepper

TO MAKE THE MANGO CUCUMBER SALSA

1. Toss the ingredients in a medium bowl until well mixed. Set aside.

TO MAKE THE SALMON

2. Preheat a grill or grill pan to medium-high. Brush the salmon with olive oil and sprinkle ½ teaspoon chili powder over each of the salmon fillets. Season with salt and pepper, and place, skin side down, onto the grill. Once the skin is crispy, about 2–3 minutes, flip, and continue to cook on other side for an additional 2 minutes, for medium rare, or 3–4 minutes, for medium. Serve alongside the salsa.

Angel Hair with Olive Oil, Garlic, and Chili Flakes

SERVES 4 TO 6 | COOK TIME: 5 MINUTES | PREP TIME: 5 MINUTES | COST: $

Easy

Like all chefs, I like a challenge in the kitchen. Regular viewers know that I take pride in doing quick, easy, and cheap meals. This simple dish might take the prize. Three minutes and less than a buck a serving!

Inspiration started with a tweet:

HEY, CHEF SYMON, THE FAMILY IS HUNGRY. PASTA, GARLIC, PARM, BUTTER, CHILI, AND A FULL SPICE CABINET—ANY IDEAS?

Any ideas? That's my middle name! Some spicy heat, some golden pan-roasted garlic, and some fresh parsley finished with Parmesan and butter make for a rich-tasting, super-fast sauce. There are two things to bear in mind: First, you only roast your garlic until it begins to color a little bit—that's the point when it has that great nutty flavor that it loses if you let it cook any longer. Second, the parsley only gets one pass with the knife—any more and you begin to squeeze out the oil, which is where the flavor in parsley lives. With herbs, my motto is "one and done."

If you make too much pasta to eat in one meal, save the noodles and use in the very next recipe.

Salt

1 pound angel hair pasta

4 tablespoons extra virgin olive oil

5 cloves garlic, sliced

1 teaspoon–1 tablespoon chili flakes

1 cup chopped parsley

½ cup freshly grated Parmesan

1 tablespoon butter

1. Bring a large pot of water to a boil and add salt.

2. Add the pasta to the water, occasionally stirring so it doesn't stick together.

3. While the pasta is cooking, heat a 12-inch skillet over low heat. Add the extra virgin olive oil and the garlic, and let cook over low heat for 3 minutes, until the garlic is tender and aromatic. Add the chili flakes.

4. Add 1 cup of the pasta water, and turn the heat up to medium and bring to simmer.

5. Cook the pasta 1 minute less than the package instructions say, then drain the pasta and add to the skillet, stirring to coat the noodles.

6. Remove from the heat. Stir in the parsley, Parmesan, and butter and serve.

Leftover Noodle Pancake with Fall Fruit Slaw

2 FER

| SERVES 6 | COOK TIME: 20 MINUTES | PREP TIME: 10 MINUTES | COST: $ |

Moderate

Like most people, I have those days when I don't feel like shopping or don't have the time, and I also don't feel like making something from scratch. So I open the fridge and see what's there and what the ingredients say to me. It's always something interesting.

One of our viewers, Jamie, sent us a list of the contents of her fridge, and then she asked us to come up with a meal. It was an average American fridge: a few pieces of fruit in the crisper, some soy sauce, half an onion (actually a bunch of halves just waiting to be tossed out because they'd never gotten used), and a bowl of noodles. When I saw those noodles, I knew I had a starting point. I'd make a crispy noodle cake like they do in Chinese restaurants, and then it seemed to me that the apples and nectarines in the fruit drawer could make a nice slaw. It's not a combination I would have come up with all on my own, but they were there and they spoke to me. Moral of the story: listen to your fridge.

IT'S MONDAY! WHAT'S FOR DINNER?

FOR THE NOODLE PANCAKE

2 tablespoons extra virgin olive oil

½ onion, sliced

Salt

2 eggs

Pepper

½ pound leftover cooked pasta noodles

2 tablespoons bread crumbs

3 scallions, chopped

1 2-inch ginger, julienned

½ serrano chili, minced

2 tablespoons soy sauce

2 tablespoons rice wine vinegar

TO MAKE THE NOODLE PANCAKE

1. Preheat the oven to 350 °F.

2. In a large ovenproof, nonstick skillet, heat the olive oil to medium heat and add the onion to sauté. Season with salt, and cook until soft, about 4 minutes.

3. Whisk the eggs gently in a large bowl, and season with salt and pepper to taste. Add the pasta to the eggs, along with the sauteed onion and bread crumbs. Add in the rest of the pancake ingredients and toss to coat.

4. Add the contents of the bowl to the large skillet and cook over medium-high heat. Cook until golden and crispy on the bottom, then place in the oven for 10 minutes. Take out of the oven and flip. Place back into the oven for 5 more minutes, until the other side is browned.

FOR THE SPICY
FRUIT SLAW

2 nectarines, peaches, or
plums, pitted and julienned

2 Granny Smith
apples, julienned

½ serrano chili, sliced

2 tablespoons almonds,
toasted and chopped

2 jarred cherry
peppers, chopped

2 scallions, sliced

2 tablespoons capers

¼ cup basil, chiffonade

Juice of 1 lime

2 tablespoons rice
wine vinegar

1 tablespoon soy sauce

Kosher salt

Freshly ground black pepper

TO MAKE THE SPICY FRUIT SLAW

5. Place the thinly sliced nectarines, apples, and serrano chili in a medium bowl. Add the rest of the ingredients and toss with the vinegar and soy. Season with salt and pepper.

6. Plate the noodle pancake on a large platter and top with the spicy fruit slaw.

Grilled Chicken Thighs with Watermelon Feta Salad

SERVES 4 WITH LEFTOVERS, OR 8 | **COOK TIME: 10 MINUTES**

PREP TIME: 5–10 MINUTES | **INACTIVE PREP TIME: 2–4 HOURS** | **COST: $**

Easy

I love this easy dish because of its enticing blend of sweet, salty, and savory: watermelon salad with feta—a classic Greek combo. My mom made it for us all the time, and we always ate the whole thing. Also from my Greek heritage: marinating in yogurt, then grilling. We do it with chicken or lamb for a tangy crust. The spices, especially the chipotle, are a bit of a New World mash-up, but the inspiration is Greek. Daphne, who is an endless source of nutritional wisdom, informed us that watermelon is a sexy food because it sends a jolt of blood to—ahem—the right places. I knew there was a reason people love watermelon. If there are any thighs left over—they are the makings of a wonderful Chicken Club (page 47).

FOR THE CHICKEN

8 boneless, skin-on chicken thighs

Kosher salt

1 cup Greek yogurt

Zest and juice of 1 orange

1 tablespoon whole coriander seeds, toasted and ground

2 teaspoons whole cumin seeds, toasted and ground

2 teaspoons chipotle powder

TO MAKE THE CHICKEN

1. Season the thighs liberally with salt. In a gallon-sized zip-top bag, combine the yogurt, orange zest and juice, coriander, cumin, and chipotle. Season with salt. Add the chicken, turn to coat, and refrigerate for 2–4 hours, or put together before work and let marinate until it's time to make dinner!

2. Let the chicken come to room temperature for 30 minutes before grilling.

3. Meanwhile, heat a charcoal or gas grill to medium.

4. Remove the chicken from the bag, wiping off and discarding any excess marinade. Put the chicken on the grill, skin side down, and cover with the lid. Grill for 4–6 minutes, open the lid, and flip the chicken. Put the lid back on, and grill for 5 minutes, until the chicken reaches an internal temp of 160 °F. If using a grill pan, cook the chicken about 5 minutes per side, until cooked in the center. Remove from the grill and let rest while you put the salad together.

FOR THE WATERMELON FETA SALAD

½ small to medium seedless watermelon, cubed

1 cup Greek feta, crumbled

¼ cup mint leaves, torn

3 scallions, sliced

1 clove garlic, grated or finely minced

3 tablespoons red wine vinegar

¼ cup extra virgin olive oil, plus more for garnish

Pepper, to taste

TO MAKE THE WATERMELON FETA SALAD

5. Combine the watermelon, feta, mint, scallions, and garlic in a bowl. Whisk together the red wine vinegar and olive oil. Pour over the salad, season with pepper, and toss to coat.

6. Plate the chicken with a side of watermelon feta salad, and finish with a drizzle of olive oil for garnish.

Grilled Chicken Club

2 FER

| SERVES 4 | COOK TIME: 10 MINUTES | PREP TIME: 10 MINUTES | COST: $ |

Easy

When it comes to chicken leftovers, I'm a thigh man. No insult meant to breasts, which are a fine body part, but the thigh is way more succulent. When we made this on the show, Leo Howard from the Disney show *Kickin' It* was my helper. It turns out this guy is more than a great young martial arts expert and comic actor. He can actually cook! When I asked him how he came to be so comfortable in the kitchen, he came up with one of the best answers: "My parents didn't cook, and I was like, 'Okay, I've got to figure out how to do something to feed myself.'" Molto practical, as we say in Italy.

As for the sandwich, bacon and avocado can make anything taste good, but if you want to go from good to great, make your own condiments instead of reaching for that old jar of ketchup or mayo in the fridge. This lime and jalapeño aioli makes everything taste so fresh and zippy. It's also great with leftover fish.

4 boneless, skin-on chicken thighs

Kosher salt

Freshly cracked black pepper

Olive oil, to brush the grill

8 tablespoons Jalapeño Aioli (recipe follows)

4 kaiser rolls, split and toasted

1 avocado, sliced

10 slices cooked bacon

2 cups arugula

FOR THE JALAPEÑO AIOLI

2 egg yolks

1 jalapeño, seeded, deveined, and minced very finely

Zest and juice of 1 lime

Salt, to taste

Pepper, to taste

1 cup extra virgin olive oil

1. Preheat a grill or grill pan to medium-high heat.

2. Season the chicken thighs with salt and pepper. Brush the grill or grill pan with the olive oil, and place the chicken thighs, skin side down, on the grill. Grill for 4–6 minutes, or until the skin releases easily, and flip and cook another 5 minutes, until the chicken is cooked through.

3. Spread 2 tablespoons of the aioli on the cut side of the top half of the kaiser roll. Stack the chicken, avocado, bacon, and arugula on the bottom half of the roll, and then sandwich with the top.

TO MAKE THE JALAPEÑO AIOLI

4. Place the egg yolks, jalapeño, lime zest, lime juice, salt, and pepper in a large bowl or the bowl of a food processor. Mix just to combine. Slowly add the olive oil until emulsified. Yields ½ cup. This will keep in the fridge for up to a week.

Chicken Marsala

SERVES 4 | COOK TIME: 5 MINUTES | PREP TIME: 10 MINUTES | COST: $

Easy

Since I started doing 5-in-5s on the show (5 ingredients in 5 minutes), viewers have been writing me, asking for tips for quick meals, like this tweet:

YO CHEF SYMON! NEED AN URGENT TIP…I HAVE CHICKEN THIGHS, BUT NOT MUCH TIME OR PATIENCE! HELP!

My answer is the Italian classic Chicken Marsala—only instead of boneless breast, which can get kind of dry, I use boneless thighs because they have nice juicy dark meat. They need to be pounded thin so that they cook quickly. Then when the chicken, mushrooms, and shallots are all cooked, I deglaze the pan with a little Marsala wine and water. You will be surprised how full flavored a sauce can be with just a few ingredients.

4 boneless, skinless chicken thighs, pounded thin

Salt, to taste

Pepper, to taste

Flour, for dredging

5 tablespoons olive oil

2 shallots, thinly sliced

1 pound cremini or white mushrooms, thinly sliced

1 cup Marsala wine

3 tablespoons butter, cubed

⅓ cup parsley, chopped, for garnish

1. Heat a large sauté pan over medium-high heat.

2. Season the chicken thighs with salt and pepper. Dip the chicken in flour on both sides, and shake off the excess flour.

3. Add the olive oil to the hot pan and add the chicken thighs. Cook for 2 minutes on each side, until golden brown and cooked through, and set aside.

4. Add the shallots and mushrooms to the pan. Season with salt and pepper. Cook over medium-high heat, letting the mushrooms brown. Once they have released all their liquid, and it has cooked off, add the Marsala wine. Reduce for a minute, cooking off the wine, then stir in the butter to emulsify. If the sauce is too thick, add a splash of water to loosen.

5. Place the chicken thighs onto a platter and cover with the Marsala mushrooms. Garnish with the chopped parsley.

Chicken Saltimbocca with Capers and Grapefruit

SERVES 6 | COOK TIME: 15 MINUTES | PREP TIME: 20 MINUTES | COST: $

Moderate

I have always loved any recipe with the word *saltimbocca*, which is Italian for "jumps in your mouth." I want something that is so good that it seems to jump onto my fork and then somersaults into my mouth. The traditional saltimbocca is made with veal scallops, prosciutto, and cheese. For my chicken dish, my aim was to pair the food with the wine. Now you know how wine experts are always using phrases like "it has delicious notes of grapefruit" or "it is green and grassy." Instead of taking that as a figure of speech, last night, when I opened a bottle of Pinot Grigio that was described in exactly those terms, I said to myself, "Mario, make something with grapefruit and, for the green part, some green olives." And that's exactly what I did. You can too. Moral of the story: let all that blah blah blah on the wine label give you some ideas on flavors to combine in your next recipe.

1 grapefruit

6 boneless, skin-on chicken thighs, pounded thin

Salt

Pepper

6 tablespoons Parmigiano-Reggiano

6 slices prosciutto

6 toothpicks

All-purpose flour, for dredging

Olive oil, for the pan

2 tablespoons butter

3 cloves garlic, minced

4 tablespoons capers

10 large green olives, cut into quarters

1 cup dry white wine

1. Peel and segment the grapefruit and reserve all the juices. Cut the segments into thirds and set aside.

2. Place a large sauté pan over medium-high heat.

3. Season the chicken thighs with salt and pepper, and place skin side down on a cutting board. Grate Parmigiano-Reggiano evenly on the flesh side of the chicken, and press a piece of prosciutto on top. Fold the thigh in half (so the skin is on the outside), and secure with a toothpick. Dredge in flour and shake off the excess. Repeat with the remaining thighs.

4. Add about 3 tablespoons of olive oil to the pan, and then add the chicken thighs. Work in batches so as not to overcrowd the pan, adding more oil as needed. Brown on each side until golden, 3–4 minutes per side.

5. Drain off the excess oil, leaving about 2 tablespoons in the pan. Add in the butter. Toss in the garlic, capers, and olives. Sauté for 1 minute. Pour in the wine, and bring to a boil. Cook for 30 seconds, and then add

1 cup chicken stock

Juice of 1 lemon

3 tablespoons flat-leaf parsley, chopped

1 endive, sliced ½ inch thick

in the reserved grapefruit juice. Add the chicken stock and swirl to emulsify. Simmer until thick.

6. Take the pan off the heat and adjust the seasoning with the lemon juice, salt, and pepper. Stir in the parsley, endive, and segmented grapefruit. Remove the chicken to a platter along with the sauce.

Drew Barrymore excitedly awaits instructions from Mario.

Hot Sauce Fried Chicken

SERVES 6 TO 8　　COOK TIME: 12–24 MINUTES　　PREP TIME: 15 MINUTES

INACTIVE PREP TIME: UP TO 12 HOURS　　COST: $

Easy

Some people dream about flying to the moon or winning an Oscar or—even better—winning the lottery! Me? I dream about bacon, as in "How can I include bacon in a dish because I know bacon makes things better?" And then, in a flash of bacon-ized inspiration one night, I thought of one of the all-time crunchiest, crispiest comfort foods—fried chicken. Before I get to the bacon part, I start by marinating my chicken in my favorite hot sauce. Then, when I am ready to rock in front of the skillet, I cook some bacon in my frying oil to add smoky, salty flavor right out of the gate. Just before serving, I top the chicken with more hot sauce, chopped bacon, and scallions. Afterward, I'm ready for a nap and, most likely, another bacon-infused dream.

3 pounds chicken thighs and legs

Kosher salt

Freshly ground black pepper

1 bottle hot sauce

3 cups buttermilk

3 cups flour, for dredging

Vegetable oil, for deep-frying

½ pound bacon

2 scallions, chopped

1. If you have time, start this recipe the night before. Season the chicken pieces generously with salt and pepper. Place the chicken in a resealable bag and pour in the hot sauce. Squeeze out the excess air, and place the bag in a casserole dish (in case the bag leaks). Massage the chicken in the bag, ensuring all the pieces are coated. Marinate in the fridge overnight or as long as you can.

2. Remove the chicken from the marinade and discard the hot sauce. Pour the buttermilk in a shallow container, and place the flour in a shallow container as well. Season the flour with salt and pepper.

3. Set up a resting rack on a sheet tray. Dip the chicken pieces in the buttermilk, and then dredge them in flour and set aside.

4. Preheat a large pot of vegetable oil to 350 °F. Place the bacon in the oil to render. Remove the bacon, once crisp, to a paper towel–lined plate. Once cool, chop.

5. Fry the chicken in batches until golden brown, about 10–12 minutes per batch. Remove the chicken with a slotted spoon to a paper towel–lined plate. Sprinkle with salt immediately. Serve topped with the chopped bacon and scallions.

Dorm Room Chicken Chili

SERVES 4 TO 6 | COOK TIME: 35–40 MINUTES | PREP TIME: 10 MINUTES | COST: $

Easy

Remember those days of microwaved ramen and leftover pizza? I sure do. It's how I put on scads of weight when I started college. As I learned from experience, though, you can eat well, conveniently, and cheaply even on a college student's budget. This chili lops off about 500 calories from traditional chili recipes, but it is still loaded with flavor. Another great thing about it is once you make it, you've got a potful that's good for a few meals throughout the week.

2 tablespoons canola oil

1 large yellow onion, chopped

4 cloves garlic, smashed

4 boneless, skinless chicken breasts, diced

Salt

Pepper

2 medium zucchini, diced

1 8-ounce bag frozen corn, thawed

2 tablespoons tomato paste

1 16-ounce can of roasted tomatoes, chopped

¼ cup chili powder

2–3 tablespoons cumin

2 bay leaves

2 tablespoons oregano

1 chipotle pepper in adobo sauce, chopped

2 15-ounce cans kidney beans, drained and rinsed

1 15-ounce can black beans, drained and rinsed

1 12-ounce bottle beer

1 cup vegetable stock

Shredded Cheddar, to serve

1 avocado, chopped, to serve

Fresh lime juice, to serve

Sour cream, to serve

1. In a large heavy pot, heat the oil over medium-high heat. Add the onion and garlic, and sauté until translucent. Season the chicken with salt and pepper, and add to the pan, cooking for 3 more minutes.

2. Add the zucchini and corn, and sauté for 5 minutes, stirring occasionally. Add the tomato paste and the roasted tomatoes, including the juice. Then add salt, pepper, and all the herbs and spices. Stir well. Add the chipotle pepper and beans.

3. Add the beer and vegetable stock until liquid covers all ingredients in the pot. Bring to a boil, and then reduce heat to medium-low. Simmer for a half hour, stirring occasionally. Remove from the heat, and adjust seasonings to taste.

4. Ladle into bowls and serve with shredded Cheddar, chopped avocado, and fresh lime juice or sour cream.

NOTE: This is great made in a slow cooker too!

60-Second Guacamole

Easy

SERVES 4 TO 6 | PREP TIME: 60 SECONDS | COST: $

On a busy weeknight, if you are looking for something to add some flavor and a little spiciness to fish, poultry, or pork, think guacamole. In Mexico, the birthplace of guacamole, they use cilantro, but I've found that not everyone loves cilantro. *No problema*, I make this one with oregano. The neat thing is that I can make this recipe in 60 seconds. Of course, when I did it on the show, I had help from Mario and Michael. Hey, it still tastes great if you don't happen to have Mario or Michael hanging around your kitchen. If it takes you 120 seconds to make, no big deal. The point is, it's quick, easy, creamy, spicy, and wonderful. Be sure to try with Dorm Room Chicken Chili (page 52).

3 sprigs fresh oregano, chopped

3 ripe avocados, pitted and cubed

3 scallions, thinly sliced

Juice of 2 limes, to taste

Salt, to taste

Freshly ground pepper, to taste

Hot sauce, to taste

1. Place all the ingredients in a bowl, and mash together with a fork or potato masher to the desired texture. Check the seasonings and enjoy. If you are not planning to eat right away, store in an airtight container covered with a piece of plastic wrap rubbed with a little lime juice. This will keep the guacamole from turning brown.

Carla brings Paula Abdul in for a hug.

Grilled Skirt Steak with Cauliflower Hash

SERVES 4 TO 6 | COOK TIME: 15–20 MINUTES | PREP TIME: 15 MINUTES | COST: $

Easy

Hash is one of those things everyone likes the minute you say the word. "Hot Salad," which is what hash essentially is, doesn't sound as laid-back and home-cooking-ish as hash. In the wintertime, when fresh vegetables are in short supply, some late-season cauliflower, potatoes, and kale, plus some take-no-prisoners seasoning, fits the bill for comfort food that is nourishing but not super fattening. The full, funky flavor of skirt steak stands up well to the hearty vegetables, but lamb, pork, salmon, or shrimp also fit the bill. It's also good all on its own as a vegetarian meal. If you don't finish all that steak, make yourself a Grilled Skirt Steak Sandwich with Charred Corn Mustard (page 57).

½ pound new potatoes, sliced into ½-inch-thick coins

2 pounds skirt steak

Salt

Freshly ground pepper

¼ cup olive oil, plus more to brush the grill

2 tablespoons butter

½ onion, peeled and diced

½ head cauliflower, cut into florets

1 bunch kale, stemmed and cut into ribbons

2 cloves garlic, sliced

1 teaspoon red chili flakes

1 tablespoon fresh rosemary (leaves only), chopped

2 tablespoons parsley (leaves only), chopped

3 tablespoons red wine vinegar

1. Blanch the potatoes in a pot of boiling salted water for 3–4 minutes. Strain and set aside.

2. Preheat a grill or grill pan to medium-high heat.

3. Season the steak generously with salt and pepper. Brush the grill with olive oil. Grill the steak for 4–5 minutes per side, for medium rare, and set aside to rest.

4. In a large skillet or sauté pan, heat the butter and 2 tablespoons of the extra virgin olive oil over medium-high heat. Add the onion and potatoes in a single even layer. Cook until the potatoes have crisped, and then flip to crisp on other side, about 4 minutes per side.

5. Add the cauliflower and cook, tossing to coat and soften the cauliflower. Add the kale and garlic, and toss so the kale begins to wilt. Add the red chili flakes, rosemary, and parsley. Toss to combine, and finish the dish with the red wine vinegar and a drizzle of olive oil. Transfer to a platter to serve alongside the steak.

Grilled Skirt Steak Sandwich with Charred Corn Mustard

MAKES 4 SANDWICHES | COOK TIME: 10 MINUTES | PREP TIME: 15 MINUTES

COST: $

Moderate

Skirt steak is one of my favorite cuts, both for its deliciousness and the fact that you can serve it well done or medium rare and it is juicy and full flavored either way. Serve on a bun with lettuce and tomato, and you have got a super sandwich. But you know I'm not going to leave it at that. You see, I live in a world where thinking up new condiments is how I keep cooking and, more important, eating more interestingly. Charring the corn develops its inner sweetness and gives a little bit of a bitter edge for contrast. We all like contrast, right, sports fans? And I am a major fan of mustard and vinaigrette. Apparently, so are my cast mates on *The Chew*. Clinton, in particular, took the biggest single bite out of a sandwich that anyone has ever taken in the history of sandwichdom. That's his way of saying *this is the real deal*!

FOR THE SKIRT STEAK

1 pound skirt steak

Salt

Freshly ground pepper

Extra virgin olive oil, to brush the grill

FOR THE CHARRED CORN MUSTARD

1 tablespoon extra virgin olive oil, plus more to brush the grill and for drizzling

2 ears corn, shucked

1 onion, sliced

Salt

Freshly ground pepper

1 tablespoon Dijon mustard

TO MAKE THE SKIRT STEAK

1. Heat a grill or grill pan to medium-high heat.

2. Season the skirt steak generously on both sides with salt and freshly ground pepper. Brush the grill or the grill pan with extra virgin olive oil. Grill the steak for 5 minutes per side, for medium rare. Allow the steak to rest for 10 minutes before slicing.

NOTE: If using leftover steak, just heat through.

TO MAKE THE CHARRED CORN MUSTARD

3. Preheat a grill to medium-high heat. Brush with olive oil. Grill the ears of corn until charred in places, about 5 minutes, rotating throughout the cooking process. Cut the corn off the cob into a bowl.

4. In a sauté pan over low heat, heat 1 tablespoon of olive oil. Add the onion, and season with salt and pepper. Cook about 20 minutes, until the onions are caramelized. Add the caramelized onions to the corn.

QUICK AND EASY MEALS TO MAKE ON BUSY WEEKNIGHTS

1 head romaine lettuce, washed and thinly sliced

2 tablespoons extra virgin olive oil

Zest and juice of 1 lemon

4 kaiser rolls, split, or 1 baguette, sliced

2 beefsteak tomatoes, sliced

5. Add the Dijon mustard to the bowl with the corn and onion, season with salt and freshly ground pepper, and mix well.

TO ASSEMBLE

6. Toss the romaine in 2 tablespoons of the olive oil and the zest and juice of the lemon.

7. Place a few slices of the steak onto each of the kaiser rolls or piece of baguette. Top with some shredded romaine, a big scoop of the corn mustard, and a slice of beefsteak tomato. Season the sandwiches with salt and pepper, and drizzle with extra virgin olive oil.

Slice it the other way

Skirt steak delivers its full juicy flavor when you carve it against the grain.

Pan-Seared Strip Steak with Mushrooms & Caramelized Onions

SERVES 2 TO 4 | COOK TIME: 15–20 MINUTES | PREP TIME: 10 MINUTES | COST: $$

Easy

These ingredients go so well together that you might think that what we have here is a classic recipe. Actually, it came from one of our Fridge Raider segments, where I looked inside an average person's refrigerator and pantry shelves to see how I could make a great piece of steak even greater. The answer? Bacon, beer, onions, garlic, and sour cream, with a little parsley on top. Food scientists will tell you that bacon, steak, and mushrooms are high in that mysterious flavor called umami. If you don't know what that word means, just remember that in the original Japanese, *umami* means "yummy."

2 8-ounce strip steaks

Salt, to taste

Pepper, to taste

3 tablespoons of olive oil, plus more for drizzling

¼ pound bacon, sliced ½ inch thick

1 8-ounce container of button mushrooms, sliced ¼ inch thick

½ onion, thinly sliced

2 cloves garlic, finely minced

½ of 1 12-ounce can of beer

¼ cup sour cream

¼ cup parsley, leaves picked

1. Take the strip steaks out of the fridge 30 minutes prior to use. Season the steaks generously with salt and pepper, and drizzle with olive oil.

2. Heat a medium-sized cast-iron pan over medium-high heat. Put the steaks in the cast-iron pan and cook 3–4 minutes on each side, or until deep golden brown. Take the steaks out of the pan and let rest for at least 10 minutes.

3. In the same pan, add about 3 tablespoons of olive oil and the bacon. Let crisp for 2–3 minutes. Add the mushrooms and toss to coat. Let brown for another 2–3 minutes. Add the onion and garlic, and season everything with salt and pepper. Toss and cook for 1–2 minutes longer, until the onions begin to wilt. Add the beer and bring to a simmer. Reduce by half.

4. Off the heat, add the sour cream and stir to emulsify. Taste and adjust for seasoning. Add the parsley, stir to incorporate.

5. When the steak has rested, slice and plate. Pour the mushroom sauce over the steak and serve.

Fight that flame!

A beautifully cooked steak wants a very hot pan. It also wants some oil to keep it from sticking to the pan. I oil the steak instead of the pan because oil in a pan that hot is a recipe for smoke and fire.

QUICK AND EASY MEALS TO MAKE ON BUSY WEEKNIGHTS

Pork Tenderloin Scallopini

2 FER

Easy

A scallopini is a thin, pounded piece of meat, usually from the tenderloin, but it can also be done with chicken breast. The cool thing about it is that you can cook it quickly. This recipe, which I made in 5 minutes on the show, is absolutely crammed with flavor. Crispy, caramelized pork, diced ham, apples, and a rich sauce of apple cider, vinegar, butter, and sage. It's pretty hard to miss with that combo. Don't worry if a little bit of flour sticks to the bottom of the pan; those are the tasty bits that'll make for a super flavorful sauce. And if you don't finish all that pork, put on your Two-Fer thinking cap, turn the page, and use it with Daphne's fried rice.

1–1½ pounds pork tenderloin, cut into 1-inch-thick medallions and pounded thin

Salt, to taste

Pepper, to taste

Flour, for dredging

6 tablespoons olive oil

¼ pound ham steak

3 Granny Smith apples

1 cup apple cider

3 tablespoons butter

2 tablespoons apple cider vinegar

5 sage leaves, plus more for garnish

1. Heat a large sauté pan over medium-high heat.

2. Season the thinly pounded pork with salt and pepper. Dredge in the flour, shaking off any excess. Add 3 tablespoons of the oil to each pan. Carefully lay the pork in the pan and cook for 2 minutes on each side, then remove to a platter and lightly cover to keep warm.

3. Dice the ham into medium-sized pieces. Add the ham to the pan and allow to cook for 1 minute, browning slightly.

4. Dice the apples and add to the ham. Cook for another minute, then add the apple cider. Reduce for 2 minutes, then add the butter. Stir to combine. Finish with the apple cider vinegar and the sage leaves. Adjust seasoning. Nestle the pork back into the sauce to warm through.

5. Plate the pork medallions and top with the sauce. Garnish with sage leaves.

Oz Family Fried Rice

SERVES 4 | COOK TIME: 7–10 MINUTES | PREP TIME: 15 MINUTES | COST: $

Easy

Michael's Pork Tenderloin Scallopini is really great, but sometimes even the great Michael's food doesn't get all gobbled up—and you have some leftovers. In the Oz family, leftovers often meant we got to make one of my favorite dishes, Oz Family Fried Rice, which basically is whatever you have in the fridge crisped up with brown rice and amped up with flavor boosters like ginger, garlic, soy, and spicy Sriracha. When my vegetarian mom made it with us on our Mother's Day show, she made it with tofu, but you can do it with pork, chicken, beef . . . whatever. And like my mom said, if you have finicky kids, chances are they're going to like it because it reminds them of fried rice that you get in a Chinese restaurant. There probably isn't a kid on the planet who doesn't love Chinese restaurant fried rice.

3 tablespoons coconut oil

1 onion, diced

½ cup leftover pork, cubed

2 carrots, peeled and diced

6 shiitake mushrooms, stems removed, sliced

1 cup snow peas, stemmed

4 scallions, chopped

2 cloves garlic, minced

2 tablespoons fresh ginger, peeled and grated

2 tablespoons soy sauce

1 tablespoon sesame oil

2 tablespoons rice vinegar

1 teaspoon hot sauce

Kosher salt, to taste

Freshly cracked black pepper, to taste

1 cup cooked rice (I prefer short grain brown rice)

2 eggs, beaten

1 bunch fresh cilantro (leaves only)

1. In a large cast-iron skillet, heat 2 tablespoons coconut oil over high heat. Stir in the onion and cook for 1 minute. Stir in the pork, and cook until golden brown, about 2 minutes.

2. Stir in the carrots, mushrooms, snow peas, scallions, garlic, and ginger, and cook for 2 minutes. In a small bowl, whisk together the soy sauce, sesame oil, rice vinegar, and hot sauce. Add to the pan and stir to coat the vegetables. Season to taste with salt and pepper.

3. Stir in the cooked brown rice and mix thoroughly.

4. In a separate nonstick pan, scramble the eggs in the remaining 1 tablespoon coconut oil and stir into the fried rice, breaking up the eggs as you stir. Adjust the seasoning and serve with the cilantro.

Daphne and Dr. Oz team up to show the *Chew* crew their family favorites.

MEXICAN TORTA | BACON PANCAKES WITH MAPLE BOURBON BUTTER | FRIED CORNISH HENS AND PAN D'ORO FRENCH TOAST | HEIRLOOM TOMATO AND RICOTTA TART

BREAKFAST + DINNER = "BRINNER!"

"**WE ALL KNOW** that when you combine the idea of breakfast and lunch, you get brunch. But many Americans love having breakfast for dinner, or, as we like to call it, "Brinner." It makes so much sense during the work week. Are you too busy to shop? *No problema.* You probably have milk, eggs, cheese, flour, and some veggies in the fridge and on your pantry shelves right now. You say you don't have a lot of time to spend cooking? Well, who does in the morning when you're throwing breakfast together? Breakfasts…and Brinners…like the **DELICIOUS DISHES** in this section, come together quickly, and they are full of satisfying and fulfilling ingredients to fuel you and ward off the hunger pangs until snack time. And speaking of combining breakfast with other food opportunities, do I hear any votes for **SNACKFAST?**"

—Clinton

Mexican Torta

SERVES 5 | COOK TIME: 5 MINUTES | PREP TIME: 5 MINUTES | COST: $

Easy

Our favorite sandwich here in the USA just might be the good ol' BLT. South of the border, though, you might find the prize taken by the ACE—that's short for avocado, chorizo, and egg. For something so delicious, it's even more satisfying to know you can whip it up in almost no time. On the show—and with Daphne helping—I made it in 3 minutes. And just like the BLT, you can have this for breakfast, lunch, or a quick dinner.

2 tablespoons extra virgin olive oil

1 pound raw chorizo

6 eggs, beaten

Kosher salt

Freshly ground pepper

5 Mexican torta rolls

2 avocados, sliced

1 bunch cilantro, for garnish

1. Heat the olive oil in a skillet over medium-high heat. Add the chorizo and fry, breaking up as it browns. Add the eggs and stir into the sausage. Season generously with salt and pepper. Cook until the eggs form soft curds. Remove from the heat.

2. Split and toast the rolls, and spoon the chorizo-egg mixture onto each of the rolls. Top with slices of avocado, and garnish with the cilantro. Enjoy!

Scramble before you salt

Whenever I make scrambled eggs, I never season them first because the salt will pull water out of the eggs, and who likes watery eggs? Cook your eggs first; salt 'em afterward.

BREAKFAST + DINNER = "BRINNER!"

Bacon Pancakes with Maple Bourbon Butter

SERVES 6 | COOK TIME: 13–15 MINUTES | PREP TIME: 15 MINUTES | COST: $

Easy

Kids, young and old, love pancakes, grown-ups love bourbon, and everyone loves maple syrup, so I've put together a heavenly combination of these basic food groups. "Aha," you say, "you've left out one important food group: the bacon group!" Not to worry. I would no more think of skipping the bacon with this than I would make a Margarita without the tequila.

FOR THE PANCAKES

8 slices bacon

2 cups all-purpose flour

2 teaspoons baking powder

1 teaspoon baking soda

½ teaspoon salt

3 tablespoons sugar

3 cups buttermilk

4 tablespoons melted butter, slightly cooled

2 large eggs, lightly beaten

FOR THE SYRUP

2 tablespoons bourbon

1 cup maple syrup

3 tablespoons butter

1. On a griddle over medium-high heat, fry the bacon until crispy, and then transfer to a paper towel–lined plate.

2. Lower the heat to medium, and remove any excess bacon fat. You want there to be a thin layer for the pancakes.

3. Chop the bacon into crumbs, and separate the crumbs into two piles

4. In a medium bowl, combine the flour, baking powder, baking soda, salt, and sugar, whisking together to thoroughly combine.

5. Add the buttermilk, butter, half of the bacon, and eggs, and whisk together until combined but still slightly lumpy.

6. In batches, drop spoonfuls of the batter onto the griddle, and cook until it bubbles, then flip over, about 3 minutes. Transfer to a warm oven while finishing the rest.

TO MAKE THE SYRUP

7. In a small saucepot, combine the bourbon and maple syrup, whisking together over medium heat until thoroughly combined and hot.

8. Cook until reduced slightly, about 5 minutes, then whisk in the butter, a tablespoon at a time, until fully incorporated.

9. Serve a stack of pancakes covered in syrup and sprinkled with the reserved bacon crumbs.

Fried Cornish Hens and Pan d'Oro French Toast

SERVES 6 | COOK TIME: 15–20 MINUTES | PREP TIME: 20 MINUTES

INACTIVE PREP TIME: 12 HOURS | COST: $

Moderate

MARIO: When I see the sign CHICKEN AND WAFFLES on any restaurant, you've got me right there. I usually pull right into the parking lot and order. I am rarely disappointed. I'm going to make mine with French toast—make that Italian toast, using the eggy holiday bread known in Verona as *pan d'oro*, and as *panettone* in Milan. This is a case of less is more, as in don't oversoak; you'll get bread that falls apart. Get it wet, but don't drown it.

MICHAEL: My contribution is spicy, crispy Cornish hen, using half the spices as a dry rub and adding the other half to season up the flour. Cornish hens are great for this because you can serve each person a whole half . . . or should I say half a whole bird? Less carving (and usually cursing) during prep than with a whole bird.

MARIO: And in honor of Daphne's decadent Maple Bourbon Butter, we're going to give the finished product a good dousing.

MICHAEL: My motto is, "Everything is better with bourbon."

FOR THE BUTTERMILK CORNISH HENS

2 tablespoons salt

1 tablespoon red chili flakes

1 tablespoon paprika

2 teaspoons cracked black pepper

2 teaspoons cayenne pepper

2 teaspoons coriander, toasted and crushed

2 quarts buttermilk

3 Cornish game hens, cut into halves

Vegetable oil, for deep-frying

2 cups flour

TO MAKE THE BUTTERMILK CORNISH HENS

1. In a small bowl, whisk the spices. Pour half into a roasting pan or 2 large Ziploc bags. Pour the buttermilk into the pan or bags. Add the Cornish hens, and move around to coat, making sure the flesh side is submerged in the mixture. Cover and place in the refrigerator overnight to marinate. If you can't find Cornish hens, buy chicken and cut into pieces.

2. Fill a Dutch oven two-thirds of the way full with vegetable oil, preheat to 350 °F.

3. Place the flour in a large baking dish and mix with the reserved spice mixture. Remove the hens from the marinade and discard the liquid. Dredge the hens in the flour mix, making sure to coat heavily.

4. Place the hens in the hot oil 2–3 at a time, depending on space. Overcrowding the pot will prevent

FOR THE PAN D'ORO FRENCH TOAST

5 eggs, beaten

1 cup heavy cream

Zest of 1 orange

1 teaspoon freshly grated nutmeg

1 pinch salt

2 pan d'oro cakes, sliced crosswise into 1½-inch pieces

FOR THE HONEY BOURBON SAUCE

½ cup honey

2 tablespoons bourbon

1 teaspoon paprika

Kosher salt

Freshly cracked black pepper

FOR THE CHIVE AND PARSLEY SALAD

Juice of 1 orange

2 tablespoons olive oil

Salt, to taste

Pepper, to taste

½ cup chives

½ cup parsley

the hens from achieving a crispy crust. Fry for 12–15 minutes, or until you achieve a dark golden crust and the hens are cooked through. Remove and allow to rest on a wire rack. Serve with the warm French toast and honey bourbon sauce.

TO MAKE THE PAN D'ORO FRENCH TOAST

5. Preheat a griddle over medium-high heat.

6. Mix together the eggs, cream, orange zest, nutmeg, and salt in a large baking dish. Place the cake in the mixture, flipping to fully coat.

7. Cook on the griddle for 1–2 minutes, flip, and continue to cook for another 1–2 minutes, or until lightly golden on both sides. Remove from the griddle and continue soaking and cooking the remaining pieces of cake.

TO MAKE THE HONEY BOURBON SAUCE

8. Whisk together all the ingredients, and adjust the seasoning with salt and pepper.

TO MAKE THE CHIVE AND PARSLEY SALAD

9. Whisk together the orange juice and olive oil, and season with salt and pepper. Toss the herbs in the vinaigrette, and then garnish the chicken and French toast with the salad.

Heirloom Tomato and Ricotta Tart

SERVES 6 | COOK TIME: 40–45 MINUTES | PREP TIME: 30 MINUTES

INACTIVE COOK TIME: 30 MINUTES | COST: $

Moderate

When you shop at farmers' markets, my advice is to let the produce speak to you. If it looks good, I buy it, and the recipe sort of builds as I shop. Apart from the fact that things taste better when they are just picked, they also tend to be cheaper. This is one of our favorite quick recipes for when tomatoes are in season. It couldn't be simpler: some dough, tomatoes, basil, ricotta, and seasoning. I like to play with heirloom tomatoes because they all look different, and they're beautiful and delicious.

FOR THE DOUGH
(CAN ALSO USE STORE-BOUGHT)

3 cups flour

Pinch of salt

1 tablespoon sugar

1½ sticks butter, cold

⅓ cup shortening

2–4 tablespoons ice water

FOR THE FILLING

½ pound heirloom tomatoes, sliced

½ bunch thyme, leaves only

2 cloves garlic, sliced

Cracked black pepper

Salt

8 ounces ricotta

¼ cup olive oil

TO MAKE THE DOUGH

1. Preheat the oven to 350 °F.

2. Place the flour, salt, and sugar into a food processor, and pulse to combine. Add the cold butter and shortening, and pulse until it resembles coarse crumbs. Add the water until a ball forms. Remove and wrap in plastic. Refrigerate for 30 minutes.

3. Roll out the dough, and press into a tart shell. Dock the dough by pricking all over the bottom. Press in a piece of foil and fill with beans or rice. "Blind" bake for 15 minutes. Remove from oven, discard beans, and let cool.

TO MAKE THE FILLING

4. In a large bowl, combine the tomatoes, thyme, garlic, a few cracks of black pepper, and a large pinch of salt, and toss to coat. Arrange the tomatoes on a baking sheet and roast for 20 minutes. Set aside to cool slightly.

5. Arrange the tomatoes in the blind-baked tart shell. Top with spoonfuls of the ricotta, drizzle with the olive oil, and bake for 15 minutes. Allow to cool slightly before serving.

DORM ROOM APPLE SNACK | POTATO CHIP COOKIES | MICROWAVE
CAKE | BANANA ALMOND GELATO | APPLE BROWN BETTY | GRILLED
PEACHES WITH ROSEMARY

SWEET TREATS
FOR THE MIDDLE
OF THE WEEK!

"WHO DOESN'T LOVE A LITTLE SWEET TREAT? Either right after dinner or a little bit before bedtime. It puts a little love in your tummy. In my book, nothing beats a homemade dessert. Think about Grandma: She didn't buy a cake at the store or a premade mix. She got into the kitchen and made it herself. Of course, you may not have the stay-at-home time that lots of grandmas had in the old days, but if you have the basics—**FLOUR, EGGS, BUTTER, SUGAR,** and a little of this and that—you can quickly and easily turn out desserts that beat anything that comes in a box, or a can, or shrink wrap. You can also control the amount of sugar to your taste, rather than the sugar overload in commercial desserts. These desserts will surely send you to bed with **SWEET DREAMS.** And there's no law that says you can't make enough dessert to have a few times during the week. In fact, I recommend it. **"**

—*Clinton*

Dorm Room Apple Snack

SERVES 4 | COOK TIME: 5 MINUTES | PREP TIME: 5 MINUTES | COST: $

Easy

If necessity is the mother of invention, my dorm room met all the motherhood requirements. There were plenty of healthy food choices, provided they were simple and didn't require a full kitchen. I discovered that there is so much you can do with a blender or, in this case, a microwave. Healthy fruit, nuts, oatmeal, and yogurt combine for a recipe that works as a light meal or a hearty dessert.

4 Empire or Granny Smith apples

2 tablespoons coconut oil

2 tablespoons brown sugar

2 tablespoons oats

1 tablespoon pecans, chopped

1 tablespoon dried cranberries

1 teaspoon cinnamon

¼ cup apple cider

4 tablespoons Greek yogurt

2 tablespoons honey

1. Using a melon baller or spoon, scoop out the core of each apple, leaving the bottom intact, to make room for the filling.

2. In a medium bowl, combine the coconut oil, brown sugar, oats, pecans, cranberries, and cinnamon. Stuff the apples with the filling. Place into a microwave-safe bowl and pour the apple cider into the bottom. Microwave on high for 5 minutes.

3. Serve with a dollop of Greek yogurt and drizzled with honey!

SWEET TREATS FOR THE MIDDLE OF THE WEEK!

Potato Chip Cookies

Easy

If you want to put the black and white cookie on a whole other level, look no further. This dessert is crunchy, crispy, and sweet, which just about covers my basic food groups. I adore it with potato chips, but let your imagination be your guide—if want to try pretzels or tortilla chips, I prom- ise they'll work too. One piece of advice: don't have Michael and Clinton standing alongside you while you mix the batter; they are liable to try to eat it all straight out of the bowl before you even get to make one cookie.

1 cup butter, softened

¾ cup granulated sugar

1¼ cups crushed potato chips

1 teaspoon vanilla

2 cups all-purpose flour

Confectioners' sugar, for dusting

1 cup chocolate chips

1. Preheat the oven to 350 °F.

2. With a hand mixer, cream the butter and sugar until fluffy. Reduce speed to low and add ¾ cup of the potato chips and mix until incorporated. Add the vanilla and mix until thoroughly combined. Add the flour and mix until just combined—do not overmix the dough!

3. Use a spoon to scoop small 1-inch balls of dough onto a lightly greased sheet pan, spacing them at least 2 inches apart. Dust each of the cookies with a bit of confectioners' sugar, and press flat.

4. Cook for 10–15 minutes, or until golden brown, and cool. Heat the chocolate chips in the microwave or a double boiler until melted, stirring often. Dip each of the cookies in melted chocolate. While the chocolate is still soft, roll the cookies in the remaining crushed potato chips. Allow to set before serving.

Carla gets her dance on in the audience!

Microwave Cake

SERVES 6 | COOK TIME: 2–4 MINUTES | PREP TIME: 5 MINUTES | COST: $

Easy

I came up with this recipe when I was getting ready for *Chopped All-Stars*, because I knew they'd throw a dessert at me that I'd really have to boogie through in a hurry. Well, how does 3 minutes sound for a gourmet chocolate dessert? Even though it's a pretty casual dessert, remember when you bake that it's important to be precise with your measurements. A roast beef is a lot more forgiving than a birthday cake. Most people think their microwave is just for reheating, but it can be a really good cooking tool, especially when you don't have a lot of extra time on your hands.

FOR THE CAKE

¾ **cup flour**

¾ **cup sugar**

Zest of ½ orange

1½ **teaspoons salt**

4 **eggs**

2 **sticks butter, softened**

1⅓ **cups chopped dark chocolate**

FOR THE WHIPPED CREAM

½ **cup heavy cream**

¼ **cup sugar**

Brandied cherries, for garnish

1. In a medium bowl, whisk together the flour, sugar, orange zest, salt, and eggs.

2. Melt the butter and chocolate together in a glass bowl in the microwave.

3. Whisk the melted chocolate mixture into the flour mixture just until combined. Divide the batter among 6 small coffee mugs. Microwave for 1–2 minutes on high and then check it. It should double in size like a soufflé. You may need to add an additional 1–2 minutes to the clock.

4. Meanwhile, whisk the heavy cream until frothy. Add the sugar and continue to whisk until medium stiff peaks form. Garnish the cakes with whipped cream and brandied cherries to serve.

Banana Almond Gelato

SERVES 4 | PREP TIME: 5 MINUTES | COST: $

Easy

4 large bananas

½ cup almond- or hazelnut-flavored liqueur

½ cup almond butter

Pinch of salt

Sliced almonds, for garnish

Amaretti cookies, to serve

1. Put the peeled and sliced bananas in a zip-top bag and place in the freezer until completely frozen.

2. In a blender, add the liqueur, almond butter, bananas, and a generous pinch of salt. Blend until completely smooth, about 2 minutes, or until everything is well combined and has the consistency of gelato.

3. Scoop out into bowls and serve with a sprinkle of almonds and amaretti cookies. Serve immediately.

IT'S MONDAY! WHAT'S FOR DINNER?

Apple Brown Betty

SERVES: 8 | COOK TIME: 30 MINUTES | PREP TIME: 10 MINUTES | COST: $

Moderate

What do you make when your guest on *The Chew* is a world-famous race car driver? Pretty simple—you make something quick, which is what we did when Danica Patrick came on the show. Danica is a pretty good cook too, having just made her family's Thanksgiving turkey on the day she visited us. My speedy recipe was one of my family's favorites: Apple Brown Betty. You can make it with yesterday's homemade or store-bought biscuits, if you are the kind of family that ever has any leftover biscuits, or you can use day-old bread or pound cake. The cookie spices give it some flavor high notes, and you can pretty much spice to taste, although I'd say go easy on the cloves because they can take over. "Who was Betty?" you ask. Beats me, but if I ever meet her, I'd give her a big Batali-sized hug.

6 medium Empire or Granny Smith apples

Zest and juice of ½ lemon

4 cups day-old biscuits (recipe follows), bread, or pound cake, cubed

½ cup cold butter

½ cup packed brown sugar

¼ teaspoon ground nutmeg (preferably freshly grated)

¼ teaspoon cloves

Vanilla ice cream, for serving

1. Preheat the oven to 300 °F.

2. Peel and core the apples, and cut them into ¾-inch slices. Transfer to a large bowl. Zest the lemon and squeeze the juice over the apple slices, and toss gently to cover the apples and keep them from browning before baking. Set aside.

3. On a 12-by-17-inch baking sheet, arrange the biscuit (or bread or cake) cubes in one layer and bake on the center rack of the oven until lightly brown, about 10 minutes.

4. Meanwhile, melt the butter in a small saucepan. When the biscuit cubes are done, transfer them to a large bowl, pour half of the melted butter into the bowl, and toss. Set aside.

5. Add the sugar, nutmeg, and cloves to the apples, and gently toss together.

SWEET TREATS FOR THE MIDDLE OF THE WEEK!

Danica Patrick dives in to the Brown Betty prep work.

6. Raise the oven temperature to 375 °F. Place one-third of the toasted biscuit cubes on the bottom of a 9-inch square baking dish. Top with half the apple slices, followed by another third of the biscuit cubes and then the remaining apples. Top the apples with the remaining biscuit cubes. Pour the remaining butter over everything. Bake on the center rack for 30 minutes, until the top is nicely browned.

7. Remove from the heat and serve warm with vanilla ice cream.

FOR THE BISCUITS

2 cups all-purpose flour

2 teaspoons salt

3 teaspoons baking powder

1 teaspoon baking soda

7 tablespoons cold
butter, cut into cubes

1¼ cups Greek yogurt

TO MAKE THE BISCUITS

1. Preheat the oven to 450 °F.

2. Combine the flour, salt, baking powder, and baking soda together in the bowl of a food processor, and pulse until combined. Add the butter, and pulse it a few more times, until the butter is thoroughly cut into the flour mixture.

3. Add the yogurt and pulse the mixture a couple more times to mix it in, just until the mixture forms a cohesive dough. Turn the dough out onto a floured surface and knead just until it comes together. If the dough is too sticky, add a little flour.

4. Press the dough to ¾-inch thickness and cut into rounds using a glass or biscuit cutter, pressing straight down without twisting. Place the biscuits on an ungreased parchment-lined sheet tray. Reshape the remaining dough and cut into biscuits. Bake for 7–9 minutes, or until the biscuits are light golden brown.

Grilled Peaches with Rosemary

| SERVES 5 | COOK TIME: 4–6 MINUTES | PREP TIME: 5 MINUTES | COST: $ |

Easy

I've never met anyone who didn't love grilled peaches. They are sooo good—beautiful, smooth texture and caramelized sweetness. You can do this recipe with many fruits (pineapple or cantaloupe, for example), but peaches get my vote. They go wonderfully with savory herbs, so I like to baste mine with honey and rosemary. You want firm peaches; in other words, they are not super-ripe yet. Save those for eating over the sink when the juice drips down your chin. My fellow Chewsters were totally turned on by this, each of them imagining their own special use for grilled peaches. Mario wanted to make these with grilled chicken. Go for it, Mario. Clinton said they would be nice on a menu with his Ginger Peach Margaritas. I'll drink to that. And Michael, whose thoughts also turn to meat, obsessed about a rib eye with grilled peaches and bleu cheese. I'm down with that too. But for me, they make a simple, yummy weeknight treat.

1 cup lavender honey

1 sprig rosemary

5 peaches, halved and pitted

Olive oil, for drizzling and the grill

1 pint vanilla ice cream, to serve

1. Heat a grill or grill pan over medium-high heat.

2. In a small saucepot, add the honey and rosemary, and simmer for 2–3 minutes over medium heat.

3. Lightly drizzle the peach halves with olive oil. Oil the grill well. Place the peaches cut side down on the grill and cook for 2–3 minutes.

4. Flip the peaches and brush on the warmed honey. Remove once the peaches are warm through.

5. To serve, top with a scoop of ice cream and an extra drizzle of honey.

SWEET TREATS FOR THE MIDDLE OF THE WEEK!

TGIF
(AND SATURDAY, SUNDAY, AND
OTHER
GOOD TIMES)

FRIDAY: PIZZA NIGHT, COCKTAIL PARTY

SATURDAY: BIRTHDAY PARTIES,

SATURDAY NIGHT SPECIALS, DATE NIGHT

SUNDAY: SIT-DOWNS

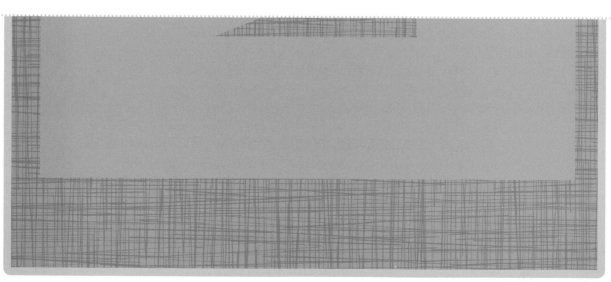

WHEN IT'S TIME TO CHILL OUT or blow it up, *The Chew* is here to help you on special days that put more fun in your food life. We've come up with some **GREAT MEALS** for cocktail parties, birthday parties, brunch, and the anchor of the week in everyone's memory . . . Sunday dinner with the family. Do you want some thoughts about how to put together a birthday menu? We can help you take care of almost everything (except the blowing-out-the-candle part—we think you can handle that without our two cents). Got a hot date? A blind date? Or just a plain good relationship date? Try these recipes and you are sure to get to first base. Need to set your sights on **SOMETHING THAT SATISFIES** your inner chef when you have the time to get down and cook your buns off? Check out our Saturday Night Specials. Cocktail parties can be costly and chaotic, or you can take down the anxiety level and follow some advice from the masters of nibbles, noshes, quenching, and quaffing. These are the recipes that **BRING PEOPLE TOGETHER** when there are no clocks to punch, no tweets to Twitter, no bosses to butter up. You are on your own time. **ENJOY IT!**

—Clinton

SHANDY | THE C&C PIZZA FACTORY (AKA CLINTON'S AND CARLA'S GRILLED PIZZAS) | TARTE FLAMBÉ | CAKE POPS

PIZZA NIGHT

"**PRETTY MUCH EVERYONE LIKES PIZZA** and pretty much everyone can agree on one thing: they want it *their* way. With sausage or pepperoni? Some onions, olives, mushrooms, or fresh garlic? Red sauce or straight white cheese? One entertaining trick that keeps pizza preferences from escalating into a food fight is to make (or buy) the raw crust and then put toppings out so people can **MIX AND MATCH** to their hearts' content. I'm pretty sure that's how pineapple first wound up in a pizza crust along with some crisp bacon. I laughed when I first heard this un-Italian idea, but guess what? **IT'S DELICIOUS.** The neat thing about putting the toppings out is that when your guests choose their own, they are already halfway to liking it, and I'll take those odds any day. Throwing together a pizza party for a Friday night with the family or a casual game night with friends is **A GREAT WAY TO END THE WEEK** and kick off the weekend."

—Clinton

Shandy

SERVES 2 | PREP TIME: 2 MINUTES | COST: $

Easy

As the grandson of a hop farmer, I was raised on the belief that beer is the great thirst quencher. When I want to "special it up," I make a shandy, which is beer and soda. Of course I prefer Italian soda—in this case, bitter orange soda finished with a splash of Aperol, which is an orange liqueur. You'll be unappetizingly interested to know that its red color comes from a dye made from beetle legs. No lie. I know it sounds weird, but I swear it sure doesn't taste like beetle legs…I think.

1 12-ounce bottle light ale, chilled

1 16-ounce can Italian orange soda, chilled

Splash of Aperol

1. Pour half of the ale and soda into each of the glasses, and top with a splash of Aperol. Serve immediately.

The C&C Pizza Factory
(aka Clinton's and Carla's Grilled Pizzas)

Easy

SERVES 4 TO 6 | COOK TIME: 15–20 MINUTES | PREP TIME: 10 MINUTES | COST: $

CLINTON: These are our favorite pizzas that we make when we're at home. Mine is topped with mozzarella, ricotta, prosciutto, and arugula. I probably make it once a weekend. It's nice hot or at room temperature.

CARLA: Mine is more of a farmers' market topping. That way the vegetables are at their peak flavor and usually their cheapest price, which is a fine combination of virtues. Here we have zucchini, sweet, smoky cherry tomatoes, and crumbled feta, because "feta makes it betta." And different from Clinton's, I'm going to go full-frontal garlic. Love that taste!

Bench flour, for dusting the table

1 ball store-bought pizza dough

½ cup olive oil

FOR CLINTON'S VERSION

2 cloves garlic

1 pound fresh mozzarella ball, sliced

½ cup fresh ricotta

¼ pound prosciutto

2 cups arugula

1. Preheat the oven to 350 °F, and a grill or grill pan to high heat.

2. First cut the pizza dough in half and let it come to room temperature. Using your hands, or a rolling pin, on a floured surface stretch the pizza dough into an oval that will fit on your grill or grill pan, about ¼ inch thick, making sure there is no lip and the dough is evenly flat.

3. Oil your grill or grill pan, and brush the top of your pizza liberally with oil. Place the dough, oiled side down, on the grill or grill pan, and let it cook until it begins to crisp and char, 6–7 minutes. Flip the dough, and begin topping the char side. Reduce the heat to medium-high, or move off the flame, while adding the desired toppings.

TO MAKE CLINTON'S VERSION

1. Rub the crust with the garlic, and then top with the mozzarella and ricotta. Bake for 5 minutes, or until the cheese melts. Remove the pizza from the oven and top with the prosciutto and arugula.

FOR CARLA'S VERSION

½ cup crumbled feta

1 zucchini, sliced
into thin coins

1 clove garlic, minced

Zest and juice of 1 lemon

Salt

Pepper

½ cup cherry
tomatoes, halved

1 bunch dill

TO MAKE CARLA'S VERSION

1. Sprinkle the crust with the feta, and top with the zucchini, garlic, lemon zest and juice, salt, pepper, and cherry tomatoes. Bake for 5 minutes, or until the cheese melts. Remove the pizza from the oven and top with the fresh dill.

Go easy on the garlic

I like a hint of garlic, but I don't want the flavor of a whole clove. The solution is simple: Smash a clove and rub it over the hot grilled dough just like you would with bruschetta. It will pick up the oils and aroma of fresh garlic but won't overpower you.

Tarte Flambé

SERVES 8   COOK TIME: 40–45 MINUTES   PREP TIME: 30 MINUTES

INACTIVE PREP TIME: 45 MINUTES   COST: $

Moderate

This cheesy onion pizza is something that French bakers used to make to check the heat of their wood-burning ovens. If the dough caught on fire (flambé), the oven was too hot. Pretty clever, those French bakers. Even cleverer: this Italian American flambés his with some grappa or kirsch. I caution you, these get gobbled up quickly. Make enough.

FOR THE PIZZA DOUGH

¼ cup white wine

¾ cup warm water

1½ ounces yeast

1 tablespoon honey

1 teaspoon kosher salt

1 tablespoon extra virgin olive oil

3 cups all-purpose flour, plus more for dusting

FOR THE TOPPING

Salt

2 russet potatoes, peeled

½ pound slab bacon, cut into lardons

1 tablespoon olive oil

1 large Spanish onion, thinly sliced

3 cloves garlic, minced

4 ounces grappa (Italian brandy) or kirsch

½ cup crème fraîche

⅓ cup Emmentaler (Swiss cheese)

TO MAKE THE PIZZA DOUGH

1. Combine the wine, water, and yeast in a large bowl, and stir until dissolved. Add the honey, salt, and olive oil, and mix thoroughly. Start by adding 1 cup of the flour and make a wet paste. Add the remaining flour and incorporate.

2. Place the dough on a lightly floured board and knead for 2–3 minutes.

3. Place the dough in a lightly oiled bowl and cover with a towel. Let rise for 45 minutes.

TO MAKE THE TOPPING

4. Preheat the oven to 400 °F.

5. Bring a pot of water to a boil and season generously with salt. Cook the potatoes until they can be pierced easily with a knife, about 20–25 minutes. Remove from the water and let cool.

6. Place the bacon in a large cast-iron skillet. Add the olive oil so the bacon doesn't stick. Cook over medium-low heat until crisp and brown. Remove the bacon from the pan and set aside on paper towels.

7. Add the onions to the pan, and season with salt. Cook until golden brown. Add the minced garlic. Remove the pan from the heat and pour in the kirsch

⅓ cup ricotta

Freshly cracked black pepper

¼ cup chives, chopped

or grappa, and add the flame to the alcohol (carefully!). Return the pan to the heat and cook off the liquid. Let the onions take on color, cooking about 10 more minutes. Once the onions are caramelized, set them aside.

8. Cut the potatoes in ⅛-inch slices. Combine the crème fraîche, Emmentaler, and ricotta. Add about 20 turns of cracked black pepper and ½ teaspoon of salt.

9. Roll the dough out to the size of a cookie sheet or a half sheet pan. Lay the dough onto the pan and cook in the oven for about 4 minutes.

10. Remove the dough from the oven. Smear the dough with the cheese mixture, and shingle the potatoes in a pinwheel pattern. Then place an even layer of the caramelized onions on the potatoes and sprinkle the bacon on top of the onions. Top with a bit more grated Emmentaler.

11. Return the dough to the oven until the dough is crisp on the bottom and the toppings are bubbly, 6–8 minutes. Sprinkle with the chives and serve.

Cake Pops

SERVES 20 TO 24 | COOK TIME: 10–15 MINUTES | PREP TIME: 1 HOUR

INACTIVE PREP TIME: 30 MINUTES | COST: $

Moderate

If you are a cake baker/maker, then you know how you get all that leftover cake when you trim the baked layers of a circular cake. Don't throw it out! What you have is the makings of a great fork-free dessert. Break up the cake, mix it with some frosting or peanut butter or anything sweet and creamy to bind it, then shape it in a little ball, roll it in some crushed nuts or coconut or chocolate bits, put it on a stick, and you have some fine individual desserts that taste supremo but don't get your hands one bit dirty.

FOR THE BASE

1 recipe boxed white cake (your favorite recipe)

1½ cups butter (room temperature)

4½ cups powdered sugar

1 tablespoon vanilla extract

2 tablespoons milk

FOR THE PEANUT BUTTER CAKE POPS

¼ cup peanut butter

2 heaping teaspoons grape jelly

1 cup dark chocolate, melted

½ cup peanuts, chopped

FOR THE COCONUT CAKE POPS

½ cup desiccated coconut, plus more to roll through

½ teaspoon coconut extract

1 tablespoon coconut milk

1 cup dark chocolate, melted

TO MAKE THE BASE

1. Make the cake according to package instructions, allow it to cool, and then crumble. The cake should be crumbs. Split into 2 batches of 5 cups of crumbs.

2. Next make the buttercream frosting. Whip the butter and powdered sugar in an electric mixer on low. Once incorporated, add the vanilla and increase speed to high, mixing until fluffy. Add 1 tablespoon of milk at a time until you've reached your desired consistency. Should yield about 3 cups of buttercream. Split the buttercream into 2 batches.

TO MAKE THE PEANUT BUTTER CAKE POPS

3. Fold the peanut butter into one of the batches of buttercream frosting and set aside.

4. Combine the peanut butter frosting and jelly, and mix into one of the batches of cake crumbs. Roll the mixture into golf ball–sized balls. Insert a Popsicle stick into each ball, and place on a parchment-lined sheet pan. Repeat until all of the mixture has been used up, and then place in the freezer to set for 30 minutes.

5. Once they have chilled, dip the pops into the melted chocolate, and then roll the chocolate-dipped pops

through the peanuts. Return to the parchment-lined sheet pan and return to the freezer until all pops have set.

TO MAKE THE COCONUT CAKE POPS

6. Stir the remaining buttercream, coconut, coconut extract, and coconut milk into the second batch of cake crumbs until it forms a uniform consistency. Form into golf ball–sized balls. Insert a Popsicle stick into each of them, and then arrange on a parchment-lined sheet pan. Repeat until all of the mixture has been used up, and then place in the freezer to set for 30 minutes.

7. Once they have chilled, dip the pops into the melted chocolate, and then roll the chocolate-dipped pops through the coconut. Return to the parchment-lined sheet pan and return to the freezer until all the pops are set.

8. Remove the pops from the freezer when set and allow to come to room temperature before serving.

FRIDAY NIGHT COCKTAIL PARTY

COCKTAILS AND CONVERSATION go hand in hand. There's nothing like having a glass of wine or having a drink and chatting with someone until the wee hours of the night. I love a cocktail party more than anything, and I also love socializing with friends.

I put a lot of thought into my cocktail parties. I think, "Where am I going to place the food? Where am I going to place the drinks?" I would never put the food in the way of the drinks. You need to separate the two so that people have some mingling room in between, because that's generally where most of the conversation takes place at a cocktail party—in between the food and the drinks.

I love that at cocktail parties you are usually standing up so **IT'S EASY TO MINGLE**. There's a real art form to navigating through a cocktail party. How do you extricate yourself from a conversation that you just think is the most boring conversation in the world? Or how do you find your way to talk to somebody on the other side of the room? I see it as a game or a challenge.

So what makes for a great cocktail party? I asked the crew.

—Clinton

"FIRST, I THINK OF THE PRACTICALITIES.
Where are you going to have it? I mean, I think the best room for a cocktail party is the kitchen, because you can always set up a little bar somewhere in the kitchen. I like being able to be by the stove so I can continue to make things while everyone is talking and kinda pass food around and talk.

Next—and I think this is the biggest question—what are you going to serve and how much? Often, the biggest mistake at a cocktail party is portions that are too big and unwieldy. Take sandwiches for instance: it's awkward, trying to hold your drink, hold your sandwich, eat it, use your napkin, talk. You need five arms. Someone is going to make a mess at some point. Instead, I like doing kebabs or any kind of food on a stick. Whatever you do, it should be one or two bites. Even sliders to me don't make any sense because it's not like you can eat a slider in a bite, it's a four-bite thing—one of the big mistakes is serving a meal instead of a bite. Baby lamb racks are two bites. If you did little lamb sausages, and put them on an end of a kebab and grilled them, that's a bite or two. If you do tempura shrimp and passed them around, that's a bite or two. My extra-special signature treat is for specialty things that I always do. For example, I do little lamb chops with lavender salt. So different, so delicious. The main thing is, think bites and go from there.**"**

—*Michael*

"AS MUCH AS I LOVE GOING TO A PARTY
that has really delicious passed hors d'oeuvres, I don't have the patience to make them, nor do I like them when I do. So I try to make things that you can serve yourself on small plates. It's a little less portion controlled than grabby passed hors d'oeuvres, but it means a lot less time in your preparation. I'll often make marinated olives, a cool cooked or lightly pickled vegetable salad in the way that the Italians do it, or a room temperature fritto misto. I love (make that LOVE!) a tortilla Española or a quiche, cut into little cubes. I'll always have some nice cured meats and cheeses and make those a center-piece with different condiments. Wine for sure, beer too.**"**

—*Mario*

"A LOT OF OUR HOME ENTERTAINING is more on the order of a cocktail party because we live in an apartment in New York City, so there's not always seating space for everyone we want to have over. Serving things on scoop chips is an ideal solution, like in my fish taco specialty: I take a little piece of fish, guacamole, and cabbage slaw and put them on a bite-sized chip.

I also like to mix sweet and savory right from the start. The dieting plus here is that when I eat sweet in the beginning of my meal, I'm less tempted to eat dessert, and when you are deep in conversation at a cocktail party, you can scarf up the brownies and the petits fours without even thinking. One of my fave sweet and savory things is a broiled date stuffed with goat cheese and pecans. I'm sure Michael would wrap it in bacon too, which is not a bad idea now that I mention it.

One house rule is you have to serve wine and juices too (that's for you, Carla!). Not everyone likes cocktails. I'd have one white wine, one red, one sparkling.

For cocktails, if I'm doing a themed party, I'll pick a favorite cocktail, like my "sombrero aloha," which is kava or tequila, lime juice, pineapple juice, and a splash of soda water. I would do the pineapple and lime juice together in a little pitcher, and then set the tequila and soda out so people can mix their own drinks. **"**

—Daphne

"I HAVE SOME PRETTY SIMPLE RULES. You have to serve about seven things. People feel like they have choices then.

1. You have something on a stick, such as chicken satay or vodka shrimp (if you put shrimp on a buffet, some shrimpaholic is going to eat 'em all).

2. Something that's not on a stick, like little grilled cheese sandwiches.

3. Something that's gooey or liquid, or soups in a demitasse (espresso cup).

4. Something that's stationary, where you serve yourself, say, a macaroni and cheese bundle, or coq au vin with the chicken deboned and in smaller pieces.

5. Something that's passed, like spanakopita. Whatever it is, keep those babies moving.

6. Meat: maybe mini beef Wellingtons. Passed or assemble your own. Instead of wrapping in pastry, you set out pastry pieces, mushrooms, gravy, etc., and guests can assemble their own. The nine-dollar word for this would be *deconstructed*.

7. Roasted vegetables in bowls nestled on a big platter so it doesn't look messy as people dig in. You can keep refilling the bowls as needed.

For dessert, although a big honkin' piece of cake looks beautiful on display, when you start to cut pieces from it, the looks kind of go downhill. I stick with smaller desserts, like tartlets in mini muffin tins, or fruit turnovers instead of big pies. A chocolate fountain with things like fresh fruit, marshmallows, and Rice Krispies Treats for dipping always scores big.**"**

—Carla

Perfect Manhattan

SERVES 1 | **PREP TIME: 5 MINUTES** | **COST: $**

Easy

The first time somebody asked me if I wanted a perfect Manhattan, I answered, "Of course." I mean, who doesn't want *perfect*? Little did I know that the word *perfect* means that you use equal parts of sweet and dry vermouth. The classic calls for rye, but the bourbon Manhattan has made a run at the Manhattan mixologist's manual. My advice is try 'em both and decide. There ain't no bad option.

Ice

2 ounces rye whiskey

¾ ounce sweet vermouth

¾ ounce dry vermouth

4 dashes angostura bitters

1 brandy-soaked or high-end Maraschino cherry, to garnish

1. Chill a martini glass in the freezer.

2. Fill a cocktail shaker with ice. Add the rye, vermouths, and bitters. Stir vigorously for 15–30 seconds.

3. Strain the liquid into the chilled glass and garnish with the cherry.

Lara Spencer shakin' it with Carla during a commercial break.

Eggnog

Moderate

Eggnog is a classic holiday party drink. I mean, you never see someone walk into a bar and say, "Gimme an eggnog…shaken, not stirred." But it's so good it seems a shame to have it once or twice and then have to wait a whole year. For my version, I threw a party for my liquor cabinet; in addition to the traditional rum, I toss in some bourbon and brandy for good measure. Guaranteed to bring you glad tidings and good cheer even when it's not Christmastime.

8 pasteurized eggs, separated

⅓ cup sugar

1 teaspoon salt

1 cup bourbon

1 cup rum

½ cup brandy

1 quart half-and-half

2 cups whipping cream

Freshly grated nutmeg

1. Beat the egg yolks, sugar, and salt until thick and lemon colored. Gradually add the bourbon, rum, and brandy, beating constantly.

2. Combine the half-and-half and whipping cream, and beat into the egg yolk mixture.

3. Whip the egg whites until soft peaks form. Gently fold into the egg yolk mixture. Stir in salt and chill thoroughly. Grate fresh nutmeg on top before serving.

Cheese Crisps

SERVES 8 TO 10 | COOK TIME: 5–8 MINUTES | PREP TIME: 5 MINUTES | COST: $

Easy

Last thing you want when you're getting reading for a cocktail party is to slave for hours and hours. As they say where I come from: "Ain't nobody got time for that." Well, I'm here to tell you that these scrumptious cheese crisps can be made super quick. Some herbs, some spices, a slice of cheese, and a few minutes in the oven. What could be simpler? They come out lacy and crisp. It works with most hard cheeses. For Cheddar, it works best with aged Cheddar; fresher Cheddars come out a little soft and oily.

1 10-ounce block Gruyère
(or other hard cheese)

Caraway seeds

Black pepper

Almonds, chopped

Sesame seeds

1. Preheat the oven to 350 °F.

2. Shave long strips of cheese with a peeler, approximately 1½ inches by 3 inches.

3. Lay the cheese on a baking sheet lined with a silicone nonstick baking mat. Sprinkle with your choice of caraway seeds, black pepper, almonds, or sesame seeds. Or combine the ingredients to make your own unique cheese stick creations.

4. Bake for about 5–8 minutes, or until the cheese is melted, bubbly and golden brown. Remove from the oven and let the cheese sticks cool until ready to handle.

TGIF (AND SATURDAY, SUNDAY, AND OTHER GOOD TIMES)

Tip:

"Hey, Clinton," one of our viewers asked in a video she sent in, "after I spend all that money on food and drinks, there isn't a lot left over for decor. Help!"

Home decor help is my middle name. This super-inexpensive tabletop tip also takes the guesswork out of which cheese is which and what's inside those stuffed hors d'oeuvres. This spells it out for your guests.

Place your cheeses and other hors d'oeuvre selections directly onto butcher paper. Then you can simply write on the paper to identify the food. Butcher paper can also be used for a tablecloth, writing your guests' names rather than using place cards or providing a kids' table with crayons to keep the younger guests occupied.

Pumpkin Fritters

SERVES 6 TO 8 | COOK TIME: 5 MINUTES | PREP TIME: 5 MINUTES | COST: $

Easy to Moderate

Sweet, savory, cheesy. What could be better than that except for having a tall supermodel like Carla Hall standing next to you when you make it? All I can give you is the recipe. You'll have to ask Carla to join you on your own. Because these fritters are fried and crispy, they are big favorites with kids, so it's a great way to get them to scarf down their vegetables. By the way, if you don't have pumpkins around, squash will do, even cabbage. You heard me: even cabbage tastes exciting in this recipe.

1½ cups fresh or canned pumpkin puree or butternut squash puree (see Note)

2 large eggs

½ cup unbleached all-purpose flour

½ teaspoon baking powder

1 teaspoon kosher salt

¾ cup grated Parmigiano-Reggiano, plus more for garnish

¼ cup fresh flat-leaf parsley, finely chopped, plus more for garnish

⅛ teaspoon freshly grated nutmeg

Finely ground black pepper, to taste

Olive oil, for deep-frying

Good balsamic vinegar, for garnish

1. Place the pumpkin puree in a medium bowl. Lightly beat the eggs with a fork and stir them into the pumpkin with a wooden spoon or spatula. In another bowl, whisk together the flour, baking powder, and salt. Add the dry ingredients to the puree mixture, along with the grated cheese, parsley, nutmeg, and a pinch of black pepper. Use the wooden spoon or fork to combine all the ingredients into a light batter; be careful not to overmix it.

2. Heat the olive oil to 360°F in a heavy-bottomed pot. Fill the pot no more than two-thirds of the way full, allowing room for the oil to expand. Drop heaping tablespoons of the batter into the oil, and cook until the fritters are golden brown. Fry in batches, cooking for about 2 minutes per side.

3. Drain the fritters on paper towels and season with salt. Garnish with Parmigiano, parsley, and balsamic vinegar.

NOTE: If you are using a fresh pumpkin, cut the pumpkin and scrape out the seeds and stringy bits. Rub the inside with olive oil (or softened butter), and season with salt. Place the cut side down on a sheet tray lined with parchment and cook in the oven at 400 °F until soft, about 40–45 minutes. Scrape out the puree and toss the skins.

FRIDAY NIGHT COCKTAIL PARTY

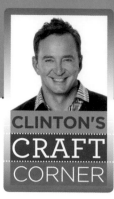

CLINTON'S CRAFT CORNER

Don't throw out the takeout

Bet you didn't know there was something you could do with used take-out containers from the Chinese place, apart from recycling or tossing in the fire. In fact, you can use them to make really neat decorative hanging lanterns for your cocktail party.

WHAT YOU NEED

Chinese food take-out containers

Pencil

Ruler

Hole punch

Paint

Brushes

Sponges

Twine or ribbon

Tea lights

HOW TO MAKE IT

1. Remove the metal handles from the containers and unfold them to lie flat.

2. Sketch the desired designs with a pencil, using a ruler to help with straight lines.

3. Using a hole punch, punch out circles along the lines of your design. Be sure to also punch out the holes from the handles so that you will be able to put string through them later.

4. If you would like to change the color of your containers, paint them in any color with a brush, using sponges to add texture. Set them aside to dry.

5. Reassemble the containers, stringing twine or ribbon through the holes where the handles once were. Put a tea light candle inside the container and hang for your celebration!

Hanky Panky

| SERVES 10 | COOK TIME: 12–15 MINUTES | PREP TIME: 5 MINUTES | COST: $ |

Easy

A midwestern Cleveland classic. There's almost no party in my hometown that doesn't start with this. It's our version of a bruschetta—a little something on toast. The "classic" is made with sausage and Velveeta. No prob—it's delicious—but my chef's version has Parmesan because, well, that's the cheese I like. I asked my parents when I was a little boy why it's called a Hanky Panky, and they said, "Ask us when you're grown up." I never did find out why, but I now know what Hanky Panky means, and I approve.

1 pound spicy Italian sausage, casing removed

2 tablespoons flour

2 cups milk

½ cup grated Parmesan

½ cup parsley, chopped, plus more for garnish

Salt

Pepper

1 baguette, sliced into 1-inch rounds

1. Preheat the broiler to high.

2. In a large skillet, sauté the sausage until cooked through, about 5–10 minutes. Be sure to break up any large chunks. When cooked, drain, reserving 2 tablespoons of the fat. Set the sausage aside.

3. Whisk the flour into the reserved fat and cook for 2 minutes. Then add the milk. Cook until the mixture thickens slightly, then add the grated Parmesan, parsley, cooked sausage, salt, and pepper. Mix to combine.

4. Heat a grill or grill pan over medium heat. Grill the slices of baguette, transfer to a sheet tray, and spoon the sausage mixture on top. Place in the oven under the broiler until golden and bubbling, about 2 minutes. Remove from the oven and garnish with chopped parsley.

Spicy Lamb Meatballs with Cucumber Dip

SERVES 8 TO 10   COOK TIME: 15–20 MINUTES   PREP TIME: 15 MINUTES

INACTIVE COOK TIME: 20–30 MINUTES   COST: $

Easy

When you think of meatballs, most folks don't think of lamb first. But it's such a good, economical meat, we ought to. My Turkish ancestors sure loved it. Michael's Greek grandparents too. It accepts aromatic spices really well and a little bit of fiery heat. Instead of pan roasting and braising, which is the classic way to go, mine are baked in the oven, which makes for a lot less fuss. And alongside them I serve a cooling yogurt dip inspired by Indian raita. It tames that first spicy kick you get from the lamb.

FOR THE MEATBALLS

2 tablespoons butter

1¼ cups white onions, finely chopped

1 tablespoon garlic, finely minced

1 jalapeño, finely chopped

1 teaspoon curry powder

1½ teaspoons ground cumin

1 teaspoon ground coriander

½ teaspoon turmeric

Salt, to taste

Freshly cracked black pepper, to taste

1½ pounds lean ground lamb

½ cup fresh whole wheat bread crumbs

⅓ cup fresh parsley, chopped

1 egg, beaten

Zest and juice of 1 orange

TO MAKE THE MEATBALLS

1. Preheat the oven to 375 °F.

2. Heat a large sauté pan over medium-high heat and add the butter. Stir in the onions and cook for 1–2 minutes, and then add the garlic and jalapeño. Cook for another 2–3 minutes, or until the onion turns soft and translucent.

3. Stir in the curry powder, cumin, coriander, and turmeric. Season with salt and pepper. Cook for another minute, or until the onion mixture is fragrant. Take off the heat and let the mixture cool to room temperature.

4. Put the lamb in a large mixing bowl and add the cooled onion mixture, bread crumbs, parsley, and egg. Add in 2 teaspoons of the orange zest and squeeze in about 1 tablespoon of the orange juice. Season with salt and pepper. Mix thoroughly and then form the mixture into meatballs, each a little smaller than a golf ball. Place onto a parchment-lined baking sheet.

5. Put the meatballs in the oven for 15–20 minutes, or until deep golden brown. When the meatballs are done, remove from the oven and let rest. Place the meatballs onto a platter and serve with the raita.

½ cup English cucumber, peeled, seeded, and diced small

Salt, to taste

1 cup Greek yogurt

2 tablespoons fresh mint, chopped

1½ teaspoons ground cumin

Pepper, to taste

TO MAKE THE RAITA

6. Sprinkle the cucumbers with an even coat of salt and transfer to a sieve. Let drain.

7. After 20–30 minutes, press the cucumbers with a spoon to release any excess water, and then stir them into the yogurt, along with the mint. Add the cumin to the yogurt, and season with salt and pepper. Chill before serving.

How to be nice to a spice

Whenever I cook with spices, I first pan roast them for 30 seconds to 1 minute to release their oils. That's where all the flavor is.

Rosemary Shrimp with Almonds

| SERVES 8 TO 10 | COOK TIME: 5–8 MINUTES | PREP TIME: 20 MINUTES | COST: $ |

Easy

I really don't know a simpler, more flavorful dish. Fast too—like 5 minutes. Skewering shrimp on rosemary stalks adds beautiful, subtle flavor. The sauce gets nuttiness from the butter, slivered almonds, and garlic, and then real brightness from the orange juice. I don't care if you are drinking cosmos or old-fashioneds at your cocktail party. The flavors will ring through. And please use real butter. It's a real food. Fake butter doesn't cut it, and you're not using so much when you consider that it's a sauce that gets spread over a number of shrimp. P.S. This sauce works with skewered fish, vegetables, and pork too.

1 pound large shrimp (about 16–20), shelled and deveined

1 bunch rosemary

Salt

Freshly ground pepper

Extra virgin olive oil, to brush the grill

3 tablespoons butter

2 cloves garlic, sliced

¼ cup slivered almonds

Zest and juice of 1 orange

1. Preheat a grill or grill pan to medium-high.

2. Skewer the shrimp on the rosemary stalks. Season generously with salt and pepper. Brush the grill with olive oil and grill the shrimp until cooked through and pink, about 2½ minutes per side.

3. In a pan over medium-high heat, melt the butter and then add the garlic, almonds, and orange zest and juice. Add some of the rosemary, stir, and pour over the shrimp to serve.

Baked Brie Bites

SERVES 9 | COOK TIME: 20–25 MINUTES | PREP TIME: 25–30 MINUTES | COST: $

Moderate

People have been serving baked brie for as long as they have been brie-ing and baking. My cocktail party twist is finger-food friendly. It doesn't get all gooey in your fingers, and adding some candied walnuts to the brie inside these pastry bundles is simply divine.

1 package puff pastry, thawed

½ pound Brie

1 cup Candied Walnuts (recipe follows), chopped

1 egg, beaten

1. Preheat the oven to 350 °F.

2. Roll out the puff pastry and cut into 3-inch squares. Cut the Brie into bite-sized pieces. Place a piece of Brie in the center of each puff pastry square, and top with the chopped candied walnuts. Pinch the opposite corners closed to form a package. Brush with the egg wash, and bake until golden brown, about 10–12 minutes.

Candied Walnuts

2 tablespoons unsalted butter

2 cups raw unsalted walnut halves

2 tablespoons firmly packed brown sugar

2 tablespoons granulated sugar

½ teaspoon cayenne pepper

⅛ teaspoon cinnamon

1 teaspoon sea salt

1. In a heavy skillet, cook the butter and nuts over medium heat, being careful not to burn. Stir frequently for about 1–2 minutes. In a separate bowl, combine the sugars and spices. Pour the spice mixture into the skillet, continue to stir, and cook, about 8 minutes, until the sugar is caramelized. Spread the nuts on a foil-lined sheet tray and cool completely. Store in an air-tight container at room temperature for up to two weeks.

CLINTON'S CRAFT CORNER

Tip:

Entertaining is a huge part of my life, and making my own decor ranks up there with cooking my own food. There's nothing more fun than having somebody over for a dinner party, or just over to watch a movie or for game night, and having them say, "Oh, I love those cool lanterns," and you get to say, "I made that!"

Once again, like so much in my life, home crafts take me back to the things I made in childhood, using the most inexpensive materials to make pretty things. It's kind of like six-year-old Clinton stepping in to lend a hand at a grown-up dinner.

I think we can make the same argument for why people like scratch decor the way they like homemade meals. It's something that's invested with your personality, and no matter how much money you spend, you can't buy that.

Butterscotch Truffles

SERVES 15 | COOK TIME: 30 MINUTES | PREP TIME: 30 MINUTES

INACTIVE PREP TIME: 20–30 MINUTES | COST: $

Moderate

The truffle was originally chocolate ganache covered in chocolate. Pretty darn good too. My little twist is to hide a ball of homemade butterscotch in the center. For all of you wondering what is so Scottish about butterscotch, the answer is: no one knows. What I do know is that way back when, it was advertised as something to rub on the chest in wintertime. I'm not sold. What I am sold on is finishing the truffles in sea salt because there are few things better on earth than salted caramel. Can I get an amen?

Cooking spray, for the baking pan

¼ cup water

1 cup granulated sugar

½ cup brown sugar

¼ cup light corn syrup

1 cup heavy whipping cream

4 tablespoons butter

1 teaspoon vanilla extract

1 teaspoon kosher salt

2 cups chocolate

Flaked sea salt, for sprinkling

1. Line an 8-inch square baking pan with parchment paper, letting the ends hang over the sides (for easy removal later), and then spray evenly with cooking spray.

2. Combine the water, sugars, and corn syrup in a medium saucepot. Bring to a boil over medium-high heat and cook until the mixture turns an amber color.

3. Meanwhile, in a second saucepot, combine the cream, butter, vanilla, and kosher salt, and heat over a medium heat. Once the mixture reaches a simmer, remove from the heat and set aside.

4. When the sugar mixture is golden, turn off the heat and slowly add the cream mixture to the sugar mixture. It will bubble, so be careful.

5. Turn the heat back on and continue cooking until the mixture reaches 245 °F on a candy thermometer. If your mixture becomes any hotter, the candy will be too firm. Pour out the mixture into the prepared pan and pop in the fridge for a few hours to cool. Once firm, turn the butterscotch out onto a cutting board. Remove parchment. Cut the butterscotch into 1-inch-long pieces, lengthwise. Roll into logs, and then cut ¾-inch pieces. Roll into balls.

6. Line a sheet tray with parchment paper. Melt the chocolate in the microwave or in a double boiler, and using two forks, dip the butterscotch balls into the chocolate and then place them on the sheet tray. Sprinkle with the flaked sea salt.

7. Once all the butterscotch is dipped, place in the fridge. When the chocolate is set, the truffles are ready to eat.

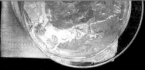

PARTY LIKE IT'S YOUR BIRTHDAY!

"**YOUR BIRTHDAY IS YOUR SPECIAL DAY** out of 365 days a year, so you should set the tone and, if you want, the menu too. If you're twelve and you want to eat cereal for dinner, then the whole family should eat cereal on your twelfth birthday. Or if you want grilled cheese sandwiches and that's your favorite food, then you should be able to have grilled cheese sandwiches.

I'm not a big birthday person myself. I don't really care about my birthday all that much, 'cause I treat every day like **I'M THE MOST SPECIAL PERSON** in the world. Well actually, there is one special thing I like: my grandmother's pear crunch pie is a must. Gotta have it!

I ask you, *Chew* Crew, what is your favorite birthday meal?"

—*Clinton*

"I LIKE TO PUT ON A SUIT AND TIE (yes, I actually own some) and go someplace special. I'm all about classic dining experiences at great restaurants. But for a family meal, at home my wife and sons make something simple that I like. It could be as easy as a turkey burger, or a nice steak, seared, grilled, and finished with a little balsamic vinegar. The real key to the success of my birthday is that my wife always makes an orange sunshine birthday cake. It's kind of like a chiffon cake with an orange buttercream and segments of mandarin oranges and strawberries. Yeah, they are completely out of season in September, but we still love it, because it's our tradition. As long as she makes that cake, we know that all is right with the world."

—Mario

"AS A GROWN-UP, I have to be honest, I usually go out to dinner for my birthday! Mario and I share the same birthday, so this year we went to dinner at one of New York's fanciest restaurants—Mario even had to shine his Crocs. We had all the great old-school dishes, including Dover sole and whole roasted duck.

I usually cook for Lizzie on her birthday. She loves seafood and prefers a more Greek-style preparation of fish: a whole roast fish with olive oil and oregano and a nice crisp salad. She was born in March, so you don't have those beautiful summer vegetables yet, so I cook down some greens with the whole fish."

—Michael

WHEN IT COMES TO BIRTHDAY DINNER, I'm just looking for the basic sort of food that makes me happy to my core—it's the simple, straightforward, and delicious flavors that just surprise you in the easiest ways. For my birthday meal, I'd begin with a huge green leafy salad with a tart, lemony dressing and a gorgeous French baguette with fresh salted butter. Then I want chicken and dumplings. I want delicious chicken stock, great chicken thighs in there, and a moist, dense dumpling. Dessert is a toss-up. I either want a German chocolate cake because I'm a huge fan of coconut pecan icing (I would actually just prefer the icing really), or, even more simple, give me a brownie à la mode. To drink, I'd start with a cava or prosecco cocktail with a splash of elderflower, then a Spanish or Portuguese white, maybe a Vinho Verde or the wine we had at our wedding, a cold crisp Albariño.

—Daphne

BEING FROM THE MIDWEST, my husband, Matthew, loves meat and potatoes, so I do him a big steak, probably a rib eye or something as fatty and yummy and delicious. I always get it from a butcher if possible, the best I can afford. And, of course, there are potatoes too, but to make the potato a little different, maybe I'll go with a sweet potato, with an herby, salty crust and *mucho* butter.

As for my special day, well, first off, I don't want to make my own dinner; I want somebody to cook for me. I like to eat bits and bobs, a little bit of this, a little bit of that…I don't wanna commit. I just want a little bit of everything. I would be perfectly happy with lots of sides like some stuffing. Or, now that I'm away from the South, you could make a bean stew with collards and some hot water corn bread on the side, and keep the vegetables coming, and I would be totally happy.

Then I'd want dessert, say, apple pie or some kind of berry cobbler with ice cream, or an ice cream sundae with salted caramel or pistachio with some hot fudge and whipped cream and toasted nuts and a cherry top, but not that funky red cherry, a real marinated maraschino. Now you've got me thinking. I could also go for a mascarpone mousse over berries with some crumbled amaretti cookies on top. I guess I'd have to make the desserts—Matthew doesn't make desserts, but he can buy the ice cream.

—Carla

Reverse Martini

SERVES 1 | **PREP TIME: 2 MINUTES** | **COST: $**

Easy

Speaking of birthdays, we made this for Julia Child's one hundredth birthday. In the years since martinis first became popular in the 1920s, the amount of gin in them has gone way up and the amount of vermouth has kind of shrunk to a wisp, if that. Julia was not from the dry martini crowd. In fact, you could say she was from the very wet martini crowd. She liked hers with two parts vermouth to one part gin. Like foie gras and pig's feet, I guess it's an acquired taste. By the way, please note that I said gin, not vodka. Nowadays, anything clear in a glass is liable to be called a martini, but to Julia or to the Don Draper crowd, martinis were made with gin.

2½ ounces dry vermouth

¾ ounce gin

Crushed ice

1. Shake the vermouth and gin in a cocktail shaker filled with ice. Strain into a small wine glass filled with crushed ice.

Jamika Pessoa joins the *Chew* crew for a birthday bonanza!

Tip If you do make something as large as a table runner, you can divide it into separate pieces so it can be easily stored. Then just assemble the pieces together on your table.

CLINTON'S CRAFT CORNER

A corking good idea

As anyone who has watched more than one episode of *The Chew* knows, I am very pro-wine. Then the question becomes: What do I do with all these corks? As far as I am concerned, old corks are a new, inexpensive decorating opportunity. Here's how to use those leftover corks to make a beautiful table runner, placemats, or coasters, depending on how many corks you have.

WHAT YOU NEED

Cigar cutter or utility knife

Wine corks (use ones you already have or get them at a craft store)

Hot glue gun

HOW TO MAKE IT

1. Using a cigar cutter or utility knife, cut your corks into four or five pieces, keeping the size of each piece consistent.

2. Lay the cork pieces out, gluing them together at the sides. Be sure to keep the glue even so that everything lays flat.

3. If you'd like to add color, you can also soak your corks overnight in any leftover red wine before assembling.

Steak House Bacon with Grilled Spring Onions

SERVES 6 TO 8 | COOK TIME: 25–30 MINUTES | PREP TIME: 15 MINUTES | COST: $

Easy

When you talk about aromas you love, nothing beats the smell of bacon. Coffee comes in as a close second, but the smell of bacon says "happy times." I know that most of you reading this agree with me, because according to research, the average American eats 18 pounds of bacon a year. Think of this dish as super thick slices of bacon or super thin smoked pork belly. Either way, it has big flavor, so it goes with a super big flavored sauce.

1 pound slab bacon

4 spring onions or scallions, sliced in half lengthwise, roots intact

Olive oil, for drizzling

Kosher salt

Freshly ground black pepper

FOR THE HOMEMADE STEAK SAUCE

2 cups balsamic vinegar

2 tablespoons red wine vinegar

1 onion, chopped

1 cup raisins

6 cloves garlic

2 anchovies

¼ cup brown sugar

1 tablespoon cumin seeds, toasted

1 tablespoon whole cloves

1 tablespoon celery seed

2 cups tomato puree

1. Preheat a grill pan to high heat.

2. Cut the slab bacon into thick slices—just shy of an inch. Arrange on the grill pan and cook until the bacon is crispy on both sides, about 3 minutes per side. Transfer to paper towel–lined plate.

3. Drizzle the spring onions lightly with olive oil, then generously season with salt and pepper and toss to coat. Grill until bright green, tender, and charred in spots, about 3 minutes.

TO MAKE THE HOMEMADE STEAK SAUCE

4. Add all the ingredients to a large saucepan and bring to a simmer. Cook until reduced by two-thirds, about 10 minutes. Strain the mixture, pressing on the solids to get maximum flavor. Discard the solids.

5. Serve the bacon with the steak sauce and spring onions.

Fail-Safe Prime Rib

SERVES 8 TO 10	COOK TIME: 2 HOURS	PREP TIME: 10 MINUTES
INACTIVE COOK TIME: 24 HOURS	COST: $$	

Moderate

A lot of people stress about making something that sounds as grand as prime rib. Don't. First of all, remember that a big cut of meat is more forgiving than a small cut. There's a bigger window of opportunity when the meat is in the right temperature range. Better yet, get an instant-read thermometer. That's the only fail-safe method I know. If the recipe book says an hour or 2 hours or whatever, that's just a rough guide. When it gets to be a half hour or 20 minutes from the time it should be done, check it. Every piece of meat is different. For medium rare, take it out of the oven at 120 °F and let it stand for 20 minutes. It will be perfect, and it goes perfectly with grated beets and horseradish. It's a slightly spicy, slightly sweet condiment that cuts the fattiness of the meat beautifully.

1 4-bone prime rib, bones removed and reserved

4 teaspoons kosher salt

Freshly ground black pepper

4 sprigs fresh rosemary

4 cloves garlic, smashed

4 whole beets, red or golden

4 ounces arugula

2 teaspoons extra virgin olive oil

2 cups Horseradish Beets (recipe follows)

1. Liberally season the prime rib with the salt and some pepper and refrigerate overnight. An hour before cooking, remove the roast from the refrigerator to allow it to come to room temperature.

2. Meanwhile, preheat the oven to 400 °F. Put the reserved ribs in a roasting pan bowed-side up. Roast the bones for about 30 minutes.

3. Remove the pan from the oven, put the rosemary sprigs on top of the bones, and then top with the meat. The ribs will be acting as the roasting rack. Put the garlic in the bottom of the pan with the trimmings. Toss in the beets, baste with the fat, and season with salt and pepper. Baste the beef with the fat drippings and return the pan to the oven. Cook for 30 minutes and then baste the roast again.

4. Reduce the heat to 350 °F and cook until the meat is medium rare (an internal temperature of 120–125 °F), about 1 hour and 15 minutes. Keep basting the roast every 30 minutes until it is done. Keep in mind that the roast will continue to cook while resting.

5. Remove the roast from the oven and put it on a cutting board to rest, uncovered, for 20 minutes. Slice the prime rib to the desired thickness, slice the whole beets, and garnish with the arugula, olive oil, and Horseradish Beets.

FOR THE HORSERADISH BEETS

4 large golden beets

4 ounces fresh grated or prepared horseradish

¼ cup sherry vinegar

2 tablespoons extra virgin olive oil

2 tablespoons Dijon mustard

Zest and juice of 1 orange

2 tablespoons honey

Large pinch of kosher salt

TO MAKE THE HORSERADISH BEETS

1. Peel the beets and grate into a large bowl. Add the rest of the ingredients and toss to combine. Adjust the seasoning and serve with the prime rib.

Racked and right

Instead of using a roasting rack, I have the butcher separate the rib eye from the bones. Then I use the bones as a roasting rack. For many people, that is the choicest part of the whole prime rib. It is a lot of fun to gnaw on.

Onion Flower Power

| SERVES 4 | COOK TIME: 5–7 MINUTES | PREP TIME: 20 MINUTES | COST: $ |

Moderate

Michael is right about people loving bacon (even vegetarians probably do in a window-shopping kind of way). I think it's just as true that people love deep-fried onion rings—so sweet, so crispy, so salty! The blooming onion that you see in restaurants is nothing more than a super jumbo fried onion. It looks really special. Just the thing to kick off a meal or as a side with a steak or pork chops.

FOR THE ONION

Vegetable oil, for deep-frying

1 sweet Vidalia onion, peeled

1 cup flour

1 teaspoon sweet paprika

1 teaspoon cayenne

1 teaspoon oregano

Salt, to taste

1 cup milk

3 eggs

FOR THE SPICY THOUSAND ISLAND DRESSING

½ cup mayo

¼ cup ketchup

1 tablespoon Thai chili hot sauce

1 tablespoon honey

TO MAKE THE ONION

1. Heat a large Dutch oven filled with oil two-thirds of the way up the sides to 360 °F.

2. Slice off the top end of the onion, leaving the root end attached. Place cut side down and begin slicing from the root down to the board, about 16 even slices around the onion, leaving the root attached.

3. Mix the flour and spices in a baking dish. Whisk the milk and eggs in another baking dish.

4. Carefully dip the onion into the flour mixture, making sure to get some inside the layers (you can also sift the seasoned flour over the entire onion), then dip into the egg mixture, and finish with the flour. Place in the oil and fry for about 5–7 minutes, until golden brown. Remove to paper towel–lined plate and season with salt.

TO MAKE THE SPICY THOUSAND ISLAND DRESSING

5. Place all the ingredients in a large bowl. Whisk together and serve alongside the onion!

Creamed Spinach

SERVES 6 | COOK TIME: 8–10 MINUTES | PREP TIME: 10 MINUTES | COST: $

Easy

One of my favorite songs from *Fiddler on the Roof* is "Tradition," and there is nothing more traditional than my favorite side: creamed spinach. I have it twice a year, so there is no reason to be shy about the butter. Bring it on! Cream too. Hey, you only have a birthday once a year.

Salt

2 pounds fresh baby spinach

1 cup whole milk

1 cup heavy cream

1 medium onion, finely chopped

½ cup (1 stick) butter

Freshly cracked black pepper

1 clove garlic, minced

½ cup flour

½ teaspoon freshly grated nutmeg

2 dashes hot sauce

1. Bring a large pot of water to a boil. Season generously with salt. Blanch the spinach for about 1–2 minutes, or until tender. Place in a fine mesh strainer, pressing to release all the liquid. Chop the spinach and set aside.

2. In a saucepan, heat the milk and cream until it's hot, but not boiling.

3. In a separate, large saucepan, over medium heat, sauté the onion in the butter until translucent. Season with salt and pepper. Add the garlic and continue sautéing, 1 more minute. Add the flour and whisk until the roux is light golden in color. Slowly whisk in the warmed milk and cream. When fully incorporated, add the nutmeg, hot sauce, and spinach, and season with salt and pepper to taste.

Boston Cream Pie

SERVES 10 TO 12 | **COOK TIME: 35 MINUTES** | **PREP TIME: 40 MINUTES** | **COST: $**

Easy

Keeping with the theme of traditional dishes, here's my take on the official dessert of the state of Massachusetts: the Boston Cream Pie, originally invented at the Parker House Hotel. That's the same place that gave us the Parker House roll. If you're keeping score, New York's famous Waldorf Astoria only has the Waldorf salad. Way to go, Boston! I give mine a little Carla twist by infusing the cream with hints of rosemary and orange. Happy birthday!

FOR THE YELLOW CAKE

2 large eggs, plus 2 large egg yolks

2 teaspoons vanilla extract

⅓ cup buttermilk

1¾ cups all-purpose flour, sifted, measured, and then sifted again

1 cup granulated sugar

1¾ teaspoons baking powder

½ teaspoon salt

4 tablespoons unsalted butter, softened

⅓ cup canola oil

½ cup heavy cream, whipped to soft peaks

FOR THE ROSEMARY ORANGE PASTRY CREAM

1 cup whole milk

1 cup heavy cream

1 sprig rosemary

4–5 2-inch strips orange peel (note: use a peeler)

TO MAKE THE YELLOW CAKE

1. Preheat the oven to 325 °F.

2. In a large liquid measuring cup, combine the eggs and vanilla with 2 tablespoons of the buttermilk.

3. In a large mixing bowl, combine the flour, sugar, baking powder, and salt, whisking well.

4. With the hand mixer on medium-low, beat in the butter, canola oil, and the remaining buttermilk into the dry mixture. Stir in the egg mixture in three parts, while scraping down the sides of the mixing bowl. Do not overmix. Fold the whipped cream into the batter.

5. Spoon the batter into three prepared cake pans. Bang the pans on the counter to release any air bubbles. Place in the oven and bake for 25–30 minutes, or until the top springs back and the cake starts to pull away from the sides of the pan.

6. Let cool for 10 minutes on a wire rack, then turn out to cool completely on the rack before frosting.

TO MAKE THE ROSEMARY ORANGE PASTRY CREAM

7. In a stainless steel pot, steam the milk and cream with the rosemary and orange peel.

½ cup sugar

¼ cup cornstarch

Pinch of fine salt

4 egg yolks

2 tablespoons butter

**FOR THE DARK
CHOCOLATE GLAZE WITH
ORANGE LIQUEUR**

9 ounces bittersweet
chocolate

2 tablespoons butter

½ cup heavy cream

1–2 tablespoons triple sec

8. Combine the sugar, cornstarch, and salt in a bowl. Pour the hot milk mixture into the bowl and whisk to combine. Return the milk mixture to the pot and bring to a low boil, continuing to whisk.

9. In another bowl, whisk the egg yolks and temper ½ cup of the hot milk mixture into the eggs. Gradually pour this back into the pot and continue to whisk as the mixture comes to a boil. Continue to cook until thick, about 3 more minutes. It should coat the back of a spoon but should not clump.

10. Strain through a fine mesh strainer into a clean bowl with the pats of butter in the bottom. Stir until the butter melts. Chill with plastic wrap directly on top of the cream.

**TO MAKE THE DARK CHOCOLATE GLAZE
WITH ORANGE LIQUEUR**

11. Put the chocolate and butter into a heatproof bowl. Heat the heavy cream and triple sec until just hot. Pour the hot cream over the chocolate and butter, and stir until smooth. Let cool slightly before pouring over the cake.

TO MAKE THE BOSTON CREAM PIE

12. Layer the cakes and the pastry cream. Drizzle the chocolate glaze over the top of the cake, just enough so the sides of the cake aren't covered completely.

BUG JUICE | SHAVED ICE | CLINTON'S CRAFT CORNER: KNOCK THE
STUFFING OUT PIÑATA | SLOPPY JOES | MOCK CHICKEN | HOMEMADE
TWINKIES | PEACH MAPLE SHERBET SANDWICHES

PARTYING WITH THE KIDS

"HEY, WHILE WE ARE ON THE SUBJECT OF BIRTHDAY PARTIES, let's not forget the kids. I think for a lot of kids, burgers and hot dogs are the way to go, but when my son, Kyle, was growing up, we had to go a little esoteric because he is allergic to red meat. Thankfully he loves spicy food, so it wasn't hard. Typically we'd do Asian-themed meals. He loved pot stickers, so we'd do different-themed pot stickers or maybe Indian samosas, but they would typically have an Asian slant for his kind of meals. More generally, there isn't anything more American than the sandwich, and you can do so many different themes on sandwiches that kids really love—eggplant parmigiana or meatballs come to mind. Or you can get a bunch of cold cuts and pickles and condiments, some good hero rolls, and let the kids invent their own sandwiches. And then there is the pizza party: this is handy in my family, where we have thirteen nephews and two nieces, mostly under twelve years old. So I make a pizza dough that I grill outside and put out the toppings, and the kids pick and choose their own custom pizzas. Mostly they go for simple stuff: tomato sauce, fresh mozzarella, sometimes pepperoni. Some of them are going through the phase where they want nothing green, so god forbid you should put some basil out there! Long story short, birthday parties are a great way for us grown-ups to show the youngsters that good food can be fun food too. **"**

—*Michael*

Bug Juice

| SERVES 8 | COOK TIME: 5 MINUTES | PREP TIME: 15 MINUTES | COST: $ |

Easy

Anyone who ever went to summer camp probably remembers bug juice. It was usually powdered fruit punch and water. Some people say it got its name because it was so sweet even the bugs stayed away. I like the little herbal taste you get when you steep a sprig of thyme in it. Now that you're a grown-up and you're not in summer camp anymore, you can always add some spirits to it—I recommend vodka!

1 cup sugar

1½ cups water

1 bunch thyme

2 pints raspberries, plus more to garnish

2 cups lemon juice

Seltzer

Lime slices, to garnish

Ice

1. In a small saucepot over medium-high heat, combine the sugar, water, and thyme to make the simple syrup.

2. Pulse the raspberries in a food processor until smooth. Strain the pureed mixture.

3. In a large pitcher, combine the raspberry puree with the lemon juice and 1–2 cups of the simple syrup, depending on the desired level of sweetness.

4. Top the pitcher with seltzer. Stir to mix, and garnish with raspberries and lime slices. Serve over ice.

Shaved Ice

| SERVES 8 | COOK TIME: 10 MINUTES | PREP TIME: 10 MINUTES | COST: $ |

Easy

What could be better than strolling down the boardwalk on a hot summer day after you've won your stuffed teddy bear? Topping it off with a cooling and refreshing shaved ice. Even if you can't get to the beach, you can still have shaved ice at home, and my bet is that you're not going to get anything as nutritious as my fresh-fruit version. Try it with a few different fruits, and let the kids choose what they want.

1 pound pitted frozen or fresh cherries, thawed and drained with the juice reserved

¼ cup lemon juice

¼ cup water

½ cup sugar

Shaved or crushed ice

1. In a blender or food processor, puree the cherries.

2. In a saucepan over medium heat, add the cherry puree, lemon juice, water, and sugar. Bring to a boil and reduce by half, about 3–4 minutes. Remove from the heat, and strain the sauce through a sieve. Allow to cool before use.

3. Drizzle over shaved or crushed ice.

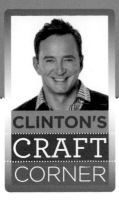

Knock the stuffing out piñata

I've yet to meet the kid who didn't love a piñata. In fact, you can add grown-ups to the legions of piñata lovers. I guess it's because we all love surprises and want to know what's inside, especially when the inside is full of treats. I don't know why it works out this way, but as each kid takes a whack at the piñata, it never seems to want to break until the shrimpiest kid picks up the stick, smacks the piñata, and out pour the goodies. You have to love that!

WHAT YOU NEED

Flour

Water

Salt

Large balloon

Newspaper, cut into 2-inch strips

4 packages of colored tissue paper

Colored construction paper

Craft glue

String, to hang the piñata

HOW TO MAKE IT

1. Combine equal parts flour and water. Add a generous pinch of salt and whisk until smooth. (The salt prevents your papier-mâché from growing mold.)

2. Inflate and tie off the balloon. Rest the balloon on an empty jar or bowl.

3. Dip the newspaper strips into the flour and water mixture, wiping off any excess. Lay the strips over the balloon, making sure all the pieces lay smoothly on the surface. (Be sure to leave a hole for filling with candy.) Once the balloon is completely covered, allow to dry. Continue this process until the entire balloon has been covered with 3–4 layers.

4. Allow the papier-mâché to dry completely. Once it has dried, pop the balloon and remove it from the interior of the piñata.

5. Cut your tissue paper into squares and crumple them to give them volume. Using craft glue, stick them to your papier-mâché in your desired design. From construction paper or other craft supplies, make and attach eyes, ears, feet, or any other features your creature may have.

6. Once it has been decorated, punch a small hole on either side and pull a string through to use to hang your piñata.

7. Finally, fill with candy, and it is ready for your celebration!

Sloppy Joes

SERVES 8 | COOK TIME: 40 MINUTES | PREP TIME: 15 MINUTES | COST: $

Easy

This recipe comes from my son Leo and was in a cookbook that he and his brother, Benno, gave me for my fiftieth birthday. When I am on the road in the summer, my boys have a Batali Boys Cookoff contest pretty much every night, and this is one of their creations. Now here I am—a big shot Iron Chef—and the most popular Batali recipe is my kids'! What's up with that? It's very cool. Of course, I had to add my own little twists, which are some beer for flavor (the alcohol cooks out) and some jalapeños for a spicy kick. I've looked and looked, in search of who this guy Joe was. No luck. But I know where the "sloppy" part of the name comes from: there's no way you can eat these without squishing some of the meat on you, usually on a piece of clothing where it really shows up well.

FOR THE PICO DE GALLO

3 tomatoes, chopped

1 jalapeño, minced

½ red onion, minced

¼ cup cilantro, chopped

Salt

Pepper

Juice of 1 lime

FOR THE SLOPPY JOES

2 tablespoons vegetable oil

1 onion, diced

1 jalapeño, sliced

1 pound ground round

2 tablespoons sugar

5 tablespoons tomato paste

½ 12-ounce beer

8 hamburger rolls

TO MAKE THE PICO DE GALLO

1. Mix all the ingredients together and set aside.

TO MAKE THE SLOPPY JOES

2. Place a skillet over medium-high heat and let it get hot for about a minute.

3. Add the oil and spread it so it covers the bottom of the pan. Add the onion and jalapeño.

4. Add the ground round and cook, breaking up the meat with the back of a spoon, until all the pink is gone, about 15 minutes.

5. Add the sugar, tomato paste, and beer, and combine.

6. When the liquid starts to simmer, reduce the heat to low, partially cover, and simmer for 25 minutes. Stir occasionally to keep the bottom from scorching.

7. Open the rolls and arrange them on a plate. Spoon the meat mixture over it, top with a spoonful of pico de gallo, and serve.

PARTYING WITH THE KIDS

Mock Chicken

SERVES 8 | COOK TIME: 8 TO 10 MINUTES | PREP TIME: 20 MINUTES

INACTIVE PREP TIME: 30 MINUTES | COST: $

Easy

Usually when I see the word *mock* in a recipe, you lose me, because it often means tofu with a lot of sauce that you hope will fool people into thinking they're eating chicken. Never fear! When a Batali makes mock chicken, he is going to use pork and veal. Actually, I should say "she," because this is a recipe my mom picked up at a neighbor's, and it became one of our household favorites. Why is it called chicken if it's made with pork and veal? Because my mom liked to squeeze the meat on the skewers so they looked like chicken legs (at least to her). They're crispy, crunchy, meaty, and well seasoned. Kids love them.

Skewers

1 pound pork shoulder

1 sleeve saltine crackers

3 eggs, lightly beaten

Flour, for dredging

Salt

Pepper

3 tablespoons extra virgin olive oil

3 tablespoons butter

2 tablespoons vermouth (optional)

Lemon wedges, for garnish

1. Soak the skewers in water for 30 minutes.

2. Cut the pork shoulder into chicken-finger-sized pieces (about 1-inch cubes).

3. Crush the saltine crackers and place into a shallow dish. Put the lightly beaten eggs into another shallow dish. Have a third dish with flour for dredging.

4. Insert the skewers into the pieces of pork as to resemble a chicken drumstick.

5. Season each "drumstick" on both sides with salt and pepper.

6. Preheat the oven to 400 °F.

7. Heat the olive oil and butter in a skillet over medium-high heat. Once smoking, dip each "drumstick" into the flour, the egg, then dredge in the cracker crumbs.

Mario's mom, Marilyn, shows the crew how Mock Chicken is done!

8. Panfry each piece lightly on both sides, then, if desired, deglaze the pan with the vermouth. Once all the pieces have been fried, transfer to a baking sheet and place in the oven to finish cooking, about 8–10 minutes. Allow to cool before serving. Garnish with a squeeze of lemon juice from the wedges.

Homemade Twinkies

| SERVES 12 | COOK TIME: 15 MINUTES | PREP TIME: 30 MINUTES | COST: $ |

Moderate

When I heard that Hostess, purveyors of the legendary Twinkie, might be going out of business, I did what any self-respecting chef would do. Did I pick up a pen and write my congressman? Did I organize like-minded Twinkie true believers to go picket my supermarket? No way! I decided to figure out my own Twinkie recipe. These have that buttery, creamy Twinkie-ness that we all love, but I actually think these are better. Not because Twinkies aren't great, but homemade is always the way I roll.

FOR THE CAKES

Nonstick cooking spray
or vegetable oil

½ cup cake flour

¼ cup all-purpose flour

1 teaspoon baking powder

½ teaspoon salt

2 tablespoons milk

4 tablespoons
unsalted butter

1 teaspoon vanilla extract

5 large eggs, separated
(room temperature)

¾ cup granulated sugar

⅓ teaspoon cream of tartar

TO MAKE THE CAKES

1. Preheat the oven to 350 °F. Adjust the oven rack to the lower-middle position.

2. Spray Twinkie molds with nonstick cooking spray or grease with vegetable oil.

3. In a mixing bowl, whisk together the cake flour, all-purpose flour, baking powder, and salt. In a small saucepan over low heat, heat the milk and butter until the butter melts. Remove from the heat and add the vanilla. Cover to keep warm.

4. In the bowl of a stand mixer, beat the egg whites on high speed until foamy. Gradually add 6 tablespoons of the sugar and the cream of tartar, and continue to beat until the whites reach soft peaks, about 6 minutes.

5. Transfer the beaten egg whites to a large bowl and add the egg yolks to the standing mixer bowl (there's no need to clean the bowl). Beat the egg yolks with the remaining 6 tablespoons of sugar on medium-high speed, until the mixture is very thick and a pale lemon color, about 5 minutes. Add the beaten egg whites to the yolks, but do not mix.

6 tablespoons unsalted butter (room temperature)

1½ cups confectioners' sugar

½ teaspoon vanilla extract

½ teaspoon salt

¾ cup marshmallow fluff

2 tablespoons heavy cream

2 tablespoons condensed milk

SPECIAL EQUIPMENT

twinkie molds

6. Sprinkle the flour mixture over the egg whites and then mix everything on low speed for just 10 seconds. Remove the bowl from the mixer, make a well in the center of the batter, and pour the melted butter mixture into the well. Fold gently with a large rubber spatula until the batter shows no trace of flour and the whites and yolks are evenly mixed, about 8 strokes.

7. Immediately scrape the batter into the prepared molds, filling each with about ¾ cup of the batter (a measuring cup can aid in this process). Bake until the cake tops are light brown and feel firm and spring back when touched, 13–15 minutes. Transfer the pan containing the molds to a wire rack and allow the cakes to cool in the molds.

TO MAKE THE FILLING

8. In the bowl of a stand mixer, beat together the butter, confectioners' sugar, vanilla extract, salt, and marshmallow fluff. Add the cream and condensed milk, and beat just until smooth. Transfer the frosting to a pastry bag fitted with a ¼-inch round tip. Pipe frosting into three spots on the underside of the Twinkie, taking care not to overfill. Serve while still warm.

Peach Maple Sherbet Sandwiches

SERVES 8	COOK TIME: 15 MINUTES	PREP TIME: 20 MINUTES

INACTIVE COOK TIME: 2 HOURS   COST: $

Easy

The only thing I like better than dessert is a dessert made with 100 percent natural, unprocessed ingredients. These sandwiches are so healthy that they make you wonder, "Could they possibly be delicious too?" The answer will become clear to you after you put out a tray of them for the kids at a birthday party.

FOR THE COOKIES

1½ cups whole wheat flour, plus extra flour for dusting

½ cup ground oats

½ teaspoon salt

½ teaspoon cinnamon

½–¾ cup coconut oil

¼ cup maple syrup

½ teaspoon vanilla

FOR THE SHERBET

3 cups fresh or frozen peaches

1⅓ cups almond milk, plus more if needed

2 tablespoons maple syrup

TO MAKE THE COOKIES

1. In a medium bowl, combine all the dry ingredients. Slowly add the coconut oil and maple syrup, mixing to combine. Finish with the vanilla. Form into a disk and place in the refrigerator for 30 minutes.

2. Preheat the oven to 350 °F.

3. Lightly dust a cutting board or counter with flour and roll the dough out to ¼ inch thick. Using a cookie cutter, cut out 3-inch rounds. Place on a parchment-lined baking sheet. Bake for 15–20 minutes. Allow the cookies to cool.

TO MAKE THE SHERBET

4. Using a blender, combine the sherbet ingredients and blend until smooth. Pour into a freezer-safe container and freeze for 2 hours or until set.

5. When ready to assemble the sandwiches, remove the sherbet from the freezer and take out of the container. Using the same cookie cutter as used with the dough, cut through the sherbet to make equal-sized cylinders. Next, slice the sherbet and sandwich each slice in between two cookies. Arrange the sandwiches on a sheet tray and refreeze until set.

SATURDAY NIGHT SPECIALS

"SITTING AROUND THE TABLE ON SATURDAY NIGHT, sharing a glass of wine with friends, for me is the "Ahhhhh" moment; it makes the whole week worthwhile. Saturday night dinner is the sparkly carrot at the end of the stick that is my exhausting workweek. But I'm not too exhausted to cook or accessorize my table. It's the day when I want to make that special meal for special people. I mean, who invites people they really don't care about a lot for **SATURDAY NIGHT DINNER?** And on Saturday, even with the errands of weekly shopping and dry cleaning drop-off, there's enough time to devote to doing it up. Sunday, I don't feel that way, maybe because the daily grind starts again the next day. I feel that on Saturdays, you should **"LIVE IT UP, BECAUSE THERE'S NO TOMORROW."** Occasionally this leads to living it up so much that tomorrow lets me know I've overdone it. Hey, so what? Enjoy your Saturday. **"**

—Clinton

Cranberry Fizz

SERVES 6 | COOK TIME: 5–10 MINUTES | PREP TIME: 2 MINUTES | COST: $

Easy

I came up with this in the Clinton Kelly Cocktail Research Institute, also known as my dressing room. I was looking for another way to get cranberries into a Thanksgiving menu, but it's so good I refuse to wait around all year to kick back and drink one, or two, or whatever. Extra bonus point: it's pretty.

½ **lemon**

½ **orange, plus slices for garnish**

Ice

2 cups gin

2 cups cranberry juice

2 cups club soda

Cranberries, for garnish

1. Cut the lemon into 4 wedges and the orange into 4 slices. Place the lemon and orange slices into a pint glass. Muddle aggressively.

2. Transfer the lemon and orange mixture to a pitcher and fill with ice. Add the gin, and then top with cranberry juice and soda. Stir. Garnish with the cranberries and orange slices.

Bruschetta with Peas and Ricotta

SERVES 8 | COOK TIME: 2–5 MINTUES | PREP TIME: 5 MINUTES | COST: $

Easy

Simple, but if the peas are fresh and local, the flavor is wow! That's because they are sweet and tender and haven't had time to turn starchy the way peas that were trucked in from far away often are. If spring peas have a best friend, it's mint. They just want to be served together. And since the flavors are so fresh and delicate, creamy and slightly sweet ricotta pulls it all together.

4 cups peas, shelled

Kosher salt

2 cups fresh sheep's milk ricotta cheese

Zest of 1 lemon

½ cup grated Parmesan

¼ cup fresh mint leaves

Freshly ground black pepper

¼ cup extra virgin olive oil

½ baguette, cut into slices at a bias

1. Fill a large bowl with ice and water. Add the peas to a well-salted, large pot of boiling water. Make sure there is way more water than peas and enough salt for it to taste like the ocean. Cook the peas for about 30 seconds. Remove the peas to the ice bath.

2. In a food processor, mix the ricotta, lemon zest, Parmesan, and mint.

3. Drain the peas and add them to the food processor. Pulse just until the mixture comes together—you want to keep a little texture and not make it totally smooth.

4. Spoon the mixture into a serving bowl, crack some black pepper over the top, and drizzle with extra virgin olive oil.

5. Heat a grill pan to medium-high. Brush the pieces of bread with olive oil and season with salt and pepper. Grill on each side until crisp and grill marks appear, about 1–2 minutes per side.

6. Serve each crostini topped with the pea mixture.

Vegetable Caponata on Sweet Potato Crisps

SERVES 6 | COOK TIME: 20–25 MINUTES | PREP TIME: 15 MINUTES | COST: $

Moderate

Everybody should have some caponata around. It's a traditional Sicilian sweet-and-sour cooked vegetable medley that serves as a halfway house between a vegetable and a condiment. It's a wonderful appetizer on crostini, or served alongside fish or a roast. I made this on the show with Fran Drescher, who really knows her onions when it comes to food, and she can cut veggies in my kitchen anytime. We're talking grown-up knife skills. My twist here is serving it on crisp sweet potato cakes that get that lacy, crunchy, crinkly crust like you achieve with potato pancakes (one of Fran's family's favorites). The secret is hot oil.

TGIF (AND SATURDAY, SUNDAY, AND OTHER GOOD TIMES)

FOR THE CAPONATA

4 tablespoons olive oil

½ cup onion, cut into ¼-inch dice

½ cup celery root, cut into ¼-inch dice

½ cup fennel, cut into ¼-inch dice and reserving the fennel fronds

½ cup sweet potato, cut into ¼-inch dice

Salt

Pepper

¼ cup apple cider vinegar

¼ cup water

2 tablespoons fresh mint, chopped

FOR THE SWEET POTATO CAKES

2 cups sweet potatoes, peeled and grated

½ cup rice flour

TO MAKE THE CAPONATA

1. In a large cast-iron skillet over medium-high heat, add the olive oil. Sauté the onion for 1–2 minutes, until soft and slightly caramelized. Add the remaining vegetables and season with salt and pepper. Cook for about 10–15 minutes, stirring occasionally.

2. Once the vegetables are caramelized and soft, deglaze with the vinegar and water, and reduce until all the liquid has evaporated. Adjust the seasoning, and, off the heat, stir in the mint.

TO MAKE THE SWEET POTATO CAKES

3. In a large mixing bowl, combine all the sweet potato cake ingredients. Season with salt and pepper.

4. In another cast-iron skillet, over medium-high heat, add about 3 tablespoons of olive oil. Once hot, use a tablespoon measure and scoop heaping tablespoons of the sweet potato mixture and press in the pan. The thickness should be about ¼ inch. It may be necessary to work in batches, depending on the size of the pan. Cook the crisps for 3–4 minutes on each side, or until golden brown.

⅓ cup almond milk

2 tablespoons cocoa powder

2 teaspoons ground cumin

Salt

Pepper

Olive oil, for frying

5. Once the sweet potato crisps are cooked through, remove to a plate lined with paper towels. Place on a platter and top the sweet potato crisps with the caponata and garnish with the fennel fronds.

Swordfish Piccata with Escarole Salad

SERVES 4 | COOK TIME: 10 MINUTES | PREP TIME: 15 MINUTES | COST: $

Moderate

I went to college in New Jersey and I am a huge fan of everything in New Jersey, from Bruce Springsteen to beefsteak tomatoes. The license plates say it's THE GARDEN STATE, but to me it's also THE OCEAN STATE, with wonderful seafood from its rich waters. Jersey swordfish is a particular favorite—it's big on flavor, which is why I like it with a quick, easy, and super flavorful pan sauce. When I want to add flavor, I think of salt, acidity, and heat—spicy heat, in this case, with the famous Bomba peppers of Calabria. They pack a punch, so they want big flavors to balance them. I look to add flavor in every step in this dish, so instead of dredging in flour, I use pulverized almonds, which give you the crispiness of flour and an extra sweet layer of ffavor. The same holds true for the escarole salad—big flavor, starting out with crushed anchovies. When I made this on the show with Daisy Fuentes, she gave me her philosophy on salad dressing—and love: "Salads, like people, are best underdressed."

Works for me.

FOR THE SWORDFISH PICCATA

4 1-inch-thick swordfish steaks, skin removed

Salt, to taste

Pepper, to taste

1 cup almond flour or ground almonds

2 tablespoons extra virgin olive oil

¼ cup dry white wine

2 tablespoons butter

Zest and juice of 2 lemons

1½ tablespoons Bomba Calabrese or red pepper paste

2 tablespoons capers, drained

2 tablespoons fresh parsley leaves, plus more for garnish

TO MAKE THE SWORDFISH PICCATA

1. Season the fish with salt and pepper. Place the almond flour or ground almonds in a baking dish and season with salt and pepper. Dredge the fish on all sides in the flour, patting off any excess.

2. In a large skillet, heat the olive oil over high heat until it just begins to smoke. Cook the fish in hot oil, flipping once to brown both sides, about 3 minutes per side. Work in batches if necessary to avoid overcrowding the pan. Remove the fish to a paper towel–lined plate.

A fishy secret

Many people are fearful of cooking fish. Don't be one of them. The secret is, don't overcook it. Overcooking is how you get that unpleasant "fishy" flavor. Moist and flaky is the way to go.

FOR THE ESCAROLE SALAD

3 anchovy fillets packed in oil, chopped to a paste

Zest and juice of 2 lemons

1 clove garlic, minced

2 tablespoons extra virgin olive oil

2 tablespoons red wine vinegar

1 head of escarole, washed and torn

3. Keeping the pan over medium heat, add the wine, butter, lemon zest and juice, and Bomba Calabrese to the pan. Toss in the capers and parsley, and season with salt and pepper, cooking just to combine flavors, about 1 minute. Plate the fish and top with the pan sauce. Garnish with the parsley and serve with the escarole salad.

TO MAKE THE ESCAROLE SALAD

4. Combine the anchovies, lemon zest and juice, and garlic in a medium bowl. Whisk in the olive oil and red wine vinegar, and toss the dressing with the escarole leaves to coat. Season with salt and pepper to taste.

CLINTON'S **CRAFT** CORNER

The upcycled tabletop

Tablecloths can be pricey. You are also limited to what the designers like. That may not always be what you like. Hey, why not roll your own? Cloth from the fabric store is very inexpensive (remnants are even cheaper), and the choices are endless. For serving trays, I like to rummage around garage sales for antique mirrors; they really dress up a table (and make it look like you have twice as much food!). And here's my numero uno tip: make friends with your florist and stop by at the end of the day and ask about any leftover flowers that didn't sell. They're always still beautiful and a real bargain.

Pan-Seared Salmon with Beet Salad

SERVES 4 | COOK TIME: 7–10 MINUTES | COST: $

Easy

Fish is a lot more fun when you get the skin nice and crispy. Even for professionals, I find that a nonstick pan is the most foolproof way to crisp up fish. Just make sure the skin is dry before you put it in the pan. When you give salmon this treatment, it is beautifully full of flavor, which means it can stand up to beets, horseradish, lemon juice, and mustard. These flavors open up the palate and are totally satisfying. If you are weight-conscious (who isn't these days?), do like I do and skip the starch side dish. This is a satisfying meal all by itself.

3 tablespoons extra virgin olive oil

4 5-ounce skin-on salmon fillets

Salt, to taste

Pepper, to taste

1 tablespoon mustard

Juice of ½ lemon, plus more for garnish

1 large beet, peeled and grated

1 tablespoon fresh horseradish, peeled and grated

¼ cup fresh parsley, leaves torn

3 scallions, sliced on a bias

1. Heat a large cast-iron skillet over medium-high heat with 2 tablespoons of the olive oil. Season the salmon with salt and pepper.

2. Cook the salmon skin side down for 3–4 minutes, making sure the skin is crispy. Flip the salmon and continue to cook for 3 minutes, for medium rare, or until the salmon reaches desired doneness.

3. Meanwhile, in a medium bowl, whisk together the remaining oil, mustard, and lemon juice. Toss in the remaining ingredients to coat lightly, and season with salt and pepper.

4. Plate the salmon skin side up with the beet salad. Garnish with the lemon juice.

Hold your horses!

This recipe calls for grating fresh horseradish. Chances are you should be able to find it in your town. I live in Cleveland, which is what they call a "mid-market" town. The way I figure it, if I can find it here, it's a good bet you can find it in most places. If not, prepared horseradish packs a punch too.

Double-Cut Pork Chops with Corn and Jalapeño Salad

| SERVES 4 TO 6 | COOK TIME: 17–20 MINUTES | PREP TIME: 15 MINUTES |

INACTIVE PREP TIME: 2–24 HOURS | COST: $

Moderate

When you see the words *pork chops* in the name of a recipe, you think that's what it's all about. Not really. For me it starts with the corn salad. When corn is sweet and just picked, this spicy, herby salad really excites me—crunchy, smoky, and fiery. I can eat it with pork chops or chicken or fish . . . don't let me forget shrimp. As for the pork chops, here's my main rule, and it holds true for everything I grill: set up your grill so that one side is very hot and the other side is a lower heat; you char it up to start and move it to the cool side to cook more gently and evenly all the way through.

TGIF (AND SATURDAY, SUNDAY, AND OTHER GOOD TIMES)

FOR THE PORK CHOPS

1 tablespoon sugar

1 tablespoon salt

1 tablespoon coriander, toasted and ground

4 double-cut pork chops

2 tablespoons olive oil, plus more to drizzle

FOR THE CORN AND JALAPEÑO SALAD

4 ears corn, shucked, with silk removed

Zest and juice of 2 limes

¼ cup cilantro (leaves only), chopped

1 pint Sweet 100 tomatoes, halved

3 scallions, chopped

1 clove garlic, minced

1 jalapeño, minced

Freshly ground black pepper

TO MAKE THE PORK CHOPS

1. Combine the sugar, salt, and coriander.

2. Rub each of the pork chops on both sides with the mixture, and refrigerate for 2 hours and up to overnight.

3. Preheat half the grill to high, and preheat the other half to low heat.

4. Drizzle the chops with olive oil and grill for 3–4 minutes per side over high heat, to sear. Once seared, transfer to the cooler part of the grill to finish cooking through, about 10 minutes, or until medium to medium well.

TO MAKE THE CORN AND JALAPEÑO SALAD

5. Grill the ears of corn till charred at parts, about 3 minutes per side. Remove the kernels from the ears to a bowl, and toss with the lime zest and juice, cilantro, tomatoes, scallions, garlic, and jalapeño. Add the 2 tablespoons of olive oil and toss to coat. Season with salt and pepper.

6. Serve the pork chops sliced and topped with the salad.

Beef Tenderloin with Pomegranate Fennel Salad

SERVES 8 | **COOK TIME: 35–45 MINUTES** | **PREP TIME: 20 MINUTES** | **COST: $$**

CLINTON: Carla, Daphne, and I put our heads together to make something special for Michael and Mario. And let this be a lesson to you about cooking for "serious" food people. Don't be intimidated: if it's good, it doesn't have to be complicated. And always remember that guys like them got in the chef business in the first place because they love food.

CARLA: Amen, sir. And we wanted to do something that was Mediterranean in spirit and in honor of Michael and Mario, so we have fennel, oranges, a rub full of herbs, lots of olive oil, and pomegranate syrup. And instead of using a roasting rack, we lay the roast right on the vegetables so that they cook in all the juices from the roast.

DAPHNE: Which got me thinking. Those vegetables and fruits are wonderful cooked, but they'd also make a great salad. That way you really explore all the texture and flavor possibilities of these ingredients.

Moderate

FOR THE RUB

2 teaspoons ground
fennel seed

1 teaspoon freshly
cracked black pepper

3 tablespoons olive oil

2 teaspoons kosher salt

2 tablespoons rosemary,
finely chopped, plus
sprigs for garnish

FOR THE BEEF TENDERLOIN

3 pounds beef tenderloin
tied with butcher's twine

2 fennel stalks, cut into
3-inch pieces with bulbs
and fronds reserved

2 sprigs thyme, plus
more for garnish

TO MAKE THE BEEF TENDERLOIN

1. Preheat the oven to 375 °F.

2. In a small bowl, mix together the ingredients for the rub, making a loose paste. Rub the tied tenderloin thoroughly with the mixture.

3. In a medium-sized bowl, toss together the fennel stalks, thyme sprigs, and orange slices. Drizzle generously with the olive oil, and season with salt and pepper. Add these to the bottom of a roasting pan, spreading evenly. Place the tenderloin on top of the fennel orange mixture. Place the roasting pan in the oven and cook until an instant-read thermometer reads 125 °F (for medium rare), about 30–40 minutes.

4. Remove the tenderloin from the pan and cut the twine off. Let rest at least 10 minutes. Transfer the vegetables to a serving platter. Garnish with the fresh rosemary sprigs.

1 orange, sliced into
rounds ¼ inch thick

3 tablespoons olive oil

Salt, to taste

Pepper, to taste

1 cup red wine

½ cup beef stock

¼ cup pomegranate syrup

2 tablespoons butter

FOR THE POMEGRANATE
FENNEL SALAD

Zest and segments of
1 orange, separated

Juice of 2 lemons

2 tablespoons olive oil

Salt

Pepper

½ cup pomegranate seeds

5. Place the roasting rack on the stove over medium heat. Add the wine and, with a wooden spoon, scrape up the bits on the bottom of the pan. Once the wine has reduced by half, add the beef stock and pomegranate syrup. Reduce only slightly, 1–2 minutes. Whisk in the butter. Pour the sauce into a gravy boat.

TO MAKE THE POMEGRANATE FENNEL SALAD

6. Shave the reserved fennel bulbs thinly into a bowl of ice water. In a small mixing bowl, whisk the orange zest, lemon juice, and about 2 tablespoons of olive oil together, and season with salt and pepper.

7. Drain the fennel well right before serving. Toss the fennel with the orange segments and coat everything in the vinaigrette. Mix in the pomegranate seeds. Plate and garnish with the reserved fennel fronds.

8. To serve, slice the tenderloin into medallions. Place some of the sauce onto a plate and top with a piece or two of beef. Top with a little of the salad.

Red Wine–Braised Short Ribs

SERVES 8 TO 10 | COOK TIME: 1 HOUR 30 MINUTES | PREP TIME: 20 MINUTES

COST: $$

Moderate

Short ribs are a true one-pot wonder. There's no comfort food that is more comforting than the aromas of slow-cooking wine-soaked beef filling up your pad. When you make it this way, it tastes so truly luxurious that you forget it's an inexpensive cut. What I love is the ease of this recipe: you cook your aromatic vegetables down, add some wine and whatever, put it in the oven at a low temperature, and voilà, a delicious dinner is ready in an hour.

6 pounds bone-in beef short ribs

Kosher salt

Freshly ground black pepper

4 tablespoons olive oil

2 stalks celery, diced

1 medium carrot, diced

1 onion, diced

6 cloves garlic

1 Fresno chili, halved

¼ cup tomato paste

5 sprigs fresh thyme (leaves only)

1 bay leaf

1 quart chicken stock

2 cups dry red wine

⅓ cup red wine vinegar

1. Season the short ribs with salt and pepper and set aside.

2. Preheat the oven to 325 °F.

3. Heat 2 tablespoons of the olive oil in a large enameled cast-iron Dutch oven over medium-high heat. Add half of the short ribs to the pan and cook on all sides until browned, about 2 minutes per side. Transfer the ribs to a plate. Repeat with the remaining ribs.

4. Pour off all but 2 or 3 tablespoons of fat from the pan. Add the celery, carrot, onion, garlic, and chili to the pan, along with a large pinch of salt, and cook over medium heat until softened, about 7 minutes. Add the tomato paste and cook, stirring, until glossy, about 2 minutes. Add the thyme sprigs and bay leaf, and cook, stirring, for 2 minutes. Scrape the bottom of the pan. Add the stock, wine, and vinegar, and bring to a boil. Return the short ribs to the pan, cover, and braise in the oven for 1 hour.

5. Remove the ribs to a serving platter and cover to keep warm while you simmer the liquid to reduce it by half. Pour the sauce over the ribs and top them with the Watercress Salad.

FOR THE WATERCRESS SALAD

1 bunch watercress, cleaned and stemmed

1 tablespoon fresh horseradish, grated, plus more for garnish

2 teaspoons chives, chopped

1 tablespoon red wine vinegar

Drizzle of olive oil, to taste

Salt, to taste

Pepper, to taste

TO MAKE THE WATERCRESS SALAD

6. Combine all the ingredients in a bowl. Serve on top of the braised short ribs. If you want, add a grating of horseradish over the completed dish before serving

NOTE: You can also use brisket or top round for this dish.

to braise a beast

The key to braising is not to drown the meat in liquid. You only want the liquid to come about three-quarters of the way up the meat so that it caramelizes while it braises.

Artichoke Scafata

SERVES 4 TO 6 | **COOK TIME: 15–20 MINUTES** | **PREP TIME: 20 MINUTES** | **COST: $**

Moderate

If you had to ask me for one dish that looks like spring, here's my vote. There's a good reason for that: it's the kind of thing that Romans make in the spring. What's their recipe? Basically you go to the market, find the things that look like they just came out of the ground, bring them home, put them in a big pot, and cook them up. There's no getting around the fact that artichokes require a little more prep time and practice than other vegetables, and, at least in the American diet, they are kind of special, so why not have them on that special day, as in Saturday, when you get down to serious cooking?

2 small lemons, halved, plus juice to garnish

15 baby artichokes

¼ cup extra virgin olive oil, plus more to garnish

1 red onion, thinly sliced

1 teaspoon hot red pepper flakes

½ cup dry white wine

1 pound fresh peas, shelled

4 bunches scallions, root ends trimmed and whites and greens cut into 2-inch pieces

Salt, to taste

Freshly ground pepper, to taste

1 bunch fresh mint leaves

1. Fill a large bowl with water, and squeeze the lemon halves into it.

2. Remove and discard the tough outer leaves of the artichokes, and trim the stems. Then cut the artichokes in half and scoop out the choke. As you work, submerge the halved artichokes in the lemon water.

3. In a Dutch oven, heat the olive oil over medium heat until hot, add the onion and cook until soft and translucent, about 4 minutes. Add the red pepper flakes, the wine, 1 cup of hot water, the peas, and the drained artichokes. Cover, and cook until the artichokes are just tender, 10–12 minutes. Add the scallions, cover, and reduce the heat to a simmer. Cook until the scallions are wilted and soft, about 4 minutes. Season with salt and black pepper.

4. Tear the mint leaves into pieces and sprinkle them over the scafata. Garnish with a drizzle of olive oil and lemon juice. Serve either warm or at room temperature.

Moderate

Crown Roast of Lamb with Quinoa Stuffing and Black Truffle Gratin

| SERVES 8 | COOK TIME: 35 TO 45 MINUTES | PREP TIME: 20 MINUTES | COST: $$ |

MARIO: This special dinner has a naughty and nice side. I made the naughty side dish with potato gratin and black truffles.

DAPHNE: Naughty just like you. I'm making a nice side of quinoa, almonds, pomegranate, and honey, proving that to be nice, you don't have to be flavorless. And quinoa is chock-full of nice health benefits.

MARIO: Just like you, Daph.

DAPHNE: Touché, chef. Very often stuffing is heavy and loaded with fat and calories, but this one is quite simple and based on quinoa. It's a beautiful grain, full of protein and minerals and easy to cook.

MARIO: I always think of naughty as taking longer than nice, but watching you make this…maybe not. My naughty side starts with a cream and Parmigiano-Reggiano sauce laced with nutmeg and Swiss cheese. And now the totally amazing black truffles. They're big-time naughty. When pigs and hounds dig them out of the dirt, they think they are following the aroma of a sex-starved lady pig or dog.

DAPHNE: Enough with the naughty, or we'll end up doing *The Chew* on the Spice Channel.

MARIO: And don't let me forget the succulent, full-flavored, fresh-off-the-hoof crown roast of lamb. Couldn't be simpler: season, put in the oven, and take a nap for 20 minutes.

DAPHNE: Now that's my idea of nice.

MARIO: But naughty if you oversleep!

FOR THE CROWN ROAST

1 2-pound crown roast of lamb (have your butcher prepare it for you)

Salt, to taste

Pepper, to taste

4 tablespoons extra virgin olive oil

TO MAKE THE CROWN ROAST

1. Preheat the oven to 400 °F.

2. Season the lamb with a generous amount of salt and pepper, drizzle with the olive oil, and set aside at room temperature.

FOR THE QUINOA STUFFING

3 tablespoons extra virgin olive oil

2 shallots, sliced

2 cloves garlic, minced

3 cups quinoa, cooked according to package instructions

Zest and juice of 3 lemons

¼ cup slivered almonds, toasted

½ cup fresh mint leaves, chiffonade

TO MAKE THE QUINOA STUFFING

3. Heat a skillet over medium-high heat with 2 tablespoons of the olive oil. Sauté the shallots and garlic just until tender, about 2–3 minutes. In a large bowl, mix the cooked quinoa, lemon zest and juice, shallots and garlic mixture, almonds, mint, coriander, and pomegranate seeds. Drizzle with the remaining olive oil and honey, and season with salt and pepper. Toss to combine.

4. In a large roasting pan, make a bed for the roast to sit on with a few large spoonfuls of the quinoa stuffing. Transfer the lamb roast to the bed and fill with the remaining quinoa mix. Drizzle with a little extra virgin olive oil and place in the preheated oven. Roast the lamb until the internal temperature reaches 130 °F, approximately 20–30 minutes.

2 teaspoons ground
coriander

½ cup pomegranate seeds

1 tablespoon honey

Salt, to taste

Pepper, to taste

FOR THE YOGURT SAUCE

1 cup strained yogurt

Zest and juice of 1 lemon

1 clove garlic, minced

1 handful of picked mint
leaves, chopped

Salt and pepper, to taste

Olive oil, to taste

5. Remove from the oven and transfer to a large platter. Top with the quinoa mix from the pan. Loosely tent with aluminum foil and allow to rest for 10 minutes before serving with the yogurt sauce.

TO MAKE THE YOGURT SAUCE

6. In a food processor, combine the ingredients and pulse until smooth. Continue to puree while drizzling the olive oil. Taste and adjust to desired seasoning.

Rinse and repeat

If you rinse your quinoa thoroughly, it gets rid of that bitter taste that some people notice.

Butter, for the baking dish

**2 pounds Yukon Gold
potatoes, peeled and
sliced crosswise into
⅛-inch-thick slices**

Salt, to taste

Pepper, to taste

3 cups heavy cream

**¾ cup grated
Parmigiano-Reggiano**

**¼ teaspoon freshly
grated nutmeg**

**1 small black truffle, plus
more for garnish (optional)**

**¾ cup grated
Emmentaler or good-
quality Swiss cheese**

TO MAKE THE BLACK TRUFFLE GRATIN

1. Place a rack in the middle of the oven and preheat to 400 °F.

2. Generously butter a gratin dish or other shallow baking dish. Layer potatoes in the casserole dish. Season with salt and pepper.

3. Put the cream in a heavy-bottomed pan and bring to a simmer. Simmer for about 5 minutes. Stir in the Parmigiano-Reggiano and grate the nutmeg and half the truffle, if using. Season the cream generously with salt and pepper.

4. Carefully pour the cream on top of the potatoes and sprinkle on the Emmentaler or Swiss cheese. Grate more truffle on top and season with more pepper.

5. Bake in the oven until the top is a deep golden brown, about 40 minutes, or until a toothpick inserted into the potatoes comes out without resistance. Let the potatoes cool slightly (this will help thicken the cream and set the gratin) for at least 20 minutes.

6. Serve the potatoes and grate fresh black truffles over each serving. Serve with the lamb.

Pear Tarte Tatin

SERVES 6 | COOK TIME: 35–40 MINUTES | PREP TIME: 10 MINUTES | COST: $

Easy

An excellent and easy dessert, provided you have one of two things: 1.) homemade puff pastry, or 2.) a good store-bought puff pastry, which means it's made with flour and real butter, and that's it. To get that real French pastry shop tatin-y taste, browned butter and sugar give a beautiful caramel color and flavor. Then caramelizing the pears in the pan will give them a super tasteful crust.

4 tablespoons butter

½ cup sugar

1 teaspoon salt

4–5 ripe and firm pears, peeled, cored, and halved lengthwise

3 tablespoons flour

1 package puff pastry, thawed

Vanilla ice cream, to serve

1. Preheat the oven to 375 °F.

2. In a large ovenproof sauté pan, melt the butter over medium-high heat. Once bubbling, sprinkle in the sugar and the salt.

3. Add the pears to the pan cut side down. Cook until the sugar begins to turn light golden brown, about 3 minutes. Flip the pears and cook for another 30 seconds.

4. Dust the counter with flour and roll out the puff pastry to the size of the sauté pan. Top the sauté pan with the puff pastry, tucking the edges into the pan.

5. Transfer to the oven and cook for 25–30 minutes, or until the pastry is golden brown. Let the tarte rest for about 5 minutes to cool enough to handle.

6. Place the serving side of a larger flat platter over the pan. The platter should be larger than the pan. Carefully flip the platter and pan to reveal the tarte. Serve with vanilla ice cream.

TGIF (AND SATURDAY, SUNDAY, AND OTHER GOOD TIMES)

Chocolate Pumpkin Cake

| SERVES 10 | COOK TIME: 35–45 MINUTES | PREP TIME: 45 MINUTES | COST: $ |

Moderate

I know many of you have never been completely sold on pumpkin as a dessert. It's just that pumpkins are so big you have to do as many things as you can with the pumpkin in the interests of keeping it out of the compost heap. So someone said, "Hey, let's convince people it's a great dessert too." This moist, sweet, creamy, chocolate-covered cake will make it hard to believe that pumpkin was ever used for anything besides dessert.

FOR THE PUMPKIN CAKE

2 cups sugar

1 cup vegetable oil

4 large eggs

2 cups all-purpose flour

2 teaspoons baking soda

1 teaspoon baking powder

3 teaspoons pumpkin pie spice

1 teaspoon salt

2 cups fresh or canned pumpkin puree (see Note page 113)

FOR THE MASCARPONE FILLING

2 cups mascarpone

1 cup fresh or canned pumpkin puree, strained of excess liquid

1 tablespoon pumpkin pie spice

2 teaspoons salt

4 cups powdered sugar

1 teaspoon vanilla extract

TO MAKE THE PUMPKIN CAKE

1. Preheat the oven to 350 °F. Grease and flour two 9-inch round layer cake pans.

2. Combine the sugar, vegetable oil, and eggs in a large mixing bowl, and mix well. Whisk the dry ingredients in a separate bowl. Stir the dry into the wet ingredients until just combined. Fold in the pumpkin puree.

3. Divide the batter between the two cake pans. Bake for 35–40 minutes, rotating the pans halfway through cooking. When a toothpick comes out clean, the cakes are done. Let cool for 5 minutes, and then turn the cakes out onto cooling racks.

TO MAKE THE MASCARPONE FILLING

4. While the cakes are cooling, make the filling. Beat the mascarpone and the pumpkin puree until blended, and then add the pumpkin spice, salt, and powdered sugar. Mix at a high speed until blended, about 1 minute. Once it's fully combined, add the vanilla and beat for another 30 seconds.

5. Once the cakes have cooled completely, cut through each cake horizontally with a serrated knife (there will now be four rounds of cake to work with).

FOR THE DARK CHOCOLATE GANACHE

3 tablespoons corn syrup

6 ounces heavy cream

12 ounces dark chocolate, chopped into small bits

½ teaspoon vanilla extract

Ginger snaps, crushed, for garnish

6. Spread the filling evenly between the layers.

7. Once assembled, transfer the cake to a cake stand with parchment paper lined around the edges (to keep the cake stand clean).

TO MAKE THE DARK CHOCOLATE GANACHE

8. In a small saucepan, combine the corn syrup and heavy cream, and bring to a simmer. Add the chocolate. Stir until smooth. Remove from the heat and add the vanilla extract.

9. Pour over the cake and use a spoon or butter knife to make sure that all of the cake is covered in chocolate.

10. Garnish with the ginger snaps. Once the ganache is set, remove the parchment. Slice and serve.

GINGER PEACH MARGARITA | GRILLED CORN SOUP WITH BASIL AND FETA | LOBSTER THERMIDOR | LOVE LETTERS (VEGETABLES, PASTA, AND CHEESE, FROM ITALY WITH LOVE) | GRILLED T-BONE LAMB CHOPS WITH FAVA BEAN AND FETA SALAD | MANGO BONBONS

DATE NIGHT!

"YOU'VE HEARD IT A MILLION TIMES: the way to a man's heart is through his stomach. I think the same thing goes for a woman's heart as well. A woman likes to be cooked for. I think there's a different kind of meal that you put together for a first date, or a third date, or a fourth for that matter. I would never cook an elaborate meal on a first date. Face it, that's a lot of time investment for somebody who might turn out to be a nut job. But if it's for someone you care about, then time or even money isn't the object. **YOU SPEND FOR THE BEST YOU CAN AFFORD** and you make it the best you can. In this case, it's the thought—the sentiment behind the meal—that really counts.

So, guys, what makes for a good date night dinner in your book?**"**

—*Clinton*

"I LIKE DINNER FOR TWO at the house, as opposed to a "romantic" expensive date. Since you're not blowing a car payment at a restaurant, you can spend a little more on the ingredients and you are still going to come out ahead and make something swanky. An old warhorse like beef Wellington may sound like a tired dish, but if you get really nice beef and get really good puff pastry and get some really good liver, you can make something really remarkable out of it. The key thing is getting the best ingredients—get to know the butchers and produce guys, even at supermarkets. If you take the time to talk with them, you are going to get VIP treatment, especially when they see that you're a regular customer, and that's true for all retail.

Now think about the wine you two will have at home. You probably rarely spend $35 for a bottle at home, but in a restaurant that's far from the most expensive wine on the list, and sometimes it's the cheapest. Look at it this way: that $35 bottle at home would cost $140 in a restaurant. Sounds like a deal, don't you think? Same goes for the beef Wellington. At $25 per person, you've got something that would easily cost twice that in a good restaurant. So stay home for your date. It's cheaper and you won't have to ask, "My place or yours?"**"**

—Mario

WHEN IT COMES TO DATE NIGHT at our house, my husband, John, and I often do a salad, but a bit fancier. I truly love a salad with sweet onions, tomato, lemon, olive oil, and feta cheese right in the dressing tossed with pomegranates and fresh field greens. And don't let me forget fish tacos. That doesn't sound that romantic, but there's nothing I love more, especially when we grill fresh fish. I often like to wing it, taking inspiration from what John is in the mood for, seeing what we have in the fridge, and taking it from there.

Really the most important thing is setting the scene. If you take the time to put out candles and flowers and set the table, it says: "This night is special for the two of us." Music too makes all the difference; I have all kinds of playlists. It depends—if we're doing old school, we'll have an Ella Fitzgerald mix. We have a great playlist that I call "boat music," because it's what I envision the Saint-Tropez yachts would play. It's sort of Brazilian, very soothing, but also kind of upbeat and lively, and now that I think about it, I don't know what it has to do with Saint-Tropez in France except, in my mind, it's all one big romantic stew.

—Daphne

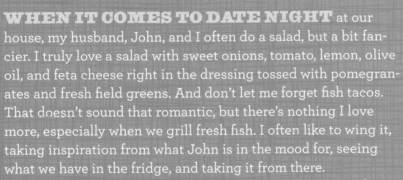

IT'S HARD TO PICK A MEAL that floats everyone's boat. Every couple is different, so my advice is more general. It's really important when cooking something special to stay in your wheelhouse. Don't go for something complicated and fancy that you've never made before. A steamed lobster or a rosy red rib eye with a nice char on the crust is simple, and both are probably at the top of everyone's wish list. Stay light instead of heavy. Nothing rivals too many heavy courses as a romantic buzzkill. Champagne is always nice, but so are plenty of less expensive sparkling wines. They all say this is a celebration. Okay, if you backed me into a corner and said, "Pick one dish right now," I might say a paella. It's a one-pot meal but full of little tastes of shellfish, sausage, and sometimes chicken. It looks amazing and most everyone likes it yet people rarely make it. Or you could always just ask your special guy or gal what they would like you to make. The important thing is that you make it. No home delivery or takeout.

—*Michael*

DATE NIGHT is about the other person. What makes them happy. Call it "fork play." For me that other person is my husband, Matthew. He loves Indian food, so I will often make him a curry with all kinds of special stuff on the side—chutneys, spices, nuts. I call those special little flavor packages "bits and bobs." They are the accents that make a dish special. One thing I never make is something heavy that puts him right to sleep. So if it's a long-cooked braise, it will be something intensely flavored, but it won't sit in your stomach like a sack of potatoes. I take my hat off to Michael Symon, who taught me a lot about brightening and emphasizing the flavor potential in my old standbys. It has helped me take what I already know and make it better. That's always my goal, Date Night and every day. You've got to better-up yourself.

—*Carla*

Ginger Peach Margarita

SERVES 1 | COOK TIME: 10 MINUTES | PREP TIME: 5 MINUTES | COST: $

Easy

The secret ingredient to this gringo's margarita is a ginger simple syrup. Take my advice and make enough to store in the fridge. It's great in iced tea or over ice cream. I researched this cocktail with great dedication (can I get an "Olé!" please?). So make sure you follow these measurements exactly . . . or not. You're the one who has to drink it. And buy the best tequila you can afford because, believe me, there is a difference the next morning.

1½ ounces silver tequila

¾ ounce lime juice

½ ounce peach schnapps

1 ounce peach puree

¾ ounce Ginger Simple Syrup

Ice

2 peaches, sliced

Champagne

1. Add all the ingredients except the peach slices and champagne to a shaker. Shake well and pour into a salt-rimmed margarita glass. Add a splash of champagne to the top of the margarita and serve with a slice of peach.

2. To make a frozen margarita, puree all the ingredients (except the peach slices and champagne) in a blender. Serve in a salt-rimmed glass, topped with champagne and garnished with a peach slice.

FOR THE GINGER SIMPLE SYRUP

1 cup sugar

1 cup water

1 large piece of fresh ginger, peeled and sliced into thin rounds

TO MAKE THE GINGER SIMPLE SYRUP

1. Bring the sugar and water to a boil in a saucepan over medium-high heat until the sugar dissolves. Add the ginger and bring to a simmer. Remove from the heat, and let steep for 1 hour. Pour the syrup through a sieve into an airtight container and discard the ginger. Refrigerate for up to 5 days.

Grilled Corn Soup with Basil and Feta

SERVES 4 | **COOK TIME: 20–30 MINUTES** | **PREP TIME: 15 MINUTES** | **COST: $**

Easy

I'm from New Jersey, the Garden State. When I was growing up, we'd all pile in the car to drive down to the Jersey Shore, and we always stopped at the farm stand for some fresh-picked corn. It was so good we'd always buy a bushel of the stuff. With apologies to Michael, who is a champion of midwestern corn, there is nothing as sweet as Jersey sweet corn. We had to find some delicious ways to use it all up, and that's where this delicious creamy corn soup comes in. It takes about 5 minutes to make, but it has deep, complex flavor. It's equally good warm or cold.

½ **head garlic, skin on, plus 2 cloves**

Extra virgin olive oil

4 **ears corn, shucked**

Salt

Freshly ground pepper

1 **quart water**

½ **onion, chopped**

2 **carrots**

½ **cup Greek yogurt**

½ **cup feta, crumbled**

Basil (leaves only), chiffonade, for garnish

1. Preheat the oven to 400 °F.

2. Place the garlic head on a sheet of aluminum foil, drizzle with 1 tablespoon of extra virgin olive oil, wrap with foil, and roast for 20 minutes until soft and caramelized.

3. Preheat a grill or grill pan to medium-high. Brush the grill with extra virgin olive oil. Season the corn with salt and pepper and grill, until charred lightly, about 10 minutes, rotating through the cooking process. Cut the kernels from the cob, reserving the cobs, and set aside.

4. Place the cobs into a pot, and top with the water. Add the onion, carrots, and garlic cloves, plus a pinch of salt and pepper. Bring to a boil, cover, and simmer. After 15 minutes, strain the corn stock, discarding the solids.

5. Add the charred corn, roasted garlic, and Greek yogurt to a blender with 1–2 cups of the corn stock, and blend until completely pureed. Add a little more of the corn stock to loosen the soup, if necessary. Check seasonings and adjust to taste.

6. Pour the puree into serving bowls and top with the crumbled feta. Garnish with the basil.

NOTE: Corn stock will last 3–5 days in the refrigerator and up to 6 months in the freezer.

Stock up on stock

Although this recipe calls for grilling instead of boiling corn, I always have some corn stock on hand made from water corn was boiled in. You can reduce it, freeze it in ice cube trays, and have a delicious soup base.

Lobster Thermidor

SERVES 4 | COOK TIME: 10–15 MINUTES | PREP TIME: 20 MINUTES | COST: $$

Easy

This is my numero uno D&D meal, as in decadent and delicious. I first had it when I was thirteen years old and went to the Clam Box in Carmel, California, with my grandparents, "Kona" and "Wild Bill." One taste was all it took. I thought it was the food of the gods (or, as Mario calls it, "an upscale casserole"). I try to have it once a year, for special occasions. Many thanks to Julia Child who inspired this, but I simplified it a bit. She has you put the cooked lobster back in the shells, but that takes time and effort, and when it's date night—or any night, for that matter—I want to get right down to business.

4 cooked lobster tails

1 stick unsalted butter, cut into pieces

½ onion, minced

1 teaspoon thyme

½ teaspoon paprika

¼ pound mushrooms, trimmed and thinly sliced

1 cup white wine

½ cup heavy cream

Juice of ½ lemon

¼ teaspoon black pepper

⅛ teaspoon salt

2 cups crushed crackers

1. Cut the lobster meat into small pieces.

2. In a sauté pan over medium heat, melt 1 tablespoon of the butter, then add the onion, thyme, paprika, and mushrooms, and sauté for 8 minutes. Add the lobster and toss, then set aside.

3. In a saucepot, reduce the wine by three-fourths, then whisk in the cream and reduce for another minute. Remove from the heat and stir in the remaining 7 tablespoons of butter, along with the lemon juice, pepper, and salt.

4. Preheat the broiler.

5. Place the lobster meat into ramekins, then add the cream sauce. Top with the crushed cracker mixture, then place under the broiler until golden brown, about 3–5 minutes. Serve.

Warming up with beurre

The crowning touch for Lobster Thermidor and many other seafood dishes is a simple sauce that the French call *beurre blanc*. It is made with butter, cream, and white wine. I ask you, with that combination, how can you go wrong?

Love Letters (Vegetables, Pasta, and Cheese, from Italy with Love)

SERVES 4 TO 6 | COOK TIME: 35–40 MINUTES | PREP TIME: 45 MINUTES | COST: $

Moderate

This is a perfect meal for a first date, but don't let that stop you if the two of you are already in a long-term relationship…even married! Why not rekindle the flames of love with a little wilted chard in a ravioli? I promise it's a lot sexier than it sounds. These lovely little pasta packages have two things going for them in the date department. First, they make for nice bites instead of long strands of pasta, which can be slurpy and sloppy, and no one wants to be slurpy and sloppy when they are trying to impress a romantic interest. And second, they are something you can make together in the kitchen. Cooking compatibility is, in my book, one of the keys to a successful love affair.

FOR THE RAVIOLI

5 tablespoons olive oil

1 red onion, finely diced

1 teaspoon chili flakes

Kosher salt

3 cups chard, washed, stemmed, and thinly sliced

Freshly ground black pepper

2 cups ricotta

⅓ cup Parmigiano-Reggiano, grated

½ teaspoon freshly grated nutmeg

1 pound fresh pasta sheets or Homemade Pasta (recipe follows)

Semolina, for dusting

TO MAKE THE RAVIOLI

1. In a large sauté pan over medium-high heat, add about 3 tablespoons of the olive oil.

2. Add the onion and chili flakes and season with salt, then cook until tender, about 6–8 minutes.

3. Add the remaining olive oil and toss in the chard. Season with salt and pepper, and cook for about 20 minutes, or until the chard is tender. Remove the chard mixture into a bowl and let cool slightly.

4. Stir in the ricotta and Parmigiano-Reggiano, and season with the nutmeg, salt, and pepper.

5. Lay out a sheet of pasta, working one at a time, and cut the sheets into 3-inch squares. Place 1 tablespoon chard filling into the center of each square.

6. Wet the edges of the pasta with warm water, and fold in half to form rectangles (or love letters). Press edges to seal. Put the finished ravioli on a cookie sheet sprinkled with semolina.

7. Bring a pot of salted water to a boil.

8. Cook the ravioli 4–5 minutes.

2 tablespoons olive oil, plus more to drizzle

½ pound bacon, chopped

1 red onion, thinly sliced

3 cloves garlic, thinly sliced

1½ teaspoons crushed red pepper

1 ½ cups store-bought tomato sauce

Salt, to taste

Pepper, to taste

½ cup freshly grated Parmigiano-Reggiano

1 large handful parsley, chopped finely

TO MAKE THE PASTA SAUCE

9. Meanwhile, in a large sauté pan over medium-high heat, add about 2 tablespoons of olive oil and cook the bacon until crisp. Add the onion and cook for about 3 minutes more. Toss in the garlic and the crushed red pepper, and cook for another minute.

10. Add about 1½ cups of tomato sauce to the pan and cook for about 5 minutes to meld the flavors. Season with salt and pepper.

11. With a slotted spoon, transfer the ravioli to the tomato sauce and toss to coat. Grate in the Parmigiano-Reggiano and a drizzle of olive oil, and toss again.

12. Plate the ravioli and top with the chopped parsley.

FOR THE HOMEMADE PASTA

3 or 4 large eggs

10 ounces all-purpose flour, plus more for dusting

TO MAKE THE HOMEMADE PASTA

1. Make a mound of flour, create a well in the middle, add 3 of the eggs, and mix with a fork, slowly incorporating the flour. (Or mix all together in a stand mixer.) If too dry, add a fourth egg yolk. If still too dry, add the white. Once the dough forms a ball, knead it for 15–20 minutes. Wrap it in plastic and let it rest for at least 30 minutes.

2. You can now cut off a portion (about a quarter) and roll it out with a pasta machine. You can also roll it out by hand, on a floured wooden board with a wooden rolling pin. Roll dough out in one direction. Flip and roll out in the other direction. Flip, turning 90 degrees, and continue. The idea is to stretch the dough until it's very thin—thin enough that you should be able to see the grains of the wooden board through the sheet.

DATE NIGHT!

Grilled T-Bone Lamb Chops with Fava Bean and Feta Salad

Moderate

| SERVES 4 | COOK TIME: 10–15 MINUTES | PREP TIME: 20 MINUTES |

INACTIVE COOK TIME: 8–24 HOURS　|　COST: $$

Lamb is a wonderful tradition among my ancestors in Greece. There's a reason for that: sheep, like many animals, have their babies in spring, so they have all summer and fall to put on some weight to weather the winter. Fava is one of the first crops of spring, so it's traditional to pair these two foods. You've probably noticed in restaurants that we chefs go nuts for favas for about a month. Finally! Something fresh and local! I use the T-bone for this rather than the more common chops because the bone runs all the way through, which gives it more flavor, and it's cheaper. I think there's a good lesson in this recipe: if you use prime local ingredients, you will often have more flavor and be satisfied with less. I'm good with 5 ounces of meat rather than a big ol' slab of a lesser grade.

FOR THE LAMB

2 tablespoons kosher salt

1 tablespoon coriander seed, toasted

1 teaspoon sugar

8 T-bone lamb chops

1 teaspoon red pepper flakes

Olive oil, to drizzle

TO MAKE THE LAMB

1. Put the salt, coriander seeds, and sugar into a mortar and pestle, and crush to blend. Place the lamb chops on a wire rack set over a baking sheet. Liberally season the chops on both sides with the spice blend. Sprinkle each side with the red pepper flakes. Allow to sit in the refrigerator, covered, for 8–24 hours before grilling, if possible. This will act as a quick cure, adding more flavor to the lamb when it's cooked.

2. Preheat a grill to medium-high heat.

3. Drizzle olive oil over the lamb and place on the grill, cooking until an instant-read thermometer inserted into the thickest part of the meat reaches 125–130 °F, for medium rare to medium, about 4–6 minutes per side, turning once. Allow the chops to rest briefly before serving.

FOR THE FAVA BEAN AND FETA SALAD

Salt

1 cup fava beans

1 shallot, minced

2 cloves garlic, smashed and minced

3 tablespoons red wine vinegar

½ cup extra virgin olive oil

Pinch of red pepper chili flakes

Freshly ground black pepper, to taste

¾ cup feta, crumbled

8–10 sprigs fresh mint leaves, torn

TO MAKE THE FAVA BEAN AND FETA SALAD

4. Fill a large bowl with ice and water. Place a large pot of water over high heat and bring to a boil. Add salt to taste. Add the fava beans to the water and blanch for about 40–50 seconds, or to al dente. Immediately plunge the beans into the ice bath to cool. Once cooled, remove the outer layer and set the shelled beans aside.

5. To a bowl, add the shallot and garlic, and season with salt to help bring out the moisture. Add the red wine vinegar, extra virgin olive oil, red pepper chili flakes, and freshly ground black pepper to taste. Add the shelled fava beans, crumbled feta, and torn mint leaves. Toss to combine. Taste for seasoning.

6. For each serving, place 2 lamb chops onto a plate. Top with the feta salad.

Spice up the spice

I like to buy spices whole and then roast them and grind them just before cooking with them. *Mucho mas* flavor!

Mango Bonbons

Easy

Date night is special. Even better is special, cheap, and delicious. And even better than that it is low-calorie too! Okay, sports fans, how about incredibly yummy, 6 cents a serving, and 8 calories. I'd like to say this recipe came about solely through a thunderbolt of inspiration. That would be only half true. The other half is I'm kind of cheap or, to use a more refined word, *economical*. Why go out and spend umpteen dollars on expensive bonbons when you can probably make something just as good or better yourself? I know what I said about 8 calories. That's only if you eat just one. But these are so good, I'd say that's not gonna happen. Okay, so eat three. That's still only 24 calories for dessert.

¾ cup Greek yogurt

⅓ cup milk

1 cup frozen mango

2 tablespoons honey

Pinch of salt

1 cup dark chocolate

¼ cup dried mango, finely chopped (optional)

SPECIAL EQUIPMENT
truffle molds

1. Add the yogurt, milk, mango, honey, and salt to a blender, and blend until smooth.

2. Pour the mixture into a silicone bonbon mold and freeze for at least 2 hours, or until firm.

3. Heat the chocolate over a double boiler just until melted. Remove from the heat. Let the chocolate cool to room temperature, but not harden.

4. Dip each frozen bonbon in the chocolate and place on a wax paper–lined cookie sheet.

5. Sprinkle dried mango over the center of each dipped bonbon, if using.

6. Place the bonbons in the freezer to set for about 10 minutes, or until ready to serve. You can make these several days in advance.

DATE NIGHT!

197

SUNDAY SIT-DOWNS

"MORE THAN ANY OTHER MEAL you will ever have, you will remember those Sunday sit-downs from when you were a young child or a teenager the most. Those meals always bring back a reverie. You eat, you sit there afterward, there's chitchat, maybe somebody brings out a deck of cards or a board game. It's pretty much the one ritual that defines family. Even after parents and grandparents are gone, it's a way to bring the spirit of those you loved back among the **PEOPLE NEAREST AND DEAREST** to them. I swear, my grandmother's spirit hovers in the steam rising from the kitchen stove. So does my grandfather's as I think about the vegetables he would pick in the garden. It's a memory that feels so real, that I even see the garden dirt he always tracked in with him. If you have grandchildren, I insist that you have them sit down and **HAVE THIS MEAL** with you. It will stay with them forever and be passed down to their children for as long as the words *roast chicken*, *prime rib*, and *leg of lamb* are spoken.**"**

—Clinton

SUNDAY DINNER is all about family. I'm not home as often as I used to be, home being Cleveland, and it ends up being a travel day now, so when I do get the chance for Sunday dinner at home, it's a big deal. For most of my life, Sunday was the day the family got together and cooked. It was typically my mom who would do the cooking, and it was always some big-style casserole dish like moussaka or the amazing Greek Calle lasagna called pastitsio. My sister, my grandparents, everyone would come over, and we would eat.

—Michael

GROWING UP, Sunday dinner in our house was always a little on the earlier side, but it was never 3 o'clock, I mean, it was 4:30 or 5, because we still had a day to enjoy. It was the one dinner during the week where you couldn't get up from the table until everyone really kind of gave it up. We always had to say, "Can I get down please?"

During football season, the day revolves around the games. I like to make food you can put on before the first game, check between the two games, and then eat after the second game (but before Sunday night football). The TV has to go off during all suppers—in and out of football season—maybe there's a little music in the background, but it's no TV, no cell phones, no text messaging, and no tweets. You eat, you talk. That's the whole deal.

—Mario

SUNDAY DINNER is not usually a big event at our house. We usually entertain Saturday night for cocktails/dinner or Sunday late morning for brunch. Sunday nights are the time John and I reserve for each other—we either go out or order in, or we cook a simpler meal that doesn't take much prep or cleanup. (I do like to cook my make-and-store meals for the week ahead during the day on Sunday—but I want the evening to relax and recharge for the week ahead.) Sometimes, if we're feeling really lazy, we just scavenge a picnic from what's in the fridge and then cozy up for a movie, or catch up with some of our favorite TV series.

—Daphne

TO ME, AND MAYBE TO MOST PEOPLE, Sunday supper means the stuff that Grandma makes. I think grandma food is pretty much what we mean when we say comfort food, because grandmas make us comfortable. In my family, we used to have at least two different meats, corn bread, homemade rolls, and no less than five sides. Grandma's house was the original all-you-can-eat buffet. Now we still love old-timey things as simple as meatloaf, mashed potatoes, and peas for Sunday dinner. Or something long braised (so you can nap and not worry about ruining dinner if you catch a few extra z's). A lot of my Sunday cooking is "dump and roll," as in you dump it in a pot and when it's done you roll it out on your plate.

—Carla

BATTLE OF THE IRON GRANDMAS

"When it's time for the ultimate Sunday dinner, who're you gonna turn to? Grandma! So, are you rarin' to roast, stoked to sauté, burstin' to braise? Get ready for the greatest throwdown in the history of food competition: *The Chew*'s Battle of the Iron Grandmas. They've had kids, changed diapers, packed school lunches, driven to music lessons, cheered their lungs out at Little League, and come home every night to cook. These are veterans of victuals, grand dames of dining, and the greatest mealtime mommas ever, ready to compete for the coveted Iron Casserole.

And not only do we have Iron Grandmas—with their very own Iron Sous Chefs Mario Batali, Michael Symon, and Carla Hall—we also have Iron Judges: Lidia Bastianich (who is an Iron Chef and a grandma), Geoffrey Zakarian, and Masaharu Morimoto.

Okay, first up, Mama T, aka the Spicy Staten Islander. Mama T, our reigning champion grandma, what do you have for us?"

—Clinton

MAMA T: I got a sausage and beef cassoulet. In Staten Island, we're happy to call it a regular old casserole. Great with a glass of wine…mmm…mmm…good!

CLINTON: Next up, the Sassy Southerner, Daisy the Dumpling Queen. The question on everyone's mind: Will the newcomer's dumplings dump the other mega matriarchs?

DAISY: You better believe it. It sticks to your ribs.

CLINTON: Say no more, I'm there! And over here, completing our holy trinity, Michael is working with Nona Arrabiata, the one and only Antoinette Lordo. What have you got for us?

ANTOINETTE: My sister Mary's melts-in-your-mouth meatloaf. I'm not a big meatloaf fan.

CLINTON: Don't oversell it, Antoinette.

ANTOINETTE: Yeah, but this meatloaf, fuggedaboutit!

CLINTON: Okay, may the best grandma win.

OKAY, JUDGES, time to chop some grandmas. And, audience, I have to tell you, it's a rare thing in the cooking-competition world that Chef Zakarian joined the Clean Plate Club with Mama T, Lidia chowed down on chicken and dumplings like she came from Alabama instead of Istria, and Morimoto, of the exquisite presentations and the teeny, tiny tweezer food, actually ate Antoinette's meatloaf with the pleasure he usually reserves for sea urchin custard. So this one is going to be hard.

Decision time, grandmas.

(Sound effect of clock ticking and suspense music, like in Psycho*)*

And which grandma will be taking home the golden casserole?

(Opens envelope)

AND THE WINNER IS…DAISY. You go home with the coveted Iron Casserole. But not to worry, our runner-up grandmas get a consolation Granny Swag Basket, complete with knitting needles, fuzzy slippers, and a mah-jongg set.

Grandmas everywhere, we learn from you, we love you, we want seconds! And, audience, try these recipes and you be the judge.

Antoinette and Mama T await the judges' decision.

Daisy's Chicken and Dumplings

Easy

SERVES 6 | **COOK TIME: 35–45 MINUTES** | **PREP TIME: 30 MINUTES** | **COST: $**

FOR THE CHICKEN

6 chicken legs (with or without skin)

6 chicken thighs (with or without skin)

1 tablespoon chicken seasoning

½ teaspoon lemon pepper

1 teaspoon garlic powder

½ tablespoon soul seasoning

Salt, to taste

2 tablespoons vegetable oil

2 stalks celery, chopped

1 small onion, chopped

3 liters chicken stock

FOR THE DUMPLINGS

2 cups self-rising flour

⅓ cup pancake mix

1 teaspoon seasoning salt

½ teaspoon onion powder

½ cup water

⅓ cup Carnation evaporated milk

2 teaspoons vegetable oil

2–3 ice cubes

TO MAKE THE CHICKEN

1. Season the chicken legs and thighs with the chicken seasoning, lemon pepper, garlic powder, soul seasoning, and salt. Prick the chicken all over with a fork to let the seasoning absorb.

2. Place 2 tablespoons of vegetable oil in a heavy-bottomed pot over medium-high heat, and sear the chicken, about 3 minutes per side. Once browned on all sides, add the celery and onion. Add about 3 liters of chicken stock, or enough to cover (about half a finger above the chicken). Bring to a boil and then reduce to a simmer. Cook for 20 minutes, or until the chicken is fully cooked.

TO MAKE THE DUMPLINGS

3. In a medium-sized bowl, add the flour, pancake mix, seasoning salt, and onion powder, and stir in the water, evaporated milk, vegetable oil, and ice cubes. The batter should be medium thick.

4. Use a soup spoon to help shape the dumplings. Start adding the dumplings to the pot of boiling chicken once the chicken is cooked through. Cover the pot and let boil for 1–2 minutes.

5. Remove from the heat and serve hot.

Carla and Daisy talk up their classic Southern cooking.

Mama T's Sausage and Beef Casserole

Easy

| SERVES 6 | COOK TIME: 1 HOUR 15 MINUTES | PREP TIME: 20 MINUTES | COST: $ |

2 tablespoons vegetable oil

1 pound beef chuck, cubed (like stew meat)

1 pound sweet Italian sausage links

1 large onion, sliced

4 cloves garlic, minced

2 red or yellow bell peppers, sliced

2 14-ounce cans kidney beans, drained and rinsed

4 russet potatoes, peeled, cut in half lengthwise, and then sliced into eighths

Salt, to taste

Pepper, to taste

Dried basil, to taste

1 cup beef stock

1. Preheat the oven to 350 °F.

2. Place vegetable oil in a large cast-iron skillet over medium-high heat, brown the beef, and set aside. In the same pan, cook the sausage, breaking it up as you cook (leaving big chunks, not crumbled), and set aside. Add the onion, garlic, and bell peppers, and cook until just tender.

3. In a large casserole dish, mix together the beef, sausage, and onion mixture. Add the kidney beans and potatoes. Season with salt, pepper, and basil to taste. Add the beef stock. Mix until everything is evenly distributed.

4. Cover and bake for about 1 hour, or until the potatoes are fork tender.

No one is tougher than Team Mama T!

Antoinette Lordo's Melt-in-Your-Mouth Meatloaf

Moderate

SERVES 10 | **COOK TIME: 1 HOUR 10 MINUTES** | **PREP TIME: 30 MINUTES** | **COST: $**

FOR THE MEATLOAF

1 large Idaho potato

1 large onion

2 tablespoons olive oil, plus more for the pan and meatloaf

Salt, to taste

Pepper, to taste

2 pounds chuck chop meat

2 cups bread crumb flakes

½ cup grated Pecorino Romano

2 eggs

4 ounces tomato sauce

1 teaspoon parsley flakes

1 teaspoon basil flakes

1 teaspoon garlic powder

8 ounces mozzarella, cubed

FOR THE GRAVY

2 cups beef broth

Salt

Pepper

3 tablespoons corn starch

1 teaspoon gravy master

1 teaspoon onion powder

1 teaspoon brewed black coffee

½ teaspoon parsley

TO MAKE THE MEATLOAF

1. Grate the potato and onion using a box grater. Heat a large frying pan with 2 tablespoons of the olive oil. Add the grated potato and onion, season with salt and pepper, then sauté until light brown, about 5–6 minutes. Set aside and allow to cool.

2. Preheat the oven to 375 °F.

3. In a large bowl, mix the meat, bread crumbs, grated cheese, eggs, tomato sauce, parsley, basil, and garlic powder. Add the cooled potato and onion mixture, and mix well with your hands.

4. Transfer the mixture onto waxed paper and flatten into a rectangle. Lay the cubed mozzarella in the middle of the loaf and fold over all sides to cover. Transfer into a greased pan, rub the meatloaf with olive oil, and bake in the oven for 1 hour, uncovered.

TO MAKE THE GRAVY

5. Heat all the ingredients in a saucepan, stirring often until it starts to boil. Continue to stir until the mixture thickens to the preferred consistency. Serve over the meatloaf.

Antoinette flexes her best cooking muscles for the competition.

Spiked Iced Tea

SERVES 4-6 | **COOK TIME: 5 MINUTES** | **PREP TIME: 10 MINUTES** | **COST: $**

Easy

Mario is right that beer is an amazing thirst-quencher, but so is iced tea—especially my iced tea. The way I look at it, any recipe that calls for a whole bottle of rum has a great party attitude. The orange or lemon garnish is optional. The rum isn't.

1 gallon black tea, brewed

5 cups spiced rum

Juice of 4 lemons, peel of one

Juice of 4 oranges, peel of 1

1 orange, thinly sliced

1 lemon, thinly sliced

Ice

1. Brew a gallon of black iced tea with the peels of 1 orange and 1 lemon.

2. In a large, 2½-gallon drink dispenser, add cooled iced tea, rum, lemon juice, and orange juice.

3. Add the orange and lemon slices and stir well. Fill with ice and serve.

"It's just as delicious without rum—promise!"

Thai Chopped Chicken Salad

SERVES 4 TO 6 | PREP TIME: 20 MINUTES | COST: $

Easy

Most of us think when we order something called "salad" that automatically means we are really eating healthfully. Think twice. Caesar salad can have 700–800 calories. A normal serving of chicken salad is 600 calories, but this light salad, made with leftover roast chicken, is hundreds less. It's also loaded with super flavorful ingredients like mangoes and soy sauce and rice vinegar, proving that healthy doesn't have to mean boring. And when you get the calorie bill, it's about half of regular chicken salad at the deli or sandwich shop. This salad is a perfect two-fer when you use leftover roast chicken from the Roast Chicken with Salsa Verde and Creamy Potatoes recipe on page 212.

4 cups roast chicken, shredded

1 mango, peeled and diced

1 cup snow peas, thinly sliced

Scallion (green and white parts), sliced

⅓ cup olive oil

1 Fresno chili, seeded and minced

1 clove garlic, minced

1 tablespoon honey

2 tablespoons light soy sauce

2 tablespoons rice vinegar

1 head Bibb Lettuce, whole leaves separated, to serve

¼ cup peanuts, chopped, to garnish

Salt, to taste

Freshly ground pepper, to taste

1. Combine the chicken, mango, snow peas, and scallion in a bowl. In another bowl, whisk the olive oil, Fresno chili, garlic, honey, soy sauce, and rice vinegar together. Pour the dressing over the chicken mix and toss to coat. Spoon into the lettuce cups and garnish with the peanuts. Season to taste.

Roast Chicken with Salsa Verde and Creamy Potatoes

| SERVES 6 | COOK TIME: 50–55 MINUTES | PREP TIME: 30 MINUTES | COST: $$ |

Easy

You've heard of steak and potatoes guys. Well, that's fine, but I'm also a chicken and potatoes guy. Really one of the measures of a chef is how well he or she makes a roast chicken. Make this one, and you'll measure up. Mine is a bunch of "nots," as in I do not brine it, and I don't stuff anything under the skin. I just put some lemon and sage inside, and oil and butter and seasoning on the outside, and let a good chicken basically cook itself. I love it with this salsa verde, which is kind of a spicy pesto made with a mix of herbs and some anchovy. That's the Michael Symon secret ingredient in a lot of his recipes, and if you do it right, it pumps the flavor big-time and no one is going to say, "Hey, Clinton, what's with the anchovies?" If they don't ask, I'm not gonna tell.

FOR THE ROAST CHICKEN

- 1 3-pound chicken
- Salt, to taste
- Pepper, to taste
- 2 lemons, halved
- 4–5 sage leaves
- 2 tablespoons extra virgin olive oil

FOR THE SALSA VERDE

- ¼ cup flat-leaf parsley
- 2 tablespoons mint
- ¼ cup tarragon
- 2 anchovy fillets, rinsed
- 1 clove garlic
- 1 tablespoon red wine vinegar
- Juice of 1 lemon

TO MAKE THE ROAST CHICKEN

1. Preheat the oven to 425 °F.

2. Remove the gizzard, heart, neck, and liver from the chicken, and then rinse it under cool water. Pat dry and then season the cavity with salt and pepper. Then stuff with the halved lemons and sage. Rub the olive oil all over the chicken, then, after washing your hands, generously season the chicken with salt and pepper.

3. Place the chicken on a rack in a roasting pan (or create a rack out of celery and carrots). Cook the chicken for 20 minutes in the oven, then reduce the heat to 325 °F and cook for 15 minutes per pound (approximately 30–45 minutes).

4. Remove the chicken from the oven and let rest at least 15 minutes.

5. While the chicken is cooking, make the salsa verde and potatoes.

1 shallot, chopped

2 tablespoons capers

1 teaspoon red chili flakes

½ cup extra virgin olive oil

Salt, to taste

Pepper, to taste

FOR THE CREAMY
POTATOES

2 pounds russet potatoes

Salt, to taste

½–1 cup heavy cream

12 ounces butter,
chilled and cubed

TO MAKE THE SALSA VERDE

6. Place all the ingredients in a food processor and pulse to combine. Adjust the seasoning with salt and pepper.

TO MAKE THE CREAMY POTATOES

7. Rub and scrub the potatoes under running water. Peel the potatoes and cut into even, large pieces. Place in a large pot and cover with cool, salted water. Bring the water to a boil, then reduce to a simmer. Cook for 15–20 minutes, or until a knife easily pierces the potatoes. Strain the potatoes.

8. In a small pot, heat the cream until scalded.

9. Using a ricer or a food mill, work the potatoes in batches over a heavy-bottomed pot. Once all the potatoes have been passed through the ricer, turn the heat on low and dry the potatoes out slightly by stirring for about 3 minutes. Stir in the butter in batches, making sure to incorporate each addition thoroughly before adding more butter. Then slowly whisk in the cream until the desired consistency. Adjust the seasoning with salt.

10. Serve the rested chicken with the salsa verde and a side of the creamy potatoes.

Swamp Thing

SERVES 6　｜　COOK TIME: 30 MINUTES　｜　PREP TIME: 20 MINUTES

INACTIVE COOK TIME: 24 HOURS　｜　COST: $

Moderate

This is my version of shrimp and grits, lightened up and without all the cheese of the traditional southern belly buster. Hey, I love it, but it doesn't love my waistline. I decided to include some of the traditional ingredients of my peeps: sweet potatoes and collards and a nice, full-flavored veggie stock. When the grits soak up all that sauce, I just want to grab my napkin and give the New Orleans version of a thumbs-up—a big old hankie wave!

FOR THE GRITS

2 cups milk

3 cups water

2 cups quick grits

1 cup fresh or frozen corn

8 tablespoons butter

Vegetable oil, for frying

FOR THE SHRIMP

3 tablespoons olive oil, plus more for the pan

1 onion, medium dice

5 cloves garlic, thinly sliced

2 carrots, medium dice

2 celery stalks, medium dice

2 cups sweet potatoes, peeled and diced

1 parsnip, peeled and diced

2 tablespoons flour

2 quarts chicken stock

4 cups collard greens, ribboned

TO MAKE THE GRITS

1. In a medium pot, heat the milk and water to a boil.

2. Slowly whisk in the grits, avoiding lumps. Cook the grits according to package time.

3. Once cooked, stir in the corn and butter until melted and incorporated.

4. Pour into a greased baking dish and allow to cool. Refrigerate overnight. Remove the grits from the refrigerator and cut into 3-inch squares.

5. Heat a nonstick pan over medium-high heat and add the vegetable oil. Fry the grits in the hot oil until golden on all sides. Remove from the pan.

TO MAKE THE SHRIMP

6. In a heavy-bottomed pot over high heat, add the olive oil. Toss in the onions and garlic, and cook for about 3 minutes.

7. Toss in the carrots, celery, sweet potatoes, and parsnip, and add more olive oil if it seems dry. Coat all the vegetables in the oil and continue to cook over high heat, just slightly browning everything.

2 teaspoons fresh thyme

1 bay leaf

½ teaspoon cayenne pepper

1 14.5-ounce can whole plum tomatoes, crushed

1 pound shrimp, peeled and deveined

Salt, to taste

Pepper, to taste

8. Sprinkle flour over the vegetables and stir. Deglaze with the chicken stock. Add the collard greens, thyme, bay leaf, and cayenne, and stir. Add in the tomatoes and bring to a boil.

9. Reduce to a simmer and cook until the vegetables are cooked through, about 15–20 minutes. Right before serving, toss in the shrimp and simmer for 2–3 minutes, or until the shrimp is just cooked through.

10. Plate in a soup bowl on top of the fried grits. Season to taste. Serve immediately.

Hold back the heat

If you want the fruitiness and some of the spiciness of a habanero chili, but not the full voltage, Bobby Flay told me to just slice the habanero and toss it in my sauce, rather than cutting it up and making the sauce super spicy.

Ham with Habanero Glaze

SERVES 10 | **COOK TIME: 2½–3 HOURS** | **PREP TIME: 20 MINUTES** | **COST: $**

Moderate

Many people only make fresh ham for the holidays, but it is such a super cut of pork and can easily feed any big family sit-down. I have been known to make them the way some folks might do a roast beef or leg of lamb for Sunday dinner. I like to start mine from scratch with a fresh ham that I brine with special spices and seasonings, then glaze with a tangy, spicy, sweet, and crispy habanero glaze, then super slow roast, and I make a sauce with the glaze that's my all-time favorite Cleveland Barbecue Sauce. If there is a flavor I left out of this, I'd be really surprised. It's got it all.

FOR THE BRINE

1 cup kosher salt

½ cup sugar

1 head garlic, halved crosswise

2 sprigs fresh rosemary

1 tablespoon black peppercorns

1 tablespoon coriander seeds

1 fresh or dried bay leaf

1 10-pound bone-in fresh ham (shank end)

FOR THE HABANERO GLAZE

1 gallon orange juice (not from concentrate)

½ cup fresh lime juice

1 habanero chili, with a slit cut in one side

1 cup packed light brown sugar

2 cups Cleveland Barbecue Sauce (recipe follows)

TO MAKE THE BRINE

1. In a large nonreactive pot over high heat, combine all the seasonings and herbs for the brine with 4 quarts of water and bring to a simmer. Whisk until the salt and sugar are completely dissolved. Remove from the heat and let cool.

2. In a container large enough to hold the ham, completely submerge the pork in the cooled brine. Weigh down the ham with a heavy plate if necessary to keep it fully submerged. Refrigerate overnight.

3. Remove the ham from the brine and pat dry with paper towels. Allow to sit out at room temperature for an hour before roasting.

4. Preheat the oven to 450 °F.

5. Score the skin, creating a diamond pattern. Transfer the ham to a roasting pan.

6. Place the ham in the oven and roast for 30 minutes to achieve a crispy skin. Reduce the heat to 350 °F and continue to roast for 1½ hours, or until the ham reaches an internal temperature of 150 °F.

7. Baste the ham with the habanero glaze and continue to cook for 45–60 more minutes, or until the ham reaches an internal temperature of 165 °F. Remove the ham from the oven and allow it to rest for 45 minutes. Slice and serve.

TO MAKE THE HABANERO GLAZE

8. Put all the glaze ingredients in a large nonreactive saucepan over medium-high heat, and boil until reduced by half. This will take about an hour.

FOR THE CLEVELAND
BARBECUE SAUCE

1½ teaspoons olive oil

½ cup red onion, minced

1 clove garlic, minced

Kosher salt

1½ teaspoons
coriander seeds

½ teaspoon cumin seeds

½ cup dark brown sugar

½ cup cider vinegar

½ cup sherry vinegar

1½ ounces chipotles
in adobo sauce

1 cup stadium-style
mustard (such as Bertman
Ball Park Mustard)

TO MAKE THE CLEVELAND BARBECUE SAUCE

1. In a nonreactive 2-quart saucepan set over medium-low heat, heat the olive oil, onion, garlic, and a good pinch of salt. Cook until the onion is translucent, about 2 minutes. Add the coriander and cumin, and cook for 1 minute. Add the brown sugar and cook for about 2 minutes, until it melts. Add the vinegars, increase the heat to medium-high, and boil for about 10 minutes, until reduced by one-quarter. Remove from the heat.

2. Puree the chipotles in adobo sauce in a blender or food processor until smooth. Stir the chipotle puree and mustard into the barbecue sauce. Let cool. Store covered in the refrigerator for up to 3 weeks.

Italian Turkey

SERVES 6 TO 8 | COOK TIME: 3 HOURS 10 MINUTES | PREP TIME: 30 MINUTES

INACTIVE PREP TIME: 24 HOURS | COST: $

Moderate

For our Thanksgiving show, in my honor, Mario made his version of a Greek-style turkey (which would probably get him arrested in Greece), while I tried my hand at an Italian-themed turkey. I've seen some spaghetti westerns that you might call Italian-themed turkeys, but that's another question altogether. I made a paste with every Italian ingredient under the Tuscan sun and piped it under the skin of the turkey so that as it roasted, it was bathed in the essence of pancetta, garlic, herbs, citrus, and spices. Then in the cavity, I put fennel, lemon, and garlic: *molto* Symon!

FOR THE TURKEY

1 12- to 15-pound turkey, rinsed and patted dry

Salt

1 pound pancetta

10 cloves garlic, minced

Zest of 3 lemons

Zest of 1 orange

½ cup parsley, chopped

4 sprigs rosemary, chopped

2 tablespoons red pepper flakes

2 tablespoons capers, rinsed and chopped

TO MAKE THE TURKEY

1. The day before roasting, rinse the turkey inside and out with cold water, set on a clean kitchen towel, and pat dry. Season the turkey inside and out with the salt. Wrap the turkey in plastic wrap and refrigerate for 24 hours.

2. Remove the turkey from the refrigerator 1–2 hours prior to roasting to bring to room temperature.

3. Put the pancetta in the bowl of a food processor and pulse until it forms a paste. Transfer to a bowl and mix in the garlic, citrus zest, parsley, rosemary, red pepper flakes, and capers by hand, until thoroughly blended.

4. Place the turkey, breast side up, on a rack set into a large roasting pan. Fold the wings and tuck the tips underneath the bird.

5. Carefully put your hands underneath the turkey skin and separate the skin from the breast. Put the pancetta mixture in a piping bag, and pipe between the skin and the turkey breast, pressing to even it out.

Baste not, want not

I am not a baster. All that opening and closing the oven makes the poor turkey crazy. It doesn't know what temperature is happening! Instead I soak a cheesecloth in Italian seasonings and olive oil and lay it over the breast. The original self-baster.

1 head of garlic, halved
through the equator

4 sprigs fresh oregano

3 sprigs thyme

1 lemon, quartered

1 onion, peeled
and quartered

1 fennel bulb, quartered, plus
¼ cup picked fennel fronds

8 tablespoons olive oil

1 cup chicken stock (or
turkey stock or water)

TO MAKE THE TURKEY AROMATICS AND BASTING

6. Preheat the oven to 425 °F.

7. In the turkey's neck cavity, place a few cloves of the garlic, a sprig of oregano, a sprig of thyme, and a quarter of the lemon. Wrap the neck skin over and around the cavity to enclose the seasoning ingredients.

8. In the body cavity, place half of the remaining garlic, half of the onion, half of the fennel, the fennel fronds, 2 lemon quarters, and half of the remaining oregano and thyme.

9. Meanwhile, in a small saucepot, combine all the remaining basting ingredients and bring to a simmer. Let cook for about 10 minutes. Remove from the heat and allow to cool slightly.

10. When cool enough to handle, soak a double layer of cheesecloth big enough to cover the bird in the basting mixture and drape it over the breast and legs of the turkey. Pour the remaining contents of the pan over the bird, pushing the pieces of vegetable and herbs into the bottom of the roasting pan. Add the neck and gizzards to the bottom of the roasting pan.

11. Place the turkey in the oven and roast for 45 minutes (there will be the distinct possibility of smoke, depending on how clean your oven is). Turn the oven temperature down to 375 °F, and continue to roast for another 15–20 minutes per pound (removing the cheesecloth for the final 10 minutes to brown, if needed), or until an instant-read thermometer inserted into the center of a thigh registers 160 °F (about 3 hours). Remove the turkey from the oven and set on a platter. Allow it to rest for 20 minutes before carving.

FOR THE GRAVY

2 links fennel sausage, removed from their casings

½ fennel bulb, finely diced

3 tablespoons flour

1 cup white wine

3 cups turkey stock, warmed

3 tablespoons butter

Salt

Pepper

TO MAKE THE GRAVY

12. Return the roasting pan to the stove and place over medium-high heat. Add the sausage and fennel, and cook until browned, about 7 minutes. Add the flour to the sausage mixture, stir in, and cook for 2–3 minutes longer. Deglaze with the wine and reduce by half. Then add in the turkey stock and bring to a simmer. Cook for a few minutes until the gravy is thickened. Whisk in the butter and adjust the seasoning.

13. Serve the gravy with the turkey.

Thou shalt not brine (this means you, Mario)

Mario is a briner; I am a seasoner. I hate brining, but don't get me started. Let's just say that I think it affects the texture of the meat. Of course, that's just me. Chef Batali couldn't disagree more. That's what makes turkey races, to coin a phrase. I season mine the night before, inside and out, so the seasoning is infused into the meat.

Greek Turkey

Moderate

Michael, if I ever doubted, that Italian Turkey is proof that there's part of you that is pure *Italiano*, but today I am channeling the Greek part, starting with something Michael never does…a brine! And just to Greek it up a bit, I add a couple of pops of ouzo. Then, to use another non-Symon technique, I baste my turkey! Actually it's a self-baster because I put thick, creamy Greek yogurt under the skin so that it melts, moistens, and tenderizes as your bird bakes; I throw in lots of dill too. There's dill and garlic and lemon—the holy trinity of the Greek kitchen—everywhere in this recipe. In the brine, in the baste, inside the cavity, and in my avgolemono Greek gravy, based on eggs and lemons. It's all so Greek tasting that I believe even Michael would concede this turkey is perfect for partying at the Parthenon!

FOR THE TURKEY

1 gallon water

1 cup sea salt

1 bunch fresh mint

¼ cup coriander seeds, toasted, plus 1 tablespoon coriander seeds, toasted and ground

1 tablespoon dried thyme

1 bunch dill

2 cups honey

10 cloves garlic

1 gallon ice water

2 cups ouzo

1 12- to 15-pound turkey

3 bulbs roasted garlic

1 lemon, quartered

2 cups Greek yogurt

TO MAKE THE TURKEY

1. In a large stockpot, combine the water, sea salt, mint, ¼ cup coriander seeds, thyme, dill, honey, and garlic. Bring to a boil, and stir frequently to be sure the salt is dissolved. Remove from the heat and let cool to room temperature.

2. When the broth mixture is cool, pour it into a clean 5-gallon bucket. Stir in the ice water and ouzo.

3. Place the turkey, breast down, into the brine. Make sure that the cavity gets filled. Place the bucket in the refrigerator overnight but no longer than 12 hours.

4. Remove the turkey. Carefully drain off the excess brine and pat dry. Discard the excess brine.

5. Preheat the oven to 425 °F. Arrange an oven rack on the lower third of the oven.

6. Place the turkey in a roasting pan on a rack. Tuck the roasted garlic cloves in the cavity of the bird, along with the lemon.

½ cup dill, chopped

Salt, to taste

Pepper, to taste

Extra virgin olive oil

FOR THE GRAVY

2 cups chicken stock

¼ cup dill

½ cup turkey drippings

Zest of 2 lemons, plus juice of 1 lemon

8 egg yolks

Salt, to taste

Pepper, to taste

7. Mix the yogurt with the chopped dill and the remaining coriander. Season with salt and black pepper. Take your hand and loosen the skin from the breast. With a piping bag, gently distribute the yogurt mixture under the skin of the turkey, in the cavity, and on the turkey skin.

8. Drizzle the olive oil over the turkey and place it in the oven. Cook for about 30 minutes, and then reduce the oven temperature to 325 °F. Continue cooking until a thermometer reads 160 °F when inserted into the thickest part of the thigh, about 2½–3 more hours.

9. Let the turkey rest for 20–30 minutes before carving.

TO MAKE THE GRAVY

10. In a small saucepan, add the stock, dill, turkey drippings, and lemon zest and juice. Bring to a simmer and slowly whisk in the eggs. Do not boil or the eggs will scramble. Adjust the seasoning with salt and pepper.

Cheesy Bacon, Butternut Squash, Mac 'n Cheese Casserole

SERVES 6 | COOK TIME: 20–25 MINUTES | PREP TIME: 15 MINUTES | COST: $

Easy

This Sunday casserole was actually born from a fridge-raider foray to a home on Long Island. The kids told me, "Anything but string beans." I let that go in one ear and out the other. The secret to kid-friendliness is the universally beloved mac and cheese. And once you've made friends—this is your opportunity to sneak in some healthy vegetables like kale, and butternut squash, and my secret flavor picker-upper, some smoky, peppery chipotle powder.

Salt, to taste

1 pound conchigliette (pasta shells) or penne

1 pound bacon, diced

3 tablespoons butter

Pepper, to taste

1 onion, diced

1 butternut squash, peeled and diced

2 cups kale, ribbed and cut into strips

2 cloves garlic, minced

3 tablespoons flour

3 cups milk

⅓ cup half-and-half

1½ cups grated gruyere

1 teaspoon freshly grated nutmeg

½ cup mascarpone or cream cheese

1½ tablespoons chipotle powder

2 cups bread crumbs

kosher salt and freshly ground black pepper, to taste

¼ cup parsley, chopped

1. Preheat the oven on broil. Bring a pot of water to a boil and season with salt. Cook the pasta 1 minute short of the package directions.

2. In a Dutch oven, cook bacon until crisp. Add the butter to the bacon fat, then sweat the onion, butternut squash, kale, and garlic until translucent.

3. Add flour to make a roux, and slowly pour in the milk and half-and-half while mixing. Bring mixture to a simmer.

4. Stir in the butternut squash puree. Cook gently until the mixture thickens, about 4-5 minutes.

5. Add in 1 cup of the gruyere and grate in the nutmeg, and constantly stir until all of the cheese is melted. Add the mascarpone or cream cheese, and mix until melted and combined. Stir in the chipotle powder and add the cooked pasta.

6. Toss pasta until it is well mixed. Turn the broiler to high. Sprinkle the bread crumbs over the casserole. Place the Dutch oven on a rack 6 inches from the heating source. Broil for about 1 minute, or until the topping is crunchy and golden. Garnish with parsley and serve in the Dutch oven.

Tip If you can't get to a craft store to buy a foam ring, you can make your own! Create a ring out of pipe insulation tubing by taping the two ends together. You can use something firm like a marker to hold the tube in place while you tape. In no time you've got a foam ring that cost under a dollar!

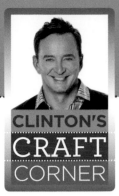

A wreath full of blessings

And now for one of the most beautiful crafty things I have ever run across. It truly looks like a painstakingly made faux floral wreath, but it's only unused coffee filters, food coloring, and some inexpensive foam piping. It takes a little time to make, but so did the needlepoint that grandmas used to do, so it seems perfect for a Sunday supper like Grandma would make. So start pinning your wreath together, and with each filter, count one of your blessings.

WHAT YOU NEED

Large, shallow bowls
Food coloring
Water
Spoons
Coffee filters
Paper towels
Straight pins
Foam ring or foam piping (see Tip)
Ribbon

HOW TO MAKE IT

1. In the bowls, add food coloring and water, and mix with spoons. Experiment with different amounts of dye to achieve the desired color.

2. Dip coffee filters into the food-coloring mixture and lay them out to dry on paper towels.

3. Once the filters have dried, begin shaping them by pinching the middle of the coffee filter and twisting to make a flower. Put a straight pin through the base of the flower and use it to attach the flower to the ring.

4. Continue creating flowers and pinning around the ring until all of the foam is covered. String a ribbon around the wreath or add a bow for a nice accent.

Scallion Chili Sweet Potato Cake

| SERVES 6 | COOK TIME: 25 MINUTES | PREP TIME: 20 MINUTES | COST: $ |

Easy

This is one of those dishes that I can eat for breakfast, lunch, dinner, or even a snack. Alongside a turkey or a pork roast or a leg of lamb, it's got the flavor oomph to stand up to those major pieces of meat, but it is all light, vegetarian ingredients so it doesn't weigh you down. Take the time to crisp the layers of sweet potato on the top and bottom so you get a firm, crunchy golden-brown effect. Chili and scallions work so well in those scallion pancakes that you get in Vietnamese restaurants, I thought, "Hey, why not with sweet potatoes?" Take it from me—there is no reason why not.

FOR THE SWEET POTATO CAKE

2⅔-pounds large sweet potatoes, peeled

½ cup extra virgin olive oil

2 Fresno chilies, sliced into rounds

1 cup fresh scallions, finely chopped

Salt

Pepper

FOR THE SALAD

½ cup scallions, sliced, plus more for garnish

1 cup parsley, leaves picked

¼ cup capers

2 tablespoons balsamic vinegar

2 tablespoons olive oil

Salt

Freshly cracked black pepper

TO MAKE THE SWEET POTATO CAKE

1. Preheat the broiler to high. Arrange a rack 6 inches away from the heating source.

2. Boil the potatoes for 20 minutes, and let them cool before slicing them into ¼-inch-thick slices.

3. Heat a couple of tablespoons of olive oil in a 6- or 8-inch cast-iron pan over medium heat. Cook the Fresno chilies and scallions for a few minutes, until softened. Remove the mixture from the pan and set aside.

4. Add as many potato slices as can fit in one layer of the pan. Cook for about 3 minutes per side, or until lightly browned. Remove the pan from the heat.

5. Arrange the remaining potatoes into even layers over the crispy potatoes, seasoning with salt and pepper and some of the Fresno chilies and scallions. Press each layer down firmly with the back of a spatula or wooden spoon.

6. Cook the sweet potato cake in the oven and brown for about 3 minutes, or until the potatoes are crispy.

TO MAKE THE SALAD

7. Toss the salad ingredients together and season with salt and pepper.

8. Cut the potato cake into wedges and serve garnished with the salad and remaining scallions.

Cranberry-Apple Cobbler

SERVES 6 | **COOK TIME: 1 HOUR** | **PREP TIME: 20 MINUTES** | **COST: $**

Easy

This past summer, I made a cobbler every weekend until I got it perfect. No sooner were those words out of my mouth than Carla, the Dominatrix of Dessert, said, "I'll be the judge of that." The first thing you want for a perfect cobbler is perfect fruit. So get it when it's in season: blackberries, blueberries, peaches, apples, pears—they all have their peak time. Start there. For me, one of the nicest things about a cobbler is that you have all the fun of a pie, but you don't have to spend all that time on the crust. It has crisp and not crust! That's what makes it foolproof.

FOR THE COBBLER FILLING

5 Granny Smith apples, peeled and chopped

1 cup cranberries

¼ cup white sugar

¼ cup brown sugar

½ teaspoon ground cinnamon

⅛ teaspoon nutmeg

2 teaspoons cornstarch

Juice of 1 lemon

Generous pinch of salt

FOR THE COBBLER TOPPING

¾ cup milk

1 cup all-purpose flour

½ cup sugar

2 teaspoons baking soda

2 pinches of salt

8 tablespoons butter

TO MAKE THE COBBLER FILLING

1. Preheat the oven to 350 °F.

2. In a large bowl, toss together all the ingredients for the cobbler filling.

TO MAKE THE COBBLER TOPPING

3. In a separate bowl, whisk together the topping ingredients.

4. Put the butter in the pie dish and place in the oven until melted. Remove the dish from the oven and fill with the fruit mixture. Pour the cobbler topping over the fruit.

5. Bake for approximately 1 hour, or until the juices are bubbling and the cobbler is golden. Tent with foil if the cobbler is getting too brown.

Lemon Pound Cake

SERVES 6 | COOK TIME: 50–60 MINUTES | PREP TIME: 20 MINUTES | COST: $

Easy

In 1998, I was named one of *Food & Wine*'s best new chefs, which, if you do the math, makes me one of the best old-ish chefs at this point. Part of the deal—I mean honor—was that they ask you to make something at the *Food & Wine* Classic in Aspen, and even though I'm not a pastry chef, I signed up for dessert. I knew it had to be kind of a foolproof one. What could be easier than pound cake? It was kind of my coming-out party, and in this dessert you can relive my virgin voyage into big-time chef-dom. I hope you find it as thrilling as I did, or at least pretty good.

½ cup yellow cornmeal

1 cup all-purpose flour

½ teaspoon baking soda

½ teaspoon salt

3 eggs, separated

½ cup butter

1¼ cups sugar

2 tablespoons grated lemon zest, plus 6 tablespoons fresh lemon juice

½ cup milk

Lavender Simple Syrup (recipe follows)

Strawberries

TO MAKE THE CAKE

1. Preheat the oven to 350 °F. Line a 9-by-5-inch loaf pan with parchment.

2. Combine the cornmeal, flour, baking soda, and salt, and set aside.

3. Beat the egg whites until stiff and set aside.

4. Cream the butter, sugar, and lemon zest until fluffy, then add the egg yolks and mix well.

5. Add the lemon juice and then milk to the egg yolk mixture. Stir in the dry ingredients.

6. Carefully fold in the beaten egg whites, and spoon the batter into the prepared pan.

7. Bake for 50–60 minutes, or until a toothpick inserted near the center of the cake comes out clean.

8. To serve, cut slices of the cake and brush with the Lavender Simple Syrup. Top with fresh strawberries.

FOR THE LAVENDER SIMPLE SYRUP

3 sprigs lavender

1 cup sugar

1 cup hot water

TO MAKE THE LAVENDER SIMPLE SYRUP

1. Steep the lavender in the sugar and water until all the sugar dissolves. Strain out the lavender and allow the syrup to cool. Store in the refrigerator.

Grilled Pineapple Upside-Down Sandwich

SERVES 5 | COOK TIME: 5 MINUTES | PREP TIME: 10 MINUTES | COST: $

2 FER

Easy

One of my all-time, all-time desserts is a pineapple upside-down cake. Even more favoriter—if I can make up a word—is when you can take something like Michael's Lemon Pound Cake on page 231 and use the leftovers. Then all you need is to make some syrup, grill some pineapple, and slather on some mascarpone cheese the way you might schmear mayo on a non-dessert sandwich.

½ cup butter

½ cup brown sugar

½ cup unsweetened pineapple juice

1 cup mascarpone

1 fresh pineapple, peeled, cored, and sliced

10 slices pound cake or challah bread

Cherries, to garnish

Toothpicks

1. Combine the butter, brown sugar, and pineapple juice in a pot. Bring to a boil, then reduce to a simmer for 2 minutes. Reserve half for brushing on the fresh pineapple. Mix the other half into the mascarpone.

2. Preheat a grill to medium heat. Place the pineapple rings on the grill. Grill both sides for 1 minute each, or until warmed through, then brush with the brown sugar mixture. Grill again quickly on each side.

3. Clean the grill, then quickly grill the cake. Smear each piece of cake with the sweetened mascarpone and place a grilled pineapple ring in between two slices.

4. Top with a cherry skewered with a toothpick to serve.

Heat and sweet

Even when fruit is not totally ripe, grilling or otherwise heating develops some of those same sugars they would get in the heat of the sun.

Stanley Tucci can hardly wait to try one of Carla's sweet treats!

Nectarine Blackberry Buckle

SERVES 8 | **COOK TIME: 40–45 MINUTES** | **PREP TIME: 20 MINUTES** | **COST: $**

Easy

Okay, to answer the question that is probably on your mind, a buckle is what you call a cross between a cake, a crumble, and a pie. It's fresh fruit in a beautiful cake batter with a crumble top. If you want to do it really old-timey (which is the best way to do anything, in my book), you bake it in a parchment-lined cast-iron skillet, just like they did back in the *Little House on the Prairie* days.

FOR THE CAKE

1½ sticks unsalted butter, plus 1 tablespoon for greasing

1½ cups all-purpose flour

2 teaspoons baking powder

¾ teaspoon salt

½ teaspoon cinnamon

½ cup sugar

½ cup light brown sugar

2 large eggs

⅔ cup buttermilk

5 nectarines, halved, pitted, and sliced

1 pint blackberries

Zest of 1 lemon

FOR THE STREUSEL

1 stick butter

¼ cup sugar

¼ cup light brown sugar

½ cup all-purpose flour

¼ teaspoon cinnamon

Pinch of salt

FOR THE WHIPPED CREAM

2 cups heavy cream

½ cup sugar

1 teaspoon vanilla

1 teaspoon cinnamon

TO MAKE THE CAKE

1. Preheat the oven to 350 °F. Line a 10-inch cast-iron skillet with parchment and grease it with 1 tablespoon of the butter.

2. Melt the remaining butter in a small saucepan over medium-low heat until light brown. Set aside to cool.

3. In a large bowl, whisk together the flour, baking powder, salt, and cinnamon.

4. In another large bowl, whisk together the cooled browned butter and sugars. Then add the eggs, one at a time. Stir in the buttermilk.

5. Add the dry ingredients into the wet. Pour the batter into the prepared pan.

6. In a large bowl, toss the nectarines and blackberries with the lemon zest and arrange them in a single layer on top of the batter.

TO MAKE THE STREUSEL

7. In a medium bowl, combine all the ingredients for the streusel. Mix together to form a crumb. Crumble over the nectarines and blackberries. Place in the oven and bake for 40–45 minutes.

TO MAKE THE WHIPPED CREAM

8. Combine the cream, sugar, and vanilla, and beat until peaks form. Fold in the cinnamon. Serve the buckle topped with whipped cream.

INDEX

The
CHEW
FOOD. LIFE. FUN.

OVER 100 DELICIOUS RECIPES
FROM *THE CHEW* KITCHEN

Edited by PETER KAMINSKY and ASHLEY ARCHER

KINGSWELL

LOS ANGELES • NEW YORK

Food photographer: Andrew Scrivani
Food stylists: Martha Tinkler, Jackie Rothong, Kevin Mendlin
Prop stylist: Francine Degni

The Chew: Food. Life. Fun. — Photographer Credits:
Craig Sjodin/ABC: headshots, ii, 124, 170; Donna Svennevik/ABC: 7, 10, 12, 14, 23, 30, 66,
67, 71, 78, 92, 98, 104, 118, 127, 135, 141, 161, 168, 169, 184, 197, 199, 201, 213; Fred Lee/ABC:
176; Heidi Gutman/ABC: 17, 110, 111, 113, 139, 145; Ida Mae Astute/ABC: 68, 69, 77, 107, 125,
180, 193, 215; Jeff Neira/ABC: 115, 117, 163; Lorenzo Bevilaqua/ABC: 3, 33, 55, 57, 58, 73, 86,
115, 126, 214; Lou Rocco/ABC: vi, 11, 12, 77, 91, 205, 216, 221

For information address Kingswell, 1101 Flower Street, Glendale, California 91201.

The Chew: Food. Life. Fun.
Book design by Vertigo Design NYC
Library of Congress Cataloging-in-Publication Data
The Chew: food, life, fun / The Chew. — 1st edition.
pages cm
ISBN 978-1-4013-1106-3
1. Cooking, American. 2. Chew (Television Program) 3. Celebrity Chefs — United States — Interviews.
I. Chew (Television Program). II. Title:
TX714.C46668 2012
641.3—dc23
2012018523

The Chew: Back 2 Back
Editorial Director: Wendy Lefkon
Executive Editor: Laura Hopper
Design by H. Clark Wakabayashi

ISBN 978-1-4847-5864-9
FAC-008598-15233

First Bind-up edition October 2015
1 3 5 7 9 10 8 6 4 2

Extreme superspecial thanks to
Kerry McConnell, without whom
this book would have been
impossible and much less fun

CONTENTS

Introduction

By Gordon Elliott, EXECUTIVE PRODUCER

The CHEW was created in about 20 minutes, like a fully formed song just waiting to be written by a hungover rock star. Brian Frons, then head of ABC daytime, a lovely man, was chatting with me one day and threw out the question, "What would you do with an hour on ABC daytime?"

Being a cable TV producer, it was rare anyone asked my opinion of anything. I had one shot and nothing to lose, so I began a stream of consciousness ramble that had been running around my head for years.

I had always imagined a group of friends with lifestyle skills, wit, and real camaraderie that could show viewers how to get a little more out of their daily routines. Not fancy stuff, not expensive, just how to get through the day with a better meal, a smarter choice, a useful tip, a few laughs. If it was done right, I hoped it would feel like a party in the kitchen. TV that made you feel the time you spent watching wasn't wasted.

Brian paused. I imagined I'd bored him rigid by this point.

"What would you call it?"

The name was pure cheek.

"Well, it's a mix of food and a group host format like *The View*, so *The Chew* seems blindly obvious."

I figured he thought I was just kidding around. Neither of us was. *The Chew* was born.

I immediately sat down with the very smart Mark Schneider, my managing director and trusted consigliere. Our usual easy collaboration made it all look doable. Without him it would have been a nightmare. I took a deep breath and made a casting note to myself. I imagined a group of friends effortlessly preparing dinner, splashing Chardonnay and laughter with each other. I wrote the type of "characters" they would be—like a scene from *The Big Chill*.

The host of the party—generous, witty, and well rounded.

The funny guy with a cheeky point of view but also something solid to him.

The curious younger woman with a mix of humility and smarts.

The "mother love" figure with life under her belt but still laughs easily.

The older guy with wisdom and skill—the father figure.

Things began to come together quickly. Randy Barone, the show's eventual godfather at ABC, rushed into my office the first week of casting with a tape of Daphne Oz. She had just made her first-ever appearance on her father's TV program, *The Dr. Oz Show*. Her poise, humor, and humility were

obvious. We had coffee. She wasn't looking to be on TV; she wanted to study and write. She was not overeager, like a presidential nominee who doesn't seem to want the gig. This only made her an even more attractive candidate.

Similar to many women, her relationship with food was complex. She had faced terrible insecurity about her body image growing up and knew that constant dieting only fed the beast—pun intended. Daphne eventually found a daily routine that helped her shed her excess 30 pounds and keep it off permanently. She then wrote a book about her search and solutions. It was a *New York Times* bestseller. Not bad for a twenty-three-year-old.

Daphne was newly married, curious, practical, and looking for balance—in her body, work, food, and career. Add a wicked sense of humor and an ability to give as good as she got and you understand why I called her the following day and offered her the job. One down, four to go.

The easy ones? Michael Symon and Mario Batali, two of the most congenial cooks ever to grace the tube. Mario—like Madonna—needs only a first name to identify him to millions of fans of his television and restaurant empire. Michael's stellar reputation was forged in the fires of *Iron Chef*, and he is the master of a heartland domain of successful and terrific restaurants. Working with them over the years, I knew what cheeky, funny men they were. Stylishly competent, they made cooking in stultifying kitchens eight days a week look sexy. Blunt but charming with hearts the size of holiday hams, they were huge TV stars in their own right. That was the problem. They had great lives and didn't need the money, the extra fame, or the time away from their families.

But I knew their weakness. Like all great chefs, they are both congenital pleasers. They live to make people happy. I explained this was their dream show. A chance to tell their stories and cook their food in real time, to hang out together and show folks how fun cooking can be. That and a couple pounds of fifty-dollar bills helped do the trick.

From the first time I saw Carla Hall on *Top Chef*, I could see she didn't cook to impress the judges as much as she grooved on her blend of food, love, and soul and the audience sensed it. Like Michael and Mario, nothing makes her happier than standing next to a new friend and showing them a long-learned recipe. She takes them into her calming, comforting world. I needed that magic on the show. I called, she screamed. I found out later she screams a lot. Her joy is high volume.

Clinton came out of the blue at the last moment. We were a week away from announcing the show and still lacked a master of ceremonies. I was starting to sweat and began checking my list of usual suspects when Randy Barone threw open my door again and walked in with Clinton Kelly, fresh from his appearance on *The View* promoting his relationship with Macy's as the company's spokesman. He walked into the room with a confident grin and a hilarious story, sweeping everyone off their feet and into party mode. I had never seen him on TV before and was staggered by how naturally he fit in. He was a true natural host. He listened carefully and, with the mental suppleness of a Russian gymnast, directed conversation to a graceful point, making people feel funnier than they really were. I was as excited as a fat boy in a bakery. I couldn't wait to bring them all together and see if they liked one another as much as I liked them individually.

They did. And the result, as they say, is in the chocolate volcano pudding: five real friends doing what they love, adding a little smarts and fun into the TV world.

You can't fake this stuff. People can tell. That's why the show is a hit.

Writing this book felt like a natural evolution. *The Chew* was always designed to be useful, but the information our hosts naturally spilled into the show soon became a flood. Beyond just recipes and cooking times, their fertile minds bore a bumper crop of life-enhancing tips that felt like a master class in useful fun. We wanted to keep the unique voice of the show intact, so we literally took the words off the screen, added some beautiful shots of the food, and threw a fellow host's side comment in here and there, just as they do on-air.

We hope we've captured the mood created on-screen and continued that spark to try something different. As Clinton says, "Small changes can make big differences in your life," so go ahead, pick one and try it out. Or just sit there and enjoy a lazy, delicious read.

I hope you enjoy the result.

The Chew icons

 Light and Healthy

Simple Italian

Viewers' Choice

Two-Fer (Two Meals in One)

 5-in-5 (5 Ingredients in 5 Minutes)

Kid Friendly

Cocktail

Each recipe includes skill level (Easy or Moderate) and price range ($ for recipes that cost under $5 to make, $$ for recipes that cost under $10, and $$$ for recipes that cost over $10).

Love at First Bite

Clinton

Sometimes one bite is all it takes to fall in love. Here's a little bit about the foods that we ate for the first time that we just fell in love with and couldn't get enough of from then on.

Carla

I was in Milan . . . I was about twenty-six years old . . . and I bit into this slice of pizza that I shared with a friend . . . it was cut with scissors and the crust was perfectly crisp with not so much topping. I remember taking a bite and going, "Oh my god, this is delicious. This is pizza! Yeah!"

Daphne

I was in Barcelona and I had something I called garlic butter-basted shrimp. You sucked them out of the head. It was a totally mind-boggling experience and the most delicious shrimp I've ever had. And I don't know what the recipe is so I can't make them for myself, which is sad.

Michael

My favorite bites of food always happened with family. And it was in the basement of my yiayia's house . . . that's where we ate dinner. She had a kitchen down there and a kitchen upstairs. The dish was her bisticchio: layered baked pasta. Oh god. I mean, I remember biting into it and thinking, "This is what I wanna cook. This is why I wanna be a chef." Food makes everybody so happy.

Mario

I was lucky enough to go to high school in Madrid. My friends and I discovered this little place where they made calamari en su tinta. Sounds complicated, but basically it's fried calamari with garlic and salt and pimento stuffed into a soft bread with a lot of crust on it and then drizzled with an aioli with black squid ink in it. So you eat it and then you look at each other and go, "Is there anything in my teeth?" They looked pretty gross—actually that's probably understating it—but boy, was it good!

Clinton

I was thirteen, with my grandparents in Carmel, California, a beautiful city, and we went to a restaurant called the Clam Box where I had lobster thermidor. It was so fancy. I thought to myself, "When I grow up, I'm gonna be fancy!"

Daphne

And here you are!

Clinton

And here I am!

Daphne

You're freakin' fancy!

Clinton

It was a life-changing moment.
Love at first bite.

FALL

Clinton

Q: **You are the host of a dinner party where a lot of people gather in the kitchen. What's required to make that happen, and how do you keep the vibe going and involve people?**

Clinton: I'm very conscious of the people who are watching the show, the people in the audience, and the people on camera with me. I try to be as welcoming as possible and nonthreatening and to keep the conversation going. There are certain things you talk about at a dinner party and there are certain things you don't talk about at a dinner party. So just like at a good dinner party, we avoid super confrontational topics and keep to the things that everybody loves: food, and family, what we did on the weekend, etc. There are many places in television where you can find disagreements, arguing, screaming. Not our style.

Q: **What's special about *The Chew*?**

Clinton: We are about more than food. We're also about family and fun, and how the average American lives his or her life. The average person eats three meals a day (maybe even four, according to some statistics I've seen about being overweight). Cooking should be part of everyone's life. So what we are doing on the show is living our lives and cooking at the same time, if that makes sense. We are not just talking about food. I do style segments that feel at home on *The Chew* because you eat every day and you put clothes on your body every day. So yes, there is nothing else like this on television. We have developed a category of our own.

11

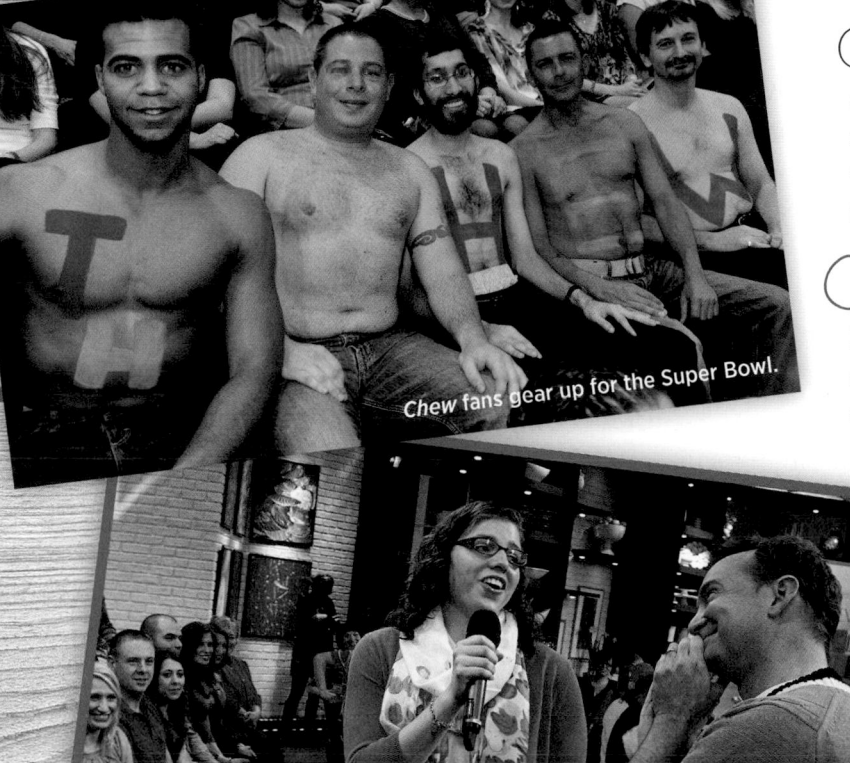

Chew fans gear up for the Super Bowl.

An audience member sings karaoke with an enchanted Clinton Kelly.

Clinton: Well, we all love performing in front of an audience. It brings life to a show. There are 150 people who have gotten up in the morning who have decided to come see us do what we do. They give us the best kind of instant feedback. If you land a good joke it feels great, it gives us a jolt of energy. Their reaction is the best guide to help us keep tabs on if we are handling the right thing, the right subjects. You can tell by the live studio audience and their reaction how the audience at home is going to be accepting of a topic. If you see a couple of people's eyes glaze over, then you know you have a million eyes glazing over at home. We are really in touch with our audience more than any other cooking show. So many cooking shows are done in a studio and you have no idea how the people are responding to it. We have a perfect idea of how they are responding because we see them.

Q: **When you invite an audience member on camera, it's like they are stepping into a friend's kitchen. There's such a level of comfort, even though they are probably on TV for the very first time. Is that something you facilitate, or is that the vibe of the show?**

Clinton: I think it's the vibe of the show. I mean, I really believe that the five of us are kind people at heart. That resonates with our audience. We love sharing recipes with people, we love making cocktails with people, we love the idea of coming together. It's not about ego, the show is not about ego—that's really the amazing thing about *The Chew*, where there are five hosts. There are no big egos, and I think that the audience gets that and they want to be a part of that because we're not intimidating.

Q: **All the hosts have had such successful careers. Are there really no egos on the set? Be honest!**

Clinton: You never know when you throw five people together how they're going to interact with each other. But we all got along beautifully from the beginning and it's kind of shocking. You know, what are your chances of putting five people in a room and having them all become great friends? Pretty rare. I can honestly say that we are not competitive with each other. Well, except maybe when it came to our chili competition (see page 92).

Q: **You are the host of the show, but you also cook and you understand food. Who's the real Clinton?**

Clinton: Well, here's the thing about me. I've been on TV now for the better part of a decade. Um, I never wanted to be a TV star. I never wanted to be a television host. I was just doing my thing and I fell into it. I've always wanted to live my life in the most pleasing way to me, and my life is not necessarily my career. My life is what I do when I'm not getting paid. That is the time that I spend with my family, that's the time I spend with my friends. Those are the most important things to me. I will choose my family, my friends, and my dog every day of the week over my career. That's my number one priority. What people have said to me over the past decade is sort of that I make people over and talk about fashion. That's not who I am. That's a part of who I am. That's my job. It's a small part of me

as a person. Who I am as a person is a lot more of a homebody, a home cook, and somebody who just enjoys entertaining. So what *The Chew* allows me to do is bring who I really am to television.

Q: **How has this group changed in the year you've been on the air?**

Clinton: The biggest change that has happened is that we are all five friends off-camera. We call each other up, we text each other, we see each other for a drink outside of the show. That has definitely made the show better, the fact that we genuinely like each other and want to spend time with each other. I look forward to coming to work and that's not been the case for me for a long time.

ROASTED AUTUMN VEGETABLES

SERVES 4 | **Skill Level: EASY** | **Cook Time: 30 mins.** | **Prep Time: 20 mins.** | **Cost: $**

This is a recipe that practically goes in one dish and comes out 30 minutes later ready to eat! With a side salad and maybe a baguette, you've got dinner. Lentils are probably the ingredient that I buy the most. I inherit that from the Turkish side of my family. We use lentils in a lot of ways to complement meat dishes but also sometimes as a substitute for meat. For vegetarians, they are a nutrient-dense, protein-dense food with the meaty consistency we all crave.

This medley features carrots and shallots, which develop a savory sweetness, and Brussels sprouts, which are at their pinnacle of flavor in the fall. When I cook for my husband after a day's work, I want to make dishes that are relatively easy and not about a whole big production. This is just that.

4 small carrots, halved lengthwise

3 shallots, halved

1 butternut squash, halved, seeded, and cut into ½-inch slices

½ pound Brussels sprouts, halved

4 cloves garlic

6 tablespoons extra virgin olive oil

Salt

Freshly ground pepper

½ cup dried black lentils, rinsed

½ an onion

1 bay leaf

3 tablespoons apple cider vinegar

1 tablespoon Dijon mustard

½ pound arugula

1. Preheat the oven to 400 °F.

2. In a large bowl, combine the carrots, shallots, squash, Brussels sprouts, and garlic. Drizzle 2 tablespoons of the extra virgin olive oil, and season with salt and pepper. Toss to coat. Pour vegetables onto a sheet tray and roast in the oven for 30 minutes, tossing once, halfway through.

3. Meanwhile, prepare the lentils by putting them into a small saucepan and covering with water by 2 inches. Add the onion and bay leaf. Bring to a boil, then simmer covered for 20 minutes, or until tender. Drain and discard the onion, season with salt and pepper, and set aside.

4. Once the vegetables are finished roasting, remove the garlic. Peel and mash the garlic in a small bowl, combine with the remaining 4 tablespoons of extra virgin olive oil, apple cider vinegar, and Dijon mustard, and whisk into a vinaigrette. Toss the lentils with the vinaigrette, fold in the arugula leaves, and then top with roasted vegetables to serve.

Some advice to new lentil lovers

With lentils, you want to add flavor while they cook. I usually boil them in water with an onion studded with cloves, some bay leaves, and a little olive oil. Then walk away and let the ingredients get to know one another. A low simmer is the way to go. Cook until they are al dente, with just a little tooth resistance. Mushy lentils are no fun. I like to use red lentils for soup because they're already cracked, they're really creamy, and they give a nice starchiness to the soup. I would use green (Puy) lentils for a salad, and I might use brown lentils for a heartier soup or casserole where I want the lentils to hold their shape.

CHESTNUT CREPES WITH MUSHROOMS & RADICCHIO SALAD

| SERVES 6 | Skill Level: MODERATE | Cook Time: 30 mins. | Prep Time: 15 mins. | Cost: $$ |

Inactive Prep Time: 20 mins. – 1 hr.

In World War I, when the supply lines were cut, the hill country folk of Emilia-Romagna, Italy, had to make everything with chestnuts, including flour for crepes. So when I opened my restaurant Babbo, I put these crepes on the menu and they have never come off it. Gwyneth Paltrow, who was first my customer and is now my friend, ordered it on her first visit and, according to her, every time since, which is why we chose to make it when Gwyneth visited The Chew. *She once paid me the highest compliment a chef can receive: My crepes always tasted the same. Now you might think a chef wants to hear "Wow! It was so delicious!" But that's not true. If someone orders something more than once, you already know they think it's great. The real thing that moves a chef's heart is to know that you can turn out something good consistently. Quick, easy, delicious, that's enough to get into my recipe Hall of Fame.*

FOR THE CREPE:

½ cup chestnut flour

¼ cup all-purpose flour

2 eggs

1 cup whole milk

Salt

Freshly ground black pepper

4 tablespoons butter, melted

FOR THE FILLING:

4 tablespoons extra virgin olive oil

3 shallots, minced

1 pound mixed mushrooms, thinly sliced

2 sprigs fresh rosemary, minced

2 sprigs thyme (leaves only)

Salt, to taste

Freshly ground black pepper, to taste

TO MAKE THE BATTER:

1. Place the two flours in a mixing bowl. Add the eggs one at a time, whisking to combine. Add the milk bit by bit, and whisk to combine, until all the milk is incorporated. Season with salt and pepper. Allow the batter to stand for 20 minutes to an hour.

TO MAKE THE FILLING:

2. In a small saucepan, heat the oil over medium heat, until smoking. Add the shallots and cook until soft, about 8–10 minutes.

3. Add the mushrooms and cook until softened, about 10 minutes.

4. Add the rosemary and thyme, and stir to combine. Season to taste with salt and pepper. Remove from the heat and set aside.

TO MAKE THE CREPES:

5. Heat a 6-inch nonstick pan over high heat until hot,

We all need a rest

Any batter with flour, eggs, and milk in it always improves if you let it rest. Leaving it overnight gives you a beautiful, smooth, silky batter.

You can make crepes in advance and store them in the freezer. Then whenever you're stuck for a meal idea, grab a few, sauté any ingredients you have on hand, and you have an interesting meal in a few minutes. Ground meat, ricotta, onions, cheese . . . let your imagination go wild.

and brush with the butter. Turn the heat down to medium and pour 1½ tablespoons of batter into the pan. Cook until pale golden on the bottom, about 1 minute. Flip and cook just 5–10 seconds on the second side. Remove and set aside. Continue the process until all the batter has been used. At this point you can freeze the crepes. Wrap crepes tightly in plastic and freeze.

FOR THE SALAD:

3 tablespoons extra virgin olive oil

3 tablespoons good balsamic vinegar

1 head radicchio lettuce, shredded

¼ cup freshly grated Parmigiano-Reggiano, to serve

TO ASSEMBLE:

6. Preheat the oven to 350 °F.

7. Use 2 tablespoons of the melted butter to coat the bottom and sides of a 10-by-8-inch ceramic baking dish. Fill each crepe with some of the mushroom mixture and fold. Put the filled crepes into the buttered dish and drizzle top with remaining butter. Put into the oven for about 15 minutes.

8. In the meantime, make a vinaigrette by slowly adding the olive oil to the balsamic vinegar, whisking to emulsify. Use the vinaigrette to dress the radicchio.

9. When the crepes are hot, remove from the oven and divide evenly among heated plates. Top the crepes with the radicchio salad and sprinkle with the grated Parmigiano-Reggiano. Drizzle with balsamic vinegar to taste and serve warm.

Mario chats with his friend Gwyneth as she takes over the stove.

17

EGGS WITH SWEET POTATO APPLE PANCAKES

| SERVES 5 | Skill Level: EASY | Cook Time: 20 mins. | Prep Time: 10 mins. | Cost: $ |

Simple, delicious, healthy, and affordable: that's my definition of a recipe worth learning. These sweet potato and apple pancakes are a good way to get your kids to eat whole, unprocessed ingredients by appealing to a child's natural sweet tooth. Come to think of it, they appeal to my grown-up sweet tooth too. The basting technique with the eggs produces a beautiful sunny-side up, with very little butter or oil required. In a time when some people say that using whole, un-processed ingredients is more expensive than fast food (not true), it's refreshing to find a meal for under two dollars that is made only with whole ingredients, including a fruit and a vegetable.

5 fresh eggs

⅓ cup olive oil, plus more if needed

1 sweet potato, peeled and grated

½ onion, peeled and grated

½ apple, peeled and grated

1 carrot, peeled and grated

2 egg whites, lightly beaten

¼ cup all-purpose flour

½ teaspoon salt

½ teaspoon pepper

TO MAKE THE EGGS:

1. Heat a large nonstick skillet over medium heat and brush or spray with olive oil. Add the eggs in batches and cook until the whites just begin to change color, about 2 minutes. Add a splash of water and steam until the whites have set but the yolk is still runny. Serve with the pancakes.

TO MAKE THE SWEET POTATO PANCAKES:

2. In a medium-sized skillet, heat ⅓ cup olive oil to medium-high heat.

3. Grate the sweet potato, onion, apple, and carrot. Wring out the liquid in a cheesecloth or paper towel (this is to ensure the pancakes won't be soggy). Then, in a large bowl, place the grated ingredients, egg whites, and flour. Add the salt and pepper. Mix well.

4. Drop enough batter into the hot oil to make 2½- to 3-inch pancakes. Add more oil, as needed, and fry cakes in batches, until golden on each side.

5. To serve, place 2 pancakes on a plate and top with a basted egg.

Wring, wring

My trick for crispy pancakes is to wrap my grated sweet potatoes and apples in cheesecloth and then wring them out by tightening the cloth. Extra added bonus: all that juice is delicious and healthful.

Steamed and stupendous

As soon as the egg whites begin to set, add a tiny bit of water to the pan and cover it. The steam will cook the eggs and leave you with a yummy runny yolk. Very little butter or oil needed.

MONTE CRISTO SANDWICH

SERVES 4 | Skill Level: EASY | Cook Time: 15 mins. | Prep Time: 20 mins. | Cost: $

First invented in the 1970s, this is the granddaddy of the gourmet grilled sandwich craze. For sure the Count of Monte Cristo never ate such a sandwich. In fact, I have heard that it was born in Disney World at a concession next to the Pirates of the Caribbean . . . but, hey, we know from watching Johnny Depp as Captain Jack Sparrow that his meals were pretty much confined to the rum food group.

After you batter the sandwich, you fry it in a skillet. To serve, I hit it with a good gob of jam, spank it with powdered sugar, garnish with a couple of jalapeños, and add a fried egg on the side. It looked so good that I swear when we took a close-up, Clinton was tempted to eat the monitor.

FOR THE MONTE CRISTO:

Vegetable oil, for frying

1 egg, lightly beaten

¾ cup milk

¾ cup flour

2 teaspoons baking powder

Salt

Pepper

4 tablespoons mustard

8 slices thick-cut white bread

4 slices Fontina cheese

4 slices ham

4 slices smoked turkey

¼ cup pickled jalapeños (optional)

Powdered sugar, for garnish

Jam (optional)

FOR THE FRIED EGGS:

1 tablespoon butter

4 eggs

1. Preheat 2 inches vegetable oil to 360 °F in a large cast-iron skillet.

2. In a shallow baking dish, whisk together the egg and milk. Stir in the flour and baking powder, and season with salt and pepper.

3. Spread mustard on the bread slices. Sandwich each piece of Fontina cheese between one slice of ham and one slice of turkey. Add a couple of pickled jalapeños, if desired, and then sandwich between two pieces of bread.

4. Coat the sandwiches evenly on all sides with the batter. Drop into the oil, and fry until golden brown and crisp. Remove to a paper towel–lined plate, and sprinkle with powdered sugar and add a spoonful of your favorite jam, if desired.

5. For the eggs, heat the butter in a nonstick skillet over medium heat. Once the butter has foamed and subsided, crack each egg into the skillet and fry until the yolk is set.

6. Serve a fried egg alongside each Monte Cristo.

CHILE CHICKEN FLAUTAS

| SERVES 6 | Skill Level: EASY | Cook Time: 1 hr. | Prep Time: 15 mins. | Cost: $ |

In Spanish, flauta means "flute," but I've never seen a flute that looks or sounds like these stuffed fried tortillas. Still, they make beautiful eating music. You can make them from scratch, as we do here, or you can fill them up with just about any leftover, including lasagna. Of course, that may just be the Italian in me speaking: I have yet to find the dish that can't be helped along with a little leftover lasagna. Okay, maybe cupcakes can't, but anything non-sweet is longing for a date with yesterday's lasagna.

As with so much Mexican food, a chile is more than just a chile. There are fresh chilies, dried chilies, smoked chilies, and pickled chilies, and all of them go into these chicken flautas for a beautiful, complex mix of flavors.

Flautas are often a big family meal in my restaurants. Our Latin chefs are extremely creative in taking leftovers and making some of the most delicious food. To tell you the truth, I often will choose their flautas over my fanciest menu items.

3 tablespoons vegetable oil, plus more for frying

6 boneless chicken thighs

Salt

1 tablespoon cumin

1 tablespoon coriander

1 tablespoon cayenne

1 onion, thinly sliced

6 cloves garlic, thinly sliced

3 red Fresno chilies, seeded and chopped

3 tablespoons tomato paste

4 ancho chilies, soaked in hot water

2 chipotles in adobo

1. Heat a large Dutch oven over medium-high heat and add 3 tablespoons oil. Season the chicken with salt, cumin, coriander, and cayenne. Add the chicken to the pot and cook until golden brown, 3 minutes per side. Remove the chicken from the pot and set aside on a plate.

2. Add the onion, garlic, and Fresno chilies, and sauté for 3 minutes. Add the tomato paste and cook for another minute.

Chilies: the miracle medicine

The chilies found in Mexican food have fiber and important vitamins. Capsaicin (the hot part) helps boost metabolism and is associated with lowering cholesterol. I think it's one of the reasons that real Mexican food is so good for you.

12 6-inch flour tortillas

2 cups Cotija cheese

1 bunch cilantro (leaves only)

Sour cream, for garnish

Lime wedges, for garnish

SPECIAL EQUIPMENT:

Toothpicks

3. Remove the ancho peppers from the water, puree with the chipotles, and add to the pot, reserving the soaking liquid.

4. Place the chicken back into the pot and add some of the reserved soaking liquid. Cook the chicken until tender, about 45 minutes.

5. Remove the chicken from the sauce and shred when cool enough to handle. Add a little of the sauce to the chicken so that it is coated but not too wet, and set aside the remaining sauce.

6. Place 2 tablespoons of the chicken into a warmed flour tortilla. Add a little cheese and cilantro. Roll the tortilla up and fasten with a toothpick. Repeat with the remaining tortillas.

7. Heat 2 inches of oil in a large cast-iron skillet to about 350 °F. Place the tortillas into the oil seam-side down, and, working in batches, fry until golden brown on each side, about 2 minutes per side. Remove to a towel-lined plate to drain. Remove the toothpicks, and serve with the remaining sauce, sour cream, cilantro, lime wedges, and cheese.

Mama T shares her family secrets with Mario.

EGGPLANT PARMIGIANINO

SERVES 8 | Skill Level: EASY | Cook Time: 50 mins. | Prep Time: 15 mins. | Cost: $

This recipe reminds me of my childhood, because my grandfather, who was Italian, had this amazing garden with wonderful eggplants. When it came time to pick them, we would get the whole family together and set up an assembly line. Pop, as I called my grandfather, would slice the eggplants. Then my sister and I would dredge them in flour, egg, and bread. My dad would fry the slices in olive oil. Finally, Mom layered the slices in a dish with tomato sauce and cheese. About half an hour later, we were in eggplant heaven.

2 cups all-purpose flour

Salt

Pepper

5 large eggs

3½ cups Italian bread crumbs

1 cup freshly grated Parmigiano-Reggiano

¾ cup olive oil, plus more if needed

3 medium eggplants, sliced lengthwise into ¼-inch slices

4 cups Mario's Basic Tomato Sauce (page 30)

1 pound fresh mozzarella, thinly sliced

1. Preheat the oven to 350 °F.

2. Stir together the flour, salt, and pepper in a large dish, and set aside. Lightly beat the eggs in a high-sided dish, and set aside. Stir together the bread crumbs and ⅓ cup Parmigiano-Reggiano in a shallow dish.

3. Heat a small amount of oil in a large nonstick skillet to medium-high heat.

4. Working with 1 slice at a time, dredge each eggplant slice in the flour mixture, shaking off excess, then dip in the egg, letting excess drip off. Dredge in the bread crumb mixture until evenly coated. Transfer the eggplant directly to hot oil.

5. Fry the eggplant 4 slices at a time, turning over once, until golden brown, 5–6 minutes per batch. Transfer with tongs to paper towels to drain. Season with salt immediately after frying.

6. Spread 1 cup tomato sauce in the bottom of a 9-by-13-inch baking dish. Arrange about a third of the eggplant slices in one layer over the sauce, overlapping slightly if necessary. Cover the eggplant with about a third of the remaining sauce and a third of the mozzarella. Continue layering with the remaining eggplant, sauce, and mozzarella. Sprinkle top with remaining Parmigiano-Reggiano.

7. Bake uncovered, until cheese is melted and golden and sauce is bubbling, 30–35 minutes.

To salt or not to salt

Some people like to salt their eggplant slices and let them sit for a while before cooking. Mario said this practice comes from an old superstition that because eggplant (like the tomato) is a member of the nightshade family, it is poisonous, and the salt somehow "unpoisons" it. Well, that's just not so. What salting does is it removes water. I don't think it's a necessary step, but if you were brought up that way, be my guest. I find that leaving it unsalted and then baking makes for a more tender result.

STUFFED MUSHROOMS

MAKES 20 | **Skill Level: EASY** | **Cook Time: 30 mins.** | **Prep Time: 15 mins.** | **Cost: $**

I made these for Thanksgiving as an appetizer that's special but not super heavy with cheesy, bacon-y calories. They don't skimp on flavor, though. Mushrooms are light, but they have that special taste called "umami" that satisfies you like a piece of beef. Some people like to fry their stuffed mushrooms, but I find if you fill them up with fresh herbs and onions sautéed to the point of creaminess, then you can just bake them in the oven and save yourself 100 calories. And who doesn't want to save 100 calories . . . especially at Thanksgiving? Oh, and did I mention they cost about twenty-seven cents apiece? It occurs to me that if enough people eat stuffed mushrooms we can solve our national weight crisis and pay down the national debt, all with the help of this one hors d'oeuvre.

20 button mushrooms, scrubbed clean and stems reserved

3 tablespoons olive oil

2 tablespoons shallots, minced

1 large clove garlic, minced

2 tablespoons almonds, chopped

Salt, to taste

3 tablespoons parsley, chopped

1 teaspoon herbes de Provence or dried thyme

2 tablespoons whole wheat bread crumbs

2–3 tablespoons vegetable stock

2 tablespoons Pecorino cheese, grated

1. Preheat the oven to 375 °F.

2. Finely chop the mushroom stems. Heat 1 tablespoon olive oil in a small nonstick skillet over medium-high heat. Sauté the chopped mushroom stems and the shallots for 4–5 minutes, stirring often.

3. Add the garlic and almonds, and season with salt. Stir well and sauté 2 more minutes. Turn off the heat and add the parsley, herbes de Provence (or thyme), and whole wheat bread crumbs.

4. Pour the vegetable stock into a food processor, then the rest of the stuffing. Pulse several times to get a fine mixture, almost a paste.

5. Toss the mushroom caps with olive oil. Fill each mushroom with the stuffing. Sprinkle grated Pecorino cheese over each mushroom and bake for 20–25 minutes, until the cheese browns a little and the mushrooms are warmed through.

Making it look like spaghetti

If you are not familiar with spaghetti squash, the way you get those spaghetti-like strands is to roast the squash and then remove the cooked flesh of the squash by scraping it with a fork.

SPAGHETTI SQUASH FRITTERS

SERVES 6 | **Skill Level: MODERATE** | **Cook Time: 35–40 mins.** | **Cost: $**

Spaghetti squash fritters, with blue cheese and nutmeg in the batter, are an intensely flavorful and ecstatically crispy appetizer or side. Just like potato latkes (pancakes) are a special treat at Hanukkah, these fritters at Thanksgiving or Christmas have that same hot, savory crispness that pretty much guarantees your guests will eat every one. If it's anything like my house, they'll start to hover around the fryer, barely able to wait until you take them from the hot oil.

1 medium spaghetti squash

1½ tablespoons fresh sage, chopped, plus whole leaves for garnish

⅛ teaspoon whole nutmeg, grated

1 scallion (green and white parts), thinly sliced on the bias

2 teaspoons garlic, minced

1 teaspoon kosher salt or coarse sea salt

½ teaspoon freshly ground pepper

4 ounces blue cheese, coarsely chopped or crumbled

Zest of 1 orange

1 large egg

3–4 tablespoons all-purpose flour

Canola oil, for deep-frying

1. Preheat the oven to 400 °F.

2. Cut the squash in half and remove the seeds. Season with salt and roast on a foil-lined half sheet pan for 30 minutes, until tender. Let cool. With a fork, scrape the squash to remove long strands and place on a towel.

3. Wrap the spaghetti squash in a kitchen towel and wring as much liquid out of it as possible, discarding the liquid.

4. In a medium bowl, combine the squash, chopped sage, nutmeg, scallion, garlic, salt, pepper, blue cheese, and all but 1 teaspoon of the orange zest. Stir in the egg and flour, and mix well until combined.

5. Add the canola oil to a large shallow pan two-thirds up the sides of the pan. Place the pan over medium-high heat. The oil should be heated to 360 °F for frying.

6. Drop spoonfuls of the squash mixture into the oil. Cook until the fritters are golden brown, about 4 minutes. After the fritters have cooked for 2 to 3 minutes, add some fresh sage leaves, but be careful because they will pop. Fry the sage leaves for a couple of minutes and remove with the fritters. Drain the fried fritters and sage leaves on paper towels and season with salt.

7. Transfer the fritters to plates and garnish with the reserved orange zest and fried sage leaves.

Sage advice

About 45 seconds before the fritters are done, put a bunch of sage leaves in the oil. Fried sage is a terrific garnish, and the flavor it releases into the frying oil (and then into the fritters) creates an insanely appetizing aroma.

WINE-STAINED PASTA WITH SAUSAGE MEATBALLS AND CAULIFLOWER

SERVES 6 | **Skill Level: EASY** | **Cook Time: 25–30 mins.** | **Prep Time: 15 mins.** | **Cost: $**

People are always blown away when I make this dish. Cooking your pasta in a whole bottle of inexpensive wine looks great, sounds brave, tastes amazing. For those of you who are hoping to get a little extra buzz from your pasta, sorry to be a buzzkill, but the alcohol just about cooks off by the time the pasta is ready. I made this on the show when Jimmy Fallon visited. Jimmy couldn't resist busting my chops with a story about the time we were in Ireland to play some golf and I took him to a market to shop for ingredients for dinner. I asked him to find a grill pan, and he comes back with one and told me there was a whole Mario Batali kitchenware aisle in the store.

"It's like going to buy Sam Adams beer with the real Sam Adams!" he said. Jimmy got extra-special pleasure making me, Mario Batali, pay for the Mario Batali grill pan. Double extra pleasure in making me relive the whole scene by telling the audience about it.

1 bottle plus 1 cup inexpensive red wine

2½ pounds sweet Italian sausage, casings removed

¼ cup extra virgin olive oil

1 medium head cauliflower, cut into small florets

2 cloves garlic, sliced

Pinch of red pepper flakes

2 cups Mario's Basic Tomato Sauce (recipe follows)

1½ pounds garganelli pasta

2 tablespoons salt

1 cup freshly grated Pecorino Romano, to serve

1. Fill a large pot with half water and half wine and bring to a boil.

2. Using your hands, form the sausage into small meatballs, about the size of marbles. In a 12- to 14-inch sauté pan, heat the oil over medium heat, until just smoking. Add the sausage balls in two batches and sauté, rolling them around, until they are browned all over, 5–6 minutes per batch. Remove, and set aside on a plate.

3. Add the cauliflower to the pan and cook until soft, about 5 minutes. Add the garlic and the red pepper flakes, cook for another minute, and add the 1 cup red wine to the cauliflower. Bring to a boil, and then add the tomato sauce and sausage balls. Bring to a boil again. Then lower the heat to a simmer and cook for 5 minutes. Remove from the heat.

4. Drop the garganelli into the boiling wine/water, season heavily with salt, and cook for 1 minute less than the package instructions indicate. Just before the pasta is done, carefully ladle ½ cup of the cooking wine/water into the sausage mixture.

5. Drain the pasta in a colander and add it to the sausage mixture. Toss until pasta is nicely coated. Pour into a serving bowl and serve immediately, with the grated Pecorino on the side.

MARIO'S BASIC TOMATO SAUCE

¼ cup extra virgin olive oil

1 yellow onion, diced

5 garlic cloves, peeled and thinly sliced

3 tablespoons fresh thyme, leaves only

½ medium carrot, shredded

2 28-ounce cans peeled whole tomatoes crushed by hand and juices reserved

Salt, to taste

1. In a 3-quart saucepan, heat the olive oil over medium heat. Add the onion and garlic and cook until soft and light golden brown, about 8 to 10 minutes.

2. Add the thyme and carrot and cook 5 minutes more, until the carrot is quite soft.

3. Add the tomatoes and juice and bring to a boil, stirring often. Lower the heat and simmer for 30 minutes until as thick as hot cereal.

4. Season with salt and serve.

Mario and Jimmy Fallon after a round of stovetop Ping Pong.

GENERAL TSO'S CHICKEN

SERVES 4 | **Skill Level: EASY** | **Cook Time: 20–25 mins.** | **Prep Time: 10 mins.** | **Cost: $**

There was a restaurant in my hometown, Port Jefferson Station, Long Island, that made me a lifelong convert to the good general's namesake chicken. Actually, in the balloon-popping department, it is my moral duty to inform you that as far as anyone can tell, there was no General Tso. The name originated from confusion with the Chinese word for "ancestral meeting house." Somehow I can't imagine anyone ordering a quart of ancestral meeting house chicken to go. So General Tso's it is. My homemade version is crispy, sweet, and uses lots less fat and salt.

FOR THE SAUCE:

1 tablespoon cornstarch

½ cup cold water

4 cloves garlic, sliced

2 tablespoons fresh ginger, grated

3 tablespoons honey

2 tablespoons low-sodium soy sauce

3 tablespoons Chinese rice wine

1 tablespoon red pepper flakes

FOR THE CHICKEN:

3 tablespoons cornstarch

½ teaspoon salt

¼ teaspoon pepper

2 tablespoons vegetable oil

1 pound boneless, skinless chicken breasts, cut into 1-inch pieces

1 pound broccoli florets, blanched

1½ cups white rice, cooked according to package instructions

4 scallions (greens only), thinly sliced, for garnish

1 teaspoon sesame seeds, for garnish

1. For the sauce, in a large bowl, mix together 1 tablespoon cornstarch and cold water until smooth. Add the garlic, ginger, honey, soy sauce, Chinese rice wine, and red pepper flakes. Set aside.

2. In a separate bowl, mix the cornstarch, salt, and pepper together until combined. Add the chicken and toss until coated.

3. Heat a large nonstick skillet with vegetable oil. Shake excess coating off the chicken and cook until golden, 4–6 minutes.

4. Add the sauce mixture and cook until the sauce has thickened. Add the steamed broccoli and toss to coat with the sauce.

5. Plate with rice. Add the scallions and sesame seeds for garnish.

ROASTED CHICKEN WITH SWEET POTATOES AND SAGE

SERVES 6 | **Skill Level: MODERATE** | **Cook Time: 1 hr.** | **Prep Time: 15 mins.** | **Cost: $**

Ask any professional chef what the measure of a great restaurant is and many will answer, "A roasted chicken." Brown and crispy on the outside, juicy and succulent meat on the inside, and a panful of roasted, caramelized vegetables. A house with a roasted chicken in the oven says, "This is a place where people love food." For me, the key is salting liberally, inside and out, the night before. Studies have shown that the salt permeates the flesh of the chicken and keeps it from drying out in the oven. My wife, Lizzie, and I make this once a week and never tire of it.

1 3- to 4-pound chicken

Salt

1 stick butter, room temperature

1 small bunch fresh sage, chopped

1 onion, peeled

2 celery roots, peeled and cubed

3 sweet potatoes, cubed

3 tablespoons cumin seeds

Drizzle of olive oil

Pepper

1. A day before cooking, rinse the chicken inside and out under cold water and pat dry. Salt it liberally, cover, and refrigerate. Remove the chicken from the refrigerator an hour before cooking it. Preheat the oven to 425 °F.

2. Combine butter and sage, and rub under the skin. Put the onion in the cavity of the chicken.

3. Toss the celery roots, potatoes, cumin seeds, olive oil, salt, and pepper.

4. Put the chicken in an ovenproof sauté pan or in a roasting pan, breast side up, on top of the sweet potato and celery root mixture. Slide it into the oven, and roast it until the thigh reaches 160 °F or until the juices run clear, about 1 hour.

5. Remove from the oven and let rest for 10–20 minutes. Cut the chicken into 8 pieces and serve with the vegetables.

Even ugly vegetables taste great

Depending on the season, I like to surround the chicken with a bed of vegetable chunks. Celery root—which gets the ugly prize—cooks up soft and sweet. Potatoes and sweet potatoes are crispy on the outside and creamy within. Onions and garlic get a golden half-crispy, half-melty soft sweetness. Just remember: the chicken takes nearly an hour to cook, so you want your vegetable pieces pretty big. That way they cook at the same rate as the chicken.

Better with butter

Add some fresh sage to soft butter and massage the skin with it. Also work some of the butter-sage mix under the skin. It keeps the meat moist, adds a deep nutty flavor, and produces a beautiful golden-brown skin.

Think twice, it's all right

It takes very little extra to roast two chickens instead of one. Then you have a week's worth of leftovers for salads, potpies, etc., or simply reheat and serve with your favorite condiments and sauces, from plain old mustard to pesto to Sriracha.

Michael gives a big hug to his one and only love, Liz.

CAST-IRON PORK PIE

| SERVES 6 | Skill Level: EASY | Cook Time: 25–30 mins. | Prep Time: 10 mins. | Cost: $ |

One of our favorite things around the Symon household is a savory pie. I have been making a pork pie for years, but when I read Keith Richards's autobiography, he gave me a new idea when he talked about how the Rolling Stones grew up in households where shepherd's pie, with its distinctive mashed potato crust, was a go-to meal. Hey, if it's cool enough for Keith, it's definitely cool enough for me. Then I wanted to health it up a little, so I included a good helping of kale. Daphne loved that idea. Anytime you can get a green leafy vegetable into a recipe, you've got a happy Daphne. And, of course, some melted Cheddar cheese on top . . . because Cheddar cheese is so good on apple pie, I figured it could go into my reinvented pork pie.

½ pound bacon, medium diced

2 pounds ground pork

Drizzle of olive oil

2 large onions

2 cups kale, roughly chopped

1 cup celery, chopped

2 cloves garlic, chopped

Pinch of ground cinnamon

Large pinch of salt

Pinch of pepper

Pinch of ground nutmeg

½ cup fresh parsley, chopped

½ cup celery leaves, chopped

3 cups mashed potatoes

1 cup aged Cheddar, grated

1. Preheat the oven to 450 °F.

2. In a cast-iron skillet, brown the bacon and pork. Remove from the pan and reserve.

3. To the same pan, add a drizzle of olive oil, onions, kale, celery, garlic, cinnamon, salt, pepper, and nutmeg, and sweat for 4–5 minutes, then add the pork and bacon back to the pan with a splash of water. Mix, then add the parsley and celery leaves, and stir in to combine. Remove from heat.

4. Spread the mashed potatoes over the pork mixture and sprinkle with grated Cheddar.

5. Bake until golden brown, about 15–20 minutes, garnish with celery leaves, and serve.

Daphne says

If you want to do a vegetarian version of this dish, eggplant, any fall squash, maybe even some portabella mushrooms will work beautifully. And, yes, don't forget the kale. Love that kale!

Straighten up and fry right

If you like to fry, get one of those home fryers with a temperature control. They take a lot of the fear out of frying, because you know your oil is always at the right temperature. If you aren't in the mood for another gadget, you can always fry in a skillet. Just remember that when things fry, the hot fat tends to burble up. To keep it from overflowing and maybe burning yourself in the process, I recommend that the oil come no more than two-thirds of the way up the pan.

Daphne's healthy hint

Frying has been getting a bad reputation that it doesn't deserve. If you fry at the right temperature and drain your fried food well, fats like olive and canola oil are actually quite healthful. Fats help your body to make use of the antioxidants in fresh vegetables. When frying, make sure you don't heat the oil until it smokes, because if you do, the fat breaks down and you lose all those healthy free radicals.

CRISPY LIME AND CILANTRO CHICKEN WINGS

SERVES 6 | Skill Level: EASY | Cook Time: 30–35 mins. | Prep Time: 20 mins.

Inactive Prep Time: 2–3 hrs. | Cost: $–$$ Cost will depend on which fat you use to fry.

Everyone loves Buffalo chicken wings. Me too. It's a perfect football-watching food. But crispy cooked wings with a delicious mix of flavors don't begin and end with the blue cheese, butter, and vinegar version of the sauce that has become a game-day mainstay. My recipe comes from my hometown in the Midwest via a marinade and dipping sauce with the bright, spicy, tangy flavors of Asia. You give up none of the powerhouse flavor of traditional Buffalo wings, but it's a much lighter dish, so you can eat more without filling up. If you are watching this when your team is playing, remember that if they score on a sixty-yard fumble recovery, don't swallow the bone while you are cheering madly.

FOR THE MARINADE:

1 tablespoon kosher salt

1 teaspoon sugar

1 tablespoon smoked paprika

Juice and zest of 2 limes (reserve zest for the wing sauce)

½ cup extra virgin olive oil

3 pounds chicken wings

4 cups duck fat or vegetable oil, for frying

FOR THE WING SAUCE:

½ cup hot sauce (such as Sriracha)

1 tablespoon apple cider vinegar

2–3 tablespoons honey

3 tablespoons unsalted butter

Reserved lime zest

½ teaspoon salt

½ cup cilantro leaves

Lime wedges, to garnish

2 jalapeños, thinly sliced, to garnish

1. In a large bowl, combine the ingredients for the marinade. Add the chicken wings, and toss to coat. Cover and marinate in the refrigerator for 2–3 hours.

2. Preheat the oven to 350 °F. Spread the wings out on a baking sheet with sides. Pour over any remaining marinade, and bake for 15–20 minutes, until just cooked through. Remove from the oven and let cool slightly, about 5 minutes.

3. Place a high-sided cast-iron pan over medium-high heat and add the duck fat or vegetable oil. Using a deep-fry thermometer to monitor the temperature, allow the fat to heat to 360 °F.

4. Carefully add the wings to the oil in batches and fry until golden brown and crispy, about 4 minutes per batch. Drain on a paper towel–lined plate and season them with salt.

5. To make the wing sauce, place a medium saucepan over medium heat. Add all the ingredients and whisk until the butter has melted, then taste and season with salt.

6. Place the chicken wings in a large bowl and pour the sauce over the top. Toss to coat the wings with the sauce. Add in the cilantro leaves, tossing one more time. Serve with lime wedges and sliced jalapeños.

FALL

Thanksgiving— The Familiest Day

Clinton

THANKSGIVING IS SUPER IMPORTANT TO ME as a time for the entire family to get together. It's always a group project. Nobody is expected to do all the work. Someone would volunteer for vegetables. Someone else for turkey. Still another for dessert. Without a lot a planning, somehow it was naturally coordinated. We all ended up having a great time without sticking Mom in the kitchen by herself for 8 hours. And don't let me forget cleanup. It's like a military process. When the meal is done—boom!—everybody gets up with five things in their hands and it all goes on an assembly line for the SWAT team in the kitchen. Thanksgiving is one of the few times when cleaning up after is actually fun! Maybe the only time.

Daphne

WE ARE A FAIRLY LARGE CLAN and we do something called the Oz Family Turkey Bowl, because, of course, my dad—Mr. Healthy—had to find a way to work activity and exercise into the biggest eating day of the year. So we get twenty-five people together and have ten-on-ten full-contact football with five subs for the people who, inevitably, pull a muscle or get a scrape. To give you some idea of how seriously we take this, my mother played this game when she was eight months pregnant with me. Of course we have a real turkey, but we also have a tofu turkey, or, as we call it, a Tofurkey.

Carla

BACK IN THE DAY (when I was in business for myself), we didn't have much money and I usually didn't have much of a Thanksgiving anyway since the holidays were big work days. One year, I decided to have my own Thanksgiving and I wanted to treat myself. My girlfriend Greta and I bought this beautiful china . . . like *totally gorgeous*, not to mention *very expensive*. We picked a few different patterns, a beautiful tablecloth. We invited people over—mostly holiday stragglers with nowhere else to go. Dinner was super—six or seven courses. It was a special night.

Michael

THANKSGIVING IS MY FAVORITE
HOLIDAY of the year by far. It's all about
food, family, friends, and football. Which
is good. My grandfather used to do it, but
we took over in the past couple of years.
All our families are there plus people
who work for us who are too far from
their families to drive home. So it can be
anywhere between twenty-five and fifty
people at our house, so it is truly a feast.
We have one ginormous table where we
seat about twenty-eight to thirty people,
and the kids sit at another one. Quite a
spectacle!

Mario

I HAD A BIG FAMILY with lots of cousins
on both the eastern side of Washington
State and the western side of the state, so
we kind of alternated hosting duties every
year. We would go to either Aunt Izzy's
or Aunt Mari's or Aunt Cheri's or Uncle
Paul's or our house. And every one of the
holidays, whether it was July Fourth or
Christmas or New Year's Day or Easter or
any of them, including Thanksgiving, got
divvied up in some secret meeting that
I never knew existed. Day of, we all just
knew where we were going. We'd figure
out with the cousins what kind of mischief
we might get in before dinner, including
some football. And then we would just
have this fabulous turkey. Because of our
round-robin hosting, each family would
have three or four years to warm up for
the next time they were on duty, so it was
always just a little bit different.

Setting the Thanksgiving Table

THANKSGIVING ISN'T JUST ABOUT THE FOOD. It's also about dressing: the turkey, the table, and you. And remember: dressing doesn't have to mean dressy. So here are two approaches to your Thanksgiving tabletop: one dressy and one a little more down home.

Casual thursday

If you are like me, you like hosting but you don't want to carry the whole burden on your shoulders, so you divvy up the work. Someone brings the stuffing, someone else the pumpkin pie, maybe your cousin brings the Brussels sprouts, and the lazybones in the crowd gets to open a can of cranberry sauce. Okay, a nice bunch of recipes, but the dishes they bring them in are a mix and match, hodgepodge. It doesn't look cohesive.

My advice is to map out the buffet. I like to use different heights to my advantage. All the veggies on one level, maybe the stuffings and mashed potatoes on another, a big turkey platter on another, and pies and cakes on another. So even if the serving dishes look different, each course gets its own level.

Now how are you going to make those levels? Stack books for each different level and cover them with gift paper, place mats, or decorative cloth remnants. Just like that, your spread has a cool design theme, and the eye is drawn to each grouping.

If the look of everyone's casseroles and platters is just too mixed up for you, use your own plates and presentation platters.

Dress-up day

My biggest piece of advice for a formal table is to keep it white and simple. No colors to match, just elegant simplicity. Use white linens and white napkins. And for Pete's sake, iron your tablecloth. Nothing ruins a table like a big crease that runs down the center of it. I'm a freak. I love to iron to relax myself. I do. I can get five shirts done in 7 minutes. I get into the Zen ironing moment, where I feel like I can do just anything while I'm ironing. I talk to people, I watch television; it's my favorite thing. But enough about me. Okay.

I'm nuts about nuts and ape for apples

Autumn fruits and vegetables add color that is literally appetizing to a table. Apples, pomegranates, nuts . . . are beautiful . . . and delicious.

Get set

The other thing you really have to do is pay attention to how you're setting the table. There is a format for your silverware and your plates. Let's all go through this together. It is fork, fork, plate, knife, spoon.

C'mon say it with me: "Fork, fork, plate, knife, spoon."

Then the water glass goes over the knife and the wineglass goes over the spoon.

Where does the water glass go?
Say it with me: "Over the knife."
Where does the wineglass go?
Say it with me: "Over the spoon."

And then your dessert fork and your coffee spoon go above the plate. I'm not going to make you say it again. But the reason for this is when you're done with the main course and you have dessert in front of you, all you have to do is reach out and your fork and spoon are right at your fingertips.

I was framed

Ordinary ninety-nine-cent picture frames with your guests' pictures in them are a thoughtful and effective place card. People never get tired of looking at themselves.

Set the people too

It's nice to tell people where to sit, because you never want to have your best conversationalists clustered together. Spread them out. If you have a bunch of duds on one side, fuggedaboutit.

The takeaway

One thing that makes a dinner memorable is a memento to take home. Around holiday time, a Christmas ornament is pretty and colorful. It's one of the two things that almost everyone likes. The other is fireworks. My advice: stay away from things that explode.

LEMON SAGE TURKEY

SERVES 10 to 14 | **Skill Level: EASY** | **Cook Time: 3–3 ½ hrs.** | **Prep Time: 20 mins.** | **Cost: $**

Inactive Prep Time: 12 hrs.

I've been eating my family's turkey for a long time. It's good, but I thought I could come up with something better . . . fresher . . . more flavorful and, most of all, moist. So, Kelly family, here's my take on turkey. I call it Lemon Sage Turkey. It's actually a lemon, sage, and garlic turkey, but lemon sage sounds more zingy to me. Aside from a good turkey—free range and organic get my vote—there are three secrets to my big bird. First, you have to brine. Not everyone believes in brining. In fact, Michael is a devout non-brining crusader, but it makes for juicier white meat.

The second secret is the compound butter of lemon and garlic. You rub it over and inside the skin and it becomes a delicious crust-helper and meat-moistener.

Finally, stuffing all those lemons in the cavity freshens everything, and the scent of the lemon oil makes a great little accent.

FOR THE BRINE:

1 gallon water

1 cup sea salt

1 bunch fresh rosemary

1 bunch sage

1 bunch fresh thyme

2 cups maple syrup

10 cloves garlic, smashed, skin on

1 gallon ice water

2 cups apple cider

MARIO'S BRINE

1. In a large stockpot, combine the water, sea salt, rosemary, sage, thyme, maple syrup, and garlic cloves. Bring to a boil, and stir frequently to be sure salt is dissolved. Remove from heat, and let cool to room temperature.

2. When the broth mixture is cool, pour it into a clean 5-gallon bucket. Stir in the ice water and cider.

3. Place the turkey, breast down, into the brine. Make sure that the cavity gets filled. Place the bucket in the refrigerator overnight but no longer than 12 hours.

4. Remove the turkey, carefully drain off the excess brine, and pat dry. Discard excess brine.

FOR THE TURKEY:

1 12- to 16-pound turkey

2 sticks unsalted butter at room temperature

1 shallot, finely minced

1 clove garlic, finely minced

3 tablespoons sage, minced, plus 1 bunch fresh sage

4 lemons

Kosher salt, to taste

Freshly ground black pepper, to taste

2 tablespoons olive oil

1. Preheat the oven to 425 °F. Arrange an oven shelf in the lower third of the oven.

2. Let the turkey come to room temperature. Remove the neck and giblets from the body and neck cavities, and reserve them for turkey broth. Drain the juices, and pat the bird dry inside and out.

3. Meanwhile, make the compound butter. In a large bowl, combine room temperature butter, shallot, garlic, minced sage, and juice and zest of 1 lemon. Stir together with a rubber spatula. Add salt and pepper to taste. Set aside.

4. Arrange the turkey breast side up in a rack (preferably a V-rack) set in a heavy, large roasting pan.

5. Season the inside of the turkey with salt and pepper to taste. Puncture two lemons with a fork and stuff inside cavity of the turkey, along with the fresh sage.

6. Carefully smooth the compound butter under the skin of the turkey, being mindful not to tear the membrane connecting the skin to the breast. Thinly slice the remaining lemon and slide slices under the skin along with butter.

7. Coat the outside of the bird with olive oil, and rub all over its skin. Season generously with kosher salt and freshly ground black pepper.

8. Roast the turkey in the lower third of the oven for 20 minutes at 425 °F. Then turn the oven down to 325 °F and roast until an instant-read thermometer inserted into the thickest part of the leg-thigh joint reads 165 °F.

9. Transfer the turkey to a platter, leaving the drippings in the pan for the gravy, and cover the turkey loosely with foil. Let the turkey rest for at least 20 minutes, preferably 30 minutes, before carving.

CHESTNUT MERGUEZ STUFFING

SERVES 6 | Skill Level: EASY | Cook Time: 50 mins. | Prep Time: 10 Mins. | Cost: $

One of the strongest Thanksgiving memories I have of growing up in my house is the aroma of roasting chestnuts. My grandma always roasted them for every holiday, and then we kids tried to figure out how to not eat them. We hid them in the couch, we put them behind her dresser. Now that I am a grown-up, I have altered my opinion of chestnuts. I love them, and to the best of my knowledge, my kids never hid them behind the furniture. I also like sausage in my stuffing, pretty much any sausage, but lately I have fallen in love with the slightly spicy North African lamb sausage known as merguez.

4 tablespoons extra virgin olive oil

1 pound merguez sausage, casings removed

1 large onion, diced

5 stalks celery, diced

1 cup chestnuts, roughly chopped

1 cup apples, peeled and diced

4 cups cornbread, toasted and cubed

1 tablespoon sage, for sprinkling

2½ cups chicken broth

½ cup butter, melted

1. In a large skillet over medium heat, heat the oil, then crumble the merguez into the pan and cook for 4 minutes. Add the onion, celery, chestnuts, and apples, and sauté, stirring occasionally, until sausage is cooked through.

2. In a large bowl, place the cubed cornbread. Add the sausage mixture, and sprinkle with the sage. Pour the broth and butter over the top, and toss to combine.

3. Spoon the mixture into a 9-by-13-inch baking dish and cover. Bake at 350 °F for 45 minutes.

Getting ready

Most people, the Batalis included, find themselves with too much to do and too little time when it comes to holiday meals. You can assemble this dressing/stuffing up to a day or two before it gets popped in the oven. Then on Turkey Day, put it into the oven for 45 minutes before you plan on serving your turkey.

Dressed or stuffed?

Some people call it dressing. Some call it stuffing. I learned that the difference is stuffing goes inside the bird and dressing gets cooked separately. Call it whatever you want, just so long as the family enjoys it.

MUSHROOM AND VEGETABLE STUFFING

SERVES 4 | Skill Level: **EASY** | Cook Time: **45–50 mins.** | Prep Time: **15 mins.** | Cost: **$**

At our family Thanksgiving, we serve a stuffing for meat eaters (turkey eaters count as carnivores) and a vegetarian stuffing. My veggie version has walnuts, apples, celery, and, most important, mushrooms. For those of you who think veggie stuffing is somehow second best, all I can say is we always run out of the vegetarian version first. It's hefty enough to satisfy like a classic dressing but way lighter on calories and fat.

½ loaf multigrain bread, torn into bite-sized pieces

1 tablespoon extra virgin olive oil

1 shallot, finely chopped

1 stalk celery, thinly sliced

½ pound shiitake mushrooms, stems removed and chopped

1 bunch kale, stems removed and cut into ribbons

Salt

Pepper

1 Granny Smith apple, cored and diced

1 clove garlic, minced

1 tablespoon fresh thyme leaves, minced

⅓ cup parsley leaves, minced

1 tablespoon fresh sage leaves, minced

½ cup walnuts, toasted and coarsely chopped

1 cup vegetable broth

1. In an oven preheated to 400 °F, bake the torn bread until crunchy, about 10 minutes.

2. Heat the extra virgin olive oil in a nonstick skillet over medium heat. Add the shallot, celery, mushrooms, and kale. Season with salt and pepper to taste. Cook for 5 minutes, stirring occasionally, and add the apple once the shallot has softened. Once the apple has softened, about 5 minutes, add the garlic, thyme, parsley, and sage. Cook for about a minute, until fragrant, then remove from heat, and mix in the walnuts and bread.

3. Add vegetable broth until moist but not soggy. Cover with foil and bake at 400 °F for 25 minutes. Remove foil, bake an additional 10 minutes, and serve.

The viewers speak

In a survey of *Chew* viewers, we asked people what was their favorite part of Thanksgiving: 50 percent said spending time with family and friends, 40 percent said cooking, and 10 percent said cleaning up, to which we answered, "What's up with that?" But when you think about it, the deep dishing (as in gossip) really gets good with the water running, everybody full and happy (and maybe lubricated with some cocktails and wine). If you want to be a fly on the wall, the cleanup kitchen is the wall for you.

PAN-SEARED TURKEY WITH GREMOLATA

SERVES 6 | Skill Level: EASY | Cook Time: 1–1 ½ hrs. | Prep Time: 10 mins. | Cost: $
Inactive Prep Time: 12 hrs.

I might never have come up with this recipe if my car hadn't broken down on the way to a catering job. My client was looking forward to my cooking turkey at her home. She was psyched about the house filling up with the aroma of it roasting in the oven. Well, it took so long to get the car fixed that by the time I arrived at her house, I wouldn't have been able to cook and serve dinner until very late. And then I remembered how often I had been told that you can think of a turkey as a big chicken, so I cut it into parts: wing, drumstick, thigh, breast. It cut down the cooking time by two-thirds, and everyone really liked the way we rescued Thanksgiving.

FOR THE BRINING LIQUID:

4 cups water

½–¾ cup kosher salt

½ cup brown sugar

10 whole allspice

10 whole cloves

10 whole black peppercorns

5 star anise

7–8 sprigs thyme

½ cup olive oil

1 12- to 15-pound turkey, cut into 8 pieces

FOR THE SPICY GREMOLATA:

1½ cups packed flat-leaf parsley

¼ cup sage leaves

4 cloves garlic, smashed

3 tablespoons lemon zest

2 teaspoons crushed red pepper flakes

2 teaspoons kosher salt

½ cup olive oil

1. Combine all the brining ingredients in a large resealable plastic bag, and shake to dissolve the salt and sugar. Place the turkey parts in the bag, and place in the refrigerator for 6 hours or overnight.

2. Remove the turkey from the brine and rinse thoroughly. Pat dry. Gently loosen the skin from the turkey pieces. Combine the spicy gremolata ingredients and liberally rub the gremolata under the skin on each part.

3. Preheat the oven to 400 °F. Heat a heavy skillet to medium-high heat. Sear each piece until golden brown on all sides. Place seared pieces on a sheet pan, and finish cooking them in the oven. Cook for 1–1½ hours until all the pieces have an internal temperature of 170 °F.

Special bonus . . . shelf space!

If you're the one making Thanksgiving, no doubt you are familiar with the problem of too much food in too small of a refrigerator. Breaking the turkey down in smaller parts is a much more compact way to store it overnight. That should help with your space problem, although refrigerators, just like people, tend to get overstuffed at holiday time.

FALL

47

BRUSSELS SPROUTS À LA "RUSS" WITH WALNUTS AND CAPERS

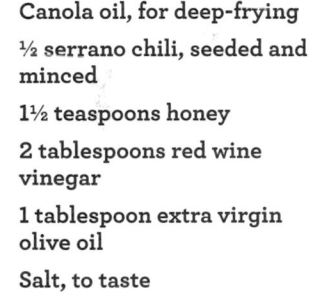

| SERVES 5 | Skill Level: EASY | Cook Time: 5 mins. | Prep Time: 5 mins. | Cost: $ |

I think one of the reasons I started doing 5-in-5 is my father-in-law, Russ. Whenever I am making Thanksgiving dinner—in fact, whenever I am in the kitchen making anything—Russ will wander into the kitchen and start picking off the plate. My way to deal with this is to get as much done as I can before he shows. Then I chill out until we're ready to make last-minute dishes.

Brussels sprouts are one of my favorite vegetables for Thanksgiving. In most of the country, they're one of the few green vegetables that you can still buy fresh and locally. Many people have included them on their Thanksgiving menu, roasting them in the oven, maybe with some diced apples and bacon. I prefer to fry them. They get very golden brown outside. Their sugars come out and get rid of any funky cabbage-y bitterness.

Canola oil, for deep-frying

½ serrano chili, seeded and minced

1½ teaspoons honey

2 tablespoons red wine vinegar

1 tablespoon extra virgin olive oil

Salt, to taste

Pepper, to taste

½ pound Brussels sprouts, trimmed and quartered lengthwise

1 tablespoon capers

¼ cup walnut pieces, toasted

1. Pour enough oil into a medium pot so that the oil comes two-thirds up the sides. Heat to 350 °F.

2. While the oil is heating, whisk together the serrano, honey, red wine vinegar, and extra virgin olive oil in a bowl large enough to toss all the Brussels sprouts. Season with salt and pepper to taste. Keep the bowl near the stovetop.

3. Fry the Brussels sprouts until the edges begin to curl and brown, about 2–3 minutes. Carefully add the capers and stand back, because they tend to splatter a bit. Fry for another minute. Remove the Brussels sprouts and the capers directly to the bowl with the vinaigrette. Toss to coat. Add salt and pepper to taste, and toss in the toasted walnuts.

Sweet and salty

Whenever I cook anything sweet, I like to put a good pinch of salt in it. It helps bring out the flavors, balancing sweet and savory. You'd be surprised how much fuller a sweet thing tastes when it gets some help in the salt department.

CHOCOLATE PUMPKIN PIE

SERVES 8 | Skill Level: **EASY** | Cook Time: **1–1 ½ hrs.** | Prep Time: **20 mins.** | Cost: **$**

Inactive Prep Time: 1 hr.

I would rather have Thanksgiving without turkey than to skip pumpkin pie. It's my favorite thing. Carla tells me people feel that way about sweet potato pie in the South, but I'm a pumpkin guy all the way. I can't imagine doing without it. But, being the kind of chef that I am, you know how I like to take traditional recipes and give them a little twist. Well, here we have a pumpkin pie enriched with rich melted chocolate. A new classic, if I do say so myself.

FOR THE CRUST:

1¼ cups all-purpose flour

2 teaspoons salt

½ teaspoon sugar

½ cup unsalted butter, very cold and cut into small pieces

2–3 tablespoons ice-cold water

FOR THE FILLING:

3 ounces bittersweet chocolate, very finely chopped

6 ounces semisweet chocolate, chopped

4 tablespoons unsalted butter, cut into small pieces

1 14-ounce can pumpkin puree

1 12-ounce can evaporated milk

¾ cup packed light brown sugar

3 large eggs

1 tablespoon cornstarch

1 teaspoon vanilla extract

¼ teaspoon salt

¾ teaspoon ground cinnamon

¾ teaspoon ground ginger

¼ teaspoon ground nutmeg

Pinch of ground cloves

Whipped cream, to serve

TO MAKE THE CRUST:

1. Combine the flour, salt, sugar, and butter in a food processor and pulse until coarse, with small marbles of butter remaining. Sprinkle in 2 tablespoons of the ice water, and pulse until crumbly and the dough holds when squeezed together. Add another sprinkle of water if too dry, but do not overmix.

2. Transfer the dough to a plastic zip-top bag, press into a disc, and refrigerate for 1 hour.

3. Preheat the oven to 425 °F.

4. Roll out the dough on a floured surface. Press into a pie plate and trim, leaving 1 inch excess around the edges. Fold under and flute the edges. Cut a piece of parchment or non-stick foil to the size of the pie, and use it to line the piecrust. Fill with pie weights or dried beans, and bake until golden, about 15 minutes.

5. Reduce heat to 325 °F.

TO MAKE THE FILLING:

6. In a double boiler, melt the bittersweet chocolate, semisweet chocolate, and butter, stirring frequently until smooth, and remove from heat.

7. In a large bowl, mix together the pumpkin puree, evaporated milk, light brown sugar, eggs, cornstarch, vanilla, salt, cinnamon, ginger, nutmeg, and cloves. Fold in the chocolate mixture, and pour into the piecrust. Place the pie pan on a baking sheet. Bake at 325 °F until center of pie has set, about an hour. Cool completely to serve with whipped cream.

FALL

BATTER FRIED APPLE RINGS

| MAKES 8 TO 10 | Skill Level: EASY | Cook Time: 15 mins. | Prep Time: 10 mins. | Cost: $ |

There are few things I like better than going back to an old family recipe and making something new and delicious from it. A few months ago, I was at home going through one of those boxes that you promise yourself that you're going to sort through but you never do. I'm glad I did, because right there in my hot little hands was a Betty Crocker box. Every month we'd get a new packet of recipes, and over the years they added up to a boxful of happiness for me. The recipe for apple pancakes got me thinking. I added in some pumpkin pie spices to give it more Thanksgiving spirit. Then I reduced some apple cider down until it was thick and sweet enough to call it syrup, and I poured it over granny smith apple fritters that I fried in my favorite childhood pancake batter. When Daphne saw how much apple was included in the recipe, she said, "Carla, I think you've got a dessert here that qualifies as a healthy serving of fruit."

1¼ cups flour

1 tablespoon baking powder

2 tablespoons sugar

1 teaspoon pumpkin pie spice

1 egg

1¼ cups buttermilk

Zest of ½ lemon

4 tablespoons butter, melted

2 medium Granny Smith apples, peeled and cored

1. Combine the dry ingredients and set aside. Whisk together the egg and buttermilk until smooth. Add the wet ingredients to the dry, and then fold in the lemon zest and stir in the butter. Cut the apples crosswise into ⅛-inch slices. Using a toothpick, dip the slices into the batter. Cook on a buttered griddle, over medium heat until golden brown, turning once. Serve hot with apple cider syrup.

APPLE CIDER SYRUP

MAKES 1 CUP | Cook time: 10 mins.

2 cups apple cider

Zest of ½ lemon

1 tablespoon cinnamon

½ cup brown sugar

In a small saucepan over medium heat add the apple cider and begin to reduce. Add the lemon zest, cinnamon, and brown sugar. Cook until liquid has reduced by half, about 10 minutes. Serve warm over batter fried apple rings.

CHEW CHEW CLUSTERS

SERVES 8 | Skill Level: EASY | Cook Time: 10 mins. | Prep Time: 25 mins. | Cost: $

Inactive Prep Time: 2–12 hrs.

If you have ever been to Nashville, Tennessee, you have probably come across a treat known as the GooGoo Cluster. It's kind of our official candy bar, a combination of chocolate, marshmallow fluff, caramel, and salted peanuts. Nashvillians revere it as the first combination chocolate and candy bar. This recipe is my made-from-scratch homage to the original. One of my big changes is to use dark chocolate, the best I can find. If you are not a peanut fancier, pecans work, as do walnuts or pine nuts. Basically, if it's a nut, go ahead and use it.

2 cups dark chocolate chips, melted

1 cup salted peanuts

1 cup caramel sauce (recipe follows)

17-ounce jar marshmallow cream

1. Place a teaspoon of melted dark chocolate in the bottom of a muffin tin. Then add a teaspoon of peanuts, a teaspoon of caramel sauce, and a teaspoon of marshmallow. Top with another teaspoon of the dark chocolate. Place in the fridge to firm up, about 2 hours and up to overnight.

CARAMEL SAUCE

1 cup sugar

½ cup heavy whipping cream

6 tablespoons butter

Heat the sugar on medium-high in a heavy-bottomed 3-quart sauce pot. As the sugar begins to brown, begin to whisk vigorously. Stop whisking as soon as the sugar is a golden amber color. In a slow stream, add the cream and whisk until the sauce is smooth. It will foam considerably during this step and the next. Remove from heat and add the butter, and whisk until the butter is incorporated. Allow the sauce to cool to room temperature before using.

FALL

TEN-GALLON APPLE PIE

SERVES 8 TO 10 | **Skill Level: EASY** | **Cook Time: 30–40 mins.** | **Prep Time: 20 mins.** | **Cost: $**

Inactive Prep Time: 1 hr.

Remember how in old cowboy movies they used to wear ten-gallon hats? They weren't really ten gallons, but the point was they were big. My Ten-Gallon Apple Pie is big in the same way. It takes more than 5 pounds of apples, and it's the most ginormous apple pie I have ever seen. It really makes an impression when you bring it to the table. And the aroma is pure heaven on a plate. It's not a hard pie to make if you cook down the apples first. That way they don't pile up so high that they won't fit in the crust.

FOR THE CRUST:

⅔ cup water

2 teaspoons salt

2 tablespoons sugar

4 cups all-purpose flour

4 sticks butter, chilled and cut into ½-inch cubes

FOR THE FILLING:

10 tablespoons unsalted butter

5¼ pounds Granny Smith apples, cored and sliced ⅛ inch thick

1¼ pounds empire or Fuji apples, cored and sliced ⅛ inch thick

2 cups sugar

2 teaspoons cinnamon

5 tablespoons bourbon or brandy

Juice of ½ lemon

1 teaspoon vanilla extract

TO FINISH:

Whites of 1 egg

1 tablespoon granulated sugar

TO MAKE THE CRUST:

1. Preheat the oven to 375 °F. Combine the water, salt, and sugar in a measuring cup. Stir and place the cup in the fridge for at least 15 minutes to chill. If possible, chill the mixing bowl and paddle attachment.

2. Combine the flour and butter pieces in the mixing bowl. On medium speed, cut the butter into the flour until the butter pieces are the size of small pebbles. With the mixer running, pour the water mixture into the flour-butter mixture. Mix until the dough comes together. Separate the dough into 2 discs. Wrap each with film and chill for at least 1 hour.

3. Roll 1 chilled pastry disc out to fit a deep-dish pie dish. Prick the dough all over with a fork. Bake 10–15 minutes, or until lightly golden. Set aside to cool.

Cooking by heart

It's very important that you taste your apples before you cook them and also after you cook them so you can be sure they have the right amount of sweetness. This is an example of "cooking by heart." That doesn't mean that you have memorized every recipe, but, instead, that you use your heart (and your taste buds) as you work through the recipe. Remember, any recipe is only a guide, and every ingredient is always a little different. Taste your food while you work. I do.

Keep your butter better

If you have ever wondered if it's important that your butter be cold when you make a crust, rest assured: it's very important. Only if the butter is cold will it release steam into the dough, which is what makes it puff up and become flaky.

TO MAKE THE FILLING:

4. In a very large skillet, melt the butter over medium-high heat, then add the apples, sugar, and cinnamon. When the apples begin to sizzle, cover and reduce to a simmer. Cook, stirring occasionally, until the apples soften and release their juices, about 10–12 minutes. Add the bourbon or brandy, cook for another minute, then stir in the lemon juice and vanilla extract, and allow to cool. If needed, cook in batches and lay the filling out on a sheet to cool.

TO MAKE THE PIE:

5. Turn the oven down to 350 °F.

6. Roll out the remaining chilled piece of piecrust large enough to cover the pie.

7. Pour the filling into par-baked crust, and cover with the second piece of piecrust. Trim the cover, and fold under the edges. Flute the edges together or use a fork to press them together. Brush the top with egg whites and sprinkle with granulated sugar. Cut four slits near the center of the pie to vent steam. Bake for 25–30 minutes, until the crust is golden brown. Allow to cool before serving.

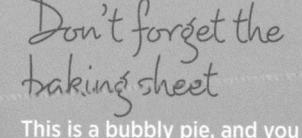

Don't forget the baking sheet

This is a bubbly pie, and you don't want it bubbling all over your oven. Make sure you put your pie plate on a baking sheet while it's cooking.

BLT BLOODY MARY

SERVES 1 | **Skill Level: EASY** | **Prep Time: 1–5 mins.** | **Cost: $**

My all-time favorite sandwich is a BLT, so I asked myself, how could you go wrong making it into a cocktail? Answer: you can't! Especially if you add some firepower with a blast of horseradish and for an exotic modern touch, coriander-infused vodka. Lotsa vodka!

FOR THE CORIANDER VODKA:

2 cups vodka

1 tablespoon coriander

FOR THE BLT BLOODY MARY:

2 ounces coriander vodka

4 ounces tomato juice

½ ounce lemon juice

¼ teaspoon hot pepper sauce

¼ teaspoon Worcestershire sauce

½ teaspoon bottled horseradish

Bacon, lettuce, and olive, for garnish

TO MAKE THE CORIANDER VODKA:

1. Combine the coriander and vodka and refrigerate overnight.

TO MAKE THE BLT BLOODY MARY:

2. Fill a cocktail shaker three-quarters full with ice. Add all the ingredients except the bacon, lettuce, and olive garnish, cover, and shake well. Strain into a highball glass filled with fresh ice. Garnish with skewer threaded with bacon, lettuce, and olive.

Clinton and Stacy London enjoying their perfectly blended cocktail.

THE STINTON

SERVES 1 | Skill Level: EASY | Prep Time: 10 mins. | Cost: $

Stacy London is my fabulous fashionista, sartorial sister, and cohost on What Not to Wear. *For those of you who think we sit around in our superstar trailer and drink gorgeous cocktails all day, I'm here to tell you that you're right.*

I wish.

Sometimes, though, we dream about what it would be like to kick back like old-time Hollywood stars and dive into a delicious cocktail. So when Stacy showed up on The Chew, *we got to live our dream—at least the cocktail-making part—and invented the Stinton, as in Stacy + Clinton = Stinton. Devilishly clever, don't you think? So add as much bourbon as you dare, cut it with some bitters, sweeten with some vermouth and a Maraschino cherry, and pretend you're Virginia Mayo.*

2 ounces bourbon

½ ounce sweet vermouth

2 dashes bitters

2 ounces seltzer

Maraschino cherry, for garnish

1. Combine the bourbon, vermouth, and bitters in a cocktail shaker. Shake well, strain into an old-fashioned glass, and top with a splash of seltzer. Garnish with a maraschino cherry.

POMEGRANATE SUNSET

SERVES 1 | Skill Level: EASY | Cook Time: 15 mins. | Prep Time: 5 mins. | Cost: $

I like to have a signature cocktail for every season. From Memorial Day to Labor Day, I'm a gin-and-tonic man. From Labor Day to Memorial Day, a Manhattan is my choice. One day, after a couple of drinks, it dawned on me that the Manhattan was getting the better of that arrangement, so I decided to invent something for fall.

Hmm…what could it be?

I thought about Daphne, and when I think about Daphne, the second thing that I think about is antioxidants (the first is I love her to pieces). And then it came to me: pomegranates are in season in the fall and they are full of antioxidants. And thus, with the assistance of a bottle of vodka, orange juice, seltzer, and mint, the Pomegranate Sunset was born.

I suppose you could get the same amount of antioxidants without the vodka, but it wouldn't be as much fun.

FOR THE POMEGRANATE SYRUP:

1 cup sugar

1 cup pomegranate juice

FOR THE POMEGRANATE SUNSET:

2 ounces vodka

2 ounces orange juice

2 ounces seltzer

1 tablespoon pomegranate syrup (recipe follows)

Mint, for garnish

TO MAKE THE POMEGRANATE SYRUP

1. Pour one part pomegranate juice to one part sugar in a small saucepan. Simmer, stirring occasionally, until it thickens, about 15 minutes. Cool and refrigerate.

TO MAKE THE POMEGRANATE SUNSET

2. Mix vodka, orange juice, and seltzer. Add pomegranate syrup. Garnish with mint.

FALL

CRANBERRY SODA

SERVES 1 | Skill Level: EASY | Cook Time: 25 mins. | Prep Time: 15 mins. | Cost: $

Inactive Prep Time: 2 – 12 hrs.

I love tartness, the really good pucker that you get from lemons, limes, rhubarb, and cranberries. Since I am not an alcohol drinker, I came up with a signature "mocktail" for my catering business. Tart cranberry, floral spicy ginger, bitter fruity cranberries in simple syrup, and ripe sweet strawberries are a killer combination. Make this for the nondrinkers in your crowd. Drinkers, feel free to add your favorite clear booze.

FOR THE GINGER SIMPLE SYRUP:

¾ cup ginger, grated

2 cups granulated sugar, plus more for coating the cranberries

1½ cups water

1 cup whole cranberries, plus extra for garnish

FOR THE CRANBERRY SODA:

2 ounces ginger simple syrup

2 ounces cranberry juice (optional)

Juice of 1 lime

2 ounces sparkling water

TO MAKE THE GINGER SIMPLE SYRUP:

1. Place the ginger, sugar, and water in a small pot.

2. Place on medium heat and simmer until the sugar dissolves, about 10 minutes, and add the cranberries.

3. Remove from the heat and let steep for 15 minutes. Strain out the cranberries and cool completely. The syrup will be slightly pink.

4. Roll the cranberries in sugar. Lay them in a single layer on a sheet pan and freeze for about 2 hours and up to overnight.

TO MAKE THE CRANBERRY SODA:

5. Combine all the ingredients and garnish with 4–5 cranberries. Serve over ice.

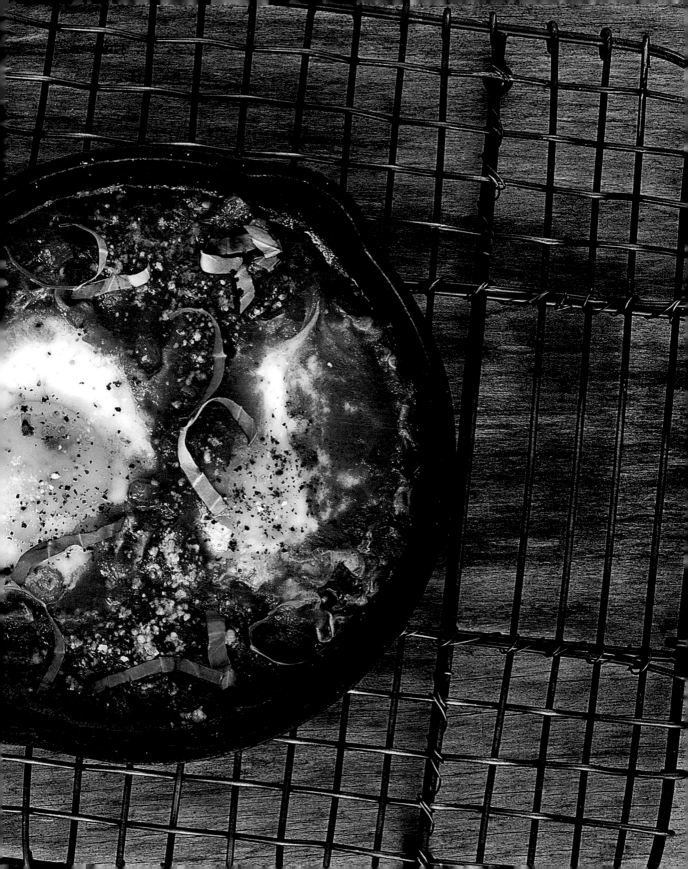

WINTER

Mario

Q: **You've done a lot of cooking on TV. How is *The Chew* different? How do you like being on the show?**

Mario: Well, the first thing I must say is that I probably never would have met these people had we not been put together in this show. Everyone is really nice; no one has any ulterior motives other than the show's success and speaking their own mind—whether it's food or fashion or crafts or whatever. The format is very easy to come into every morning—they hand us notes the night before. Whether you read them or not, you will not be quizzed or tested. If you want to sound smart, you can; if you want to sound silly or goofy, you can. And there're no rules, so we can't possibly break them. It's a very refreshing and relaxing format that allows us to chitchat, so we feel a lot more like we do in our kitchens, as opposed to some giant studio, and in the relaxing moments when it's really gelling and everyone's cooking and really digging what everyone else does— it's very informative, without being like a talking textbook.

Q: *The Chew* **is like one big dinner party, with everyone gathering in the kitchen. The food is so relaxed and accessible. Is it different from the fancier kitchens you're used to?**

Mario: Our kitchen is our living room, so when people are at our house for dinner, I'm in the kitchen just like this, so it doesn't look very much different at all from my daily experience in my house. *The Chew* appeals to people who are comfortable in the kitchen. They just need some new ideas. Many of them have basically rounded their wagon around a campfire of ten or fifteen dishes that they make slight variations on all the time. And seeing new kinds of food presented in a less-than-fifteen-minutes kind of real cooking time empowers and inspires them to look at ingredients in a different way. Our goal is "Let's help people get in the kitchen; let's remove the obstacles from them and just inspire people to be happy in their kitch-

ens, to create delicious and healthy food without being heavy-handed or 'this is the only way.'" It's just, "Look, this is quick. This is easy. This is how we like to do it. Don't overthink it, but make something delicious work."

Q: **When Michael does his 5-in-5s, he'll sometimes stop to do little asides in the middle of it. And you'll say, just like on *Iron Chef*, "Uh, 2 minutes and 43 seconds, Chef." And he's just as cool as can be. Do you ever worry that he won't make it?**

Mario: He slows down on purpose because he knows he's going to get there. And that, to his credit, is probably why he is one of the most top-winning Iron Chefs. And also why he's a compelling instructor. Because for him, there is no rush. You're just going to get it done—just stay on it.

Q: **You did a series in Spain with Gwyneth Paltrow and Mark Bittman. Spanish cooking is so influential in the world today. Would you like to bring that, or any other global influences, to *The Chew*?**

Mario: I think the Iberian Peninsula and Portuguese food isn't really hot yet with the cooking public, but it's going to be pretty soon. I love their kind of fantasy Catalan mind-set that people like Salvador Dalí and Picasso and Miró brought to painting. They have always lived on the vanguard.

I don't think we'll create balls of olive oil juice here, but we're definitely going to cook certain traditional Spanish food or even more thought-provoking modern Spanish food. But basically, *The Chew* is going to be about cooking at home; that's the story. As weird as the stuff is that I bring back, I still want it to reference what people can actually do in their home.

WARRIOR SALAD

SERVES 4 | Skill Level: EASY | Cook Time: 15 mins. | Prep Time: 10 mins. | Cost: $

Everybody has—or at least should have—some ingredients on hand that they can toss together for a quick and delicious meal. I always have some cooked quinoa in my fridge. Quinoa is very high in protein. For the same reason, I also have a few kinds of beans on hand. These ingredients are like flavor sponges. They pick up the flavors of whatever you combine them with. I looked over the shelves to see what other ingredients I could gather together. Mustard, maple syrup, olive oil, and dried cranberries all called out to me. I imagined the flavors my mom would combine and this is the result. I call it Warrior Salad because it's full of protein and complex carbs and low in fat: just the thing for a warrior going into battle, or an average American just returned from a day of corporate combat and looking for something quick and healthy for dinner.

FOR THE DRESSING:

3 tablespoons extra virgin olive oil

Juice of ½ lemon

½ teaspoon maple syrup

1 teaspoon whole grain mustard

Salt, to taste

Pepper, to taste

FOR THE SALAD:

2 cups cooked quinoa, cooked to package instructions

¾ cup chickpeas, drained and rinsed

¼ cup dried cranberries

¼ cup scallions, thinly sliced

1. For the dressing, combine the olive oil, lemon juice, maple syrup, and mustard. Season with salt and pepper to taste. Stir well. Combine all the remaining ingredients in a bowl, and toss with the dressing.

Quinoa quick fact

Quinoa is one of the many gifts of the New World to the food world. A thousand years ago, the Incas cultivated it as a source of protein and complex carbs (the good kind). It is very easy to cook: just add liquid and salt and simmer. It will keep in the fridge for days and goes well in soups and salads or reheated with some sautéed onions and served on the side like mashed potatoes.

WINTER GREEN SALAD WITH PEARS, AGED CHEDDAR, AND ALMONDS

SERVES 6 | Skill Level: EASY | Prep Time: 20 mins. | Cost: $

Summer salads make me think of light tastes and textures. A winter salad, like winter food, wants to be assertive. It needs to pull you by the palate and say, "Hey, you're gonna pay attention." I made this salad with pears from the green market and some local Cheddar. Watercress adds crunchiness, and so do the almonds. Serve it with roasted chicken and your chicken will say, "Thank you."

4 medium heads Belgian endive

2 medium shallots, finely diced

1 tablespoon red wine vinegar

Salt

2 tablespoons extra virgin olive oil

Freshly ground black pepper

1 bunch watercress, thick stems trimmed, cut into 3-inch sprigs

1 large pear, thinly sliced

1 tablespoon chives, cut at an angle into ¼-inch lengths

1 tablespoon flat-leaf parsley, coarsely chopped

⅓ cup almonds, toasted and coarsely chopped

¼ cup aged NY Cheddar cheese, crumbled

1. Remove the outer leaves of the endives and cut in half lengthwise. Cut into 1-inch-thick slices on the bias. Set aside.

2. Next, mix the shallots, vinegar, and salt in a bowl. Set aside for 5 minutes to allow the flavors to marry. Whisk the olive oil into the vinegar mixture and season with pepper. Taste and adjust seasoning.

3. Combine the endives, watercress, pear, chives, parsley, and vinaigrette in a large bowl and toss to coat. Arrange on a platter, and top with the almonds and cheese.

WINTER

71

BRAISED PORK SHANKS

| SERVES 4 with leftovers | Skill Level: MODERATE | Cook Time: 4–5 hrs. | Cost: $$ |

Prep Time: 15 mins. | Inactive Prep time: 12 hrs.

This is a super succulent, deeply flavored main course. With some mashed potatoes, parsnips, or polenta, it is a great winter meal to have after a snow-shoveling session. We made this on the show as one of our two-fer segments: how to get more than one meal out of a recipe. You can make the recipe with any braised meat, but on The Chew I did it with pork. But before we get to that second meal, first you have to make your braise for your first meal.

FOR THE BRINE:

1 gallon water

1 cup kosher salt

½ cup sugar

1 head garlic, halved

2 sprigs fresh rosemary

1 tablespoon black peppercorns

1 tablespoon coriander

1 bay leaf

6 pork shanks

FOR THE BRAISE:

Canola oil

Flour, for dredging

3 cups celery, roughly chopped

2 cups carrots, roughly chopped

1 Spanish onion, chopped

3 cloves garlic, smashed

Large pinch of salt

1 sprig rosemary

1 small bundle of thyme

2 cups white wine

2 cups apple cider

4 quarts chicken stock

1. In a large nonreactive pot, combine all the brine ingredients and bring to a simmer. Whisk until the salt and sugar are completely dissolved. Remove from heat and let cool. In a container large enough to hold the shanks, completely submerge them in the cooled brine. Weigh down the shanks with a heavy plate, if necessary, to keep them fully submerged. Refrigerate overnight.

2. The next day, preheat the oven to 300 °F.

3. Remove the shanks from the brine, discarding the liquid. Heat a large Dutch oven over medium-high heat. Pour in enough canola oil to completely coat the bottom of the pot. Dredge the shanks in flour, shaking off any excess. In batches, begin browning the shanks, cooking a few minutes on each side. When browned, transfer the shanks to a plate, and begin browning the next batch.

4. Pour off all but 2 or 3 tablespoons of fat from the pot. Add the celery, carrots, onion, and garlic cloves, along with a large pinch of salt. Cook the vegetables until tender, about 7 minutes. Add the rosemary and thyme, and cook for another minute. Deglaze the pot with the white wine, and reduce by three-quarters. Add the apple cider and reduce by half. Add the chicken stock and bring the braising liquid up to a simmer. Taste and adjust for seasoning.

5. Return the shanks to the pot, cover, and place in the oven until the meat is tender, about 4–5 hours. Strain the braising liquid and serve with the shanks. Store any leftovers in their liquid. Refrigerate.

6. Use any remaining pork to make White Beans, Pork, and Collard Greens Soup (see page 74).

Michael and Rachael Ray whip up some trouble.

WHITE BEANS, PORK, AND COLLARD GREENS SOUP

| SERVES 8 | Skill Level: EASY | Cook Time: 45 mins. | Prep Time: 20 mins. | Cost: $ |

Comfort food is just another way of saying, "I like this, it makes me kind of smile, and it doesn't take a lot of fussing to throw together." This bowl of heartwarming comfort fits the bill. It's really one of my favorite stay-at-home wintry meals. Even though winter has its challenges, I kind of hope our recent warm winters aren't a trend. I like an occasional midwestern cold snap, battening down the hatches, hanging around the fire, and smelling the house fill up with aromas on a winter afternoon.

Leftover Braised Pork Shanks, shredded (see page 72)

¼ cup olive oil

2½ cups onion, diced small

Salt

½ pound sweet Italian sausage, casings removed and filling broken up

1 teaspoon chili flakes

2 cups low-sodium chicken stock

½ pound (1 cup) dried navy beans or great northern beans, soaked

1 bay leaf

1 15.5-ounce can cannellini beans

8 cups collard greens leaves, washed and roughly chopped

Pepper

Pecorino Romano, grated, for garnish

1. Place a soup pot over medium-high heat and add the olive oil. When the oil is hot, add the onions with a large pinch of salt. Cook the onions until they start to soften, about 3 minutes.

2. Next add the sausage, breaking it up into smaller pieces as you add it to the pot. When the sausage starts to brown, add the chili flakes, and cook for another minute.

3. Add the chicken stock, navy or great northern beans, and bay leaf, and bring the liquid up to a gentle boil. After the soup comes up to a boil, reduce it to a simmer and cook for an hour on medium-low heat, stirring occasionally.

4. After an hour, add the can of cannellini beans with their liquid. Bring to a simmer.

5. Add all the collard greens to the pot with a little more salt and pepper. Cook for another 30 minutes. Stir in the shredded pork and cook just to warm through.

6. To serve, ladle the soup into bowls, and grate a good amount of cheese over the top.

There is no such thing as a quick collard

Collard greens want to be cooked for a good long while. They are one of the few greens that actually improve from long cooking. In the wintertime, they are also one of the only local, fresh green leafy vegetables available. Apart from being good for you, they give you the chance to say, "I'm making a mess o' greens."

'Tis the Season for Parties

THERE ARE A MILLION THINGS to think about when you are hosting a get-together. Since I host a lot of parties, I thought I'd share some of my favorite home entertaining tips (and one cool trick).

Lighting

The best thing you can to do is invest in an electrician. Every light in your house should always be on a dimmer. Why? Because everyone looks better in dim light. You do not want overhead lighting at your party. It's very harsh. If you can't afford an electrician right now, get yourself a whole bunch of candles, because candles make everybody look good.

Can(dle) do

Keep candles about 9 inches away from the edge of anything that you are putting them on, because I found out once the hard way with a friend who was wearing an angora sweater. That thing went right up. So keep them 9 inches away from the edge. Never put candles between people and anything they might want to reach for, like food or drink. And no scented candles near the food! However, do put a scented candle in the bathroom, because, well . . . you know why.

Napkin notes

If I'm having a big party, I use paper napkins. But if you want to be environmentally correct (I sure do), then if I'm having a smaller party, I put out cloth napkins. Washcloths—four for a dollar—work as napkins or hand towels. If you have a restaurant supply store nearby, you can sometimes buy cloth napkins cheaply and in bulk. Tie each napkin or towel in a ribbon or a little bit of raffia.

Don't forget the hamper

People will need someplace to discard used napkins. Put a sign up: DIRTY NAPKINS GO HERE. And while you're at it, put a hamper right under that sign. Ditto for used hand towels in the bathroom.

Ice is nice

If you do not have enough ice at the party, you will kill it. That's the worst thing, because when latecomers show up, all you'll have to offer is room temperature rum and Coke. That's not fun. Get enough ice: 1 pound per person for most of the year, but I bump it to 2 pounds in summer.

Also, remember, ice melts, and no one likes to slosh around a cold puddle with a pair of tongs. Put ice cubes in a colander or strainer over a bowl. That way, the ice melt drips into the bowl and the cubes stay relatively dryish.

Trash tips

Have you ever woken up after a party and found a bunch of olive pits in your potted plants? I once found shrimp tails in my bedroom and watermelon pits in a bowling trophy. Make sure you leave out some bowls for discards and, just like with the towels and napkins, put up a sign so people know what to do.

Marbles. yes, marbles.

Put some marbles in your medicine cabinet before the party starts. The first person to go snooping for drugs is in for a surprise. When the marbles fall on the floor, you'll hear the *ping ping, ping* over the loudest Jay-Z track. You'll also learn something about your friends in the process.

Do yourself a favor

Everyone likes a gift. I always put a big bowl of something special at the door. Sometimes I make peanut brittle and put it in little bags. Or brownies, or wine charms. It doesn't have to be much. It really is the thought that counts: one last nice thing you can do as host that your guests can enjoy after they have gone home, and you have cleaned the kitchen . . . and collapsed.

The Rockettes get a kick out of *The Chew* crew.

Stay smooth

The key to making nice, smooth scrambled eggs is to whisk them as they cook. The chef's term is an *even curd*, which means ultrasmooth and creamy. Also, you could use store-bought tortilla chips for this, but you will get a wonderful mix of chewy and crispy if you start with fresh tortillas and crisp them yourself.

CHILAQUILES

SERVES 4 | **Skill Level: EASY** | **Cook Time: 5 mins.** | **Prep Time: 10 mins.** | **Cost: $**

I made this on President's Day when we all dressed up as our favorite president. I picked Benjamin Franklin. Yeah, yeah, I know, he wasn't a president, but he is on the hundred-dollar bill, which will get you a lot further in New York than being a member of the Herbert Hoover Fan Club. I chose a very American dish— by that I mean something we owe to our immigrant heritage. In this case, the heritage is Mexican-American: chilaquiles, otherwise known as fried tortilla chips, eggs, cheese, and spiciness. I'm told that President Obama loves this for breakfast. When I made this on the show, Michael said whenever they ask me how long a recipe takes I always say 2 minutes. Guess what? This one actually took me 2 minutes!

4 tablespoons extra virgin olive oil

6 blue corn tortillas

1 tablespoon kosher salt

4 tablespoons unsalted butter

6 eggs, lightly beaten

2 cups store-bought roasted tomatillo salsa

1½ cups white Cheddar cheese, grated, to serve

½ cup sour cream, to serve

¼ cup fresh cilantro leaves, chopped, to garnish

2 limes, cut into wedges, to garnish

1. Heat the olive oil in a 10-inch nonstick pan over medium-high heat. Cut the tortillas into 8 pieces each, like a pie. Carefully add the tortillas to the hot oil and cook until crisp, about 3–4 minutes, stirring constantly. Remove pieces to a paper towel to drain and sprinkle with a little salt.

2. Pour out any excess oil from the pan and reduce heat to medium. Add the butter to the pan and swirl until light golden brown. Add the eggs and the tomatillo salsa, season with salt and pepper, and cook slowly, stirring constantly with a whisk, until soft curds form. Add the cooked tortillas and half of the cheese, and stir through until just set.

3. To serve, place some of the eggs on each plate and top with some Cheddar cheese and a dollop of the sour cream. Garnish each serving with a tablespoon of the chopped cilantro leaves and a lime wedge.

EGGS IN HELL

SERVES 4 | **Skill Level: EASY** | **Cook Time: 20 mins.** | **Prep Time: 5 mins.** | **Cost: $**

If you can poach an egg, sauté vegetables, and throw some tomatoes in a skillet, you already know all the cooking techniques you need to make this dish. It's nothing more than poached eggs in a spicy tomato sauce. How spicy? That's where the "hell" part comes in. I like mine molto spicy, as in I use fresh jalapeños with all of their fiery seeds. If you don't like yours so spicy, then cut back on the hot stuff. Maybe you could call it Eggs in Purgatory, then.

This is a perfect brunch recipe. I am major league into brunch, because it's a time when people actually chill. No one is on the clock. And in terms of value received for time spent, it takes the least amount of worry and rush, and with the proper amount of Bloody Marys or mimosas, you can linger over it all afternoon and follow it up with a well-deserved nap.

4 tablespoons extra virgin olive oil

1 medium onion, coarsely chopped

6 cloves garlic, thinly sliced

4 jalapeño peppers, cut into ¼-inch dice

1 teaspoon hot chili flakes

3 cups Mario's Basic Tomato Sauce (see page 30)

½ cup water

8 large eggs

¼ cup Parmigiano-Reggiano or Pecorino, grated

Salt

Pepper

¼ cup basil, shredded

1. Place a skillet over medium-high heat. Add the oil and heat until just smoking.

2. Add the chopped onion, garlic, jalapeños, and chili flakes, and cook until softened and light brown, about 7 minutes.

3. Add the tomato sauce and water and bring to a boil. Immediately lower the heat to a simmer and carefully crack the eggs, one by one, into the tomato sauce. Season with salt and pepper. Cover and cook until the whites set but the yolks are still quite runny, about 5–6 minutes.

4. Remove the pan from the heat and sprinkle with cheese and some shredded basil. Allow to cool, about 3–4 minutes. Garnish with basil and serve.

In praise of old black skillets

This is a dish for your trusty black skillet. And if you don't have a trusty black skillet, take this as your excuse to go get one. Among its many virtues—such as even heating—it also looks nice. You can cook and serve in it, which makes for one less platter to clean.

EGGS IN HEAVEN

SERVES 6 | **Skill Level: EASY** | **Cook Time: 30–40 mins.** | **Prep Time: 10 mins.** | **Cost: $**

Mario made Eggs in Hell, which inspired me to make Eggs in Heaven. If you're from the South, you can be forgiven for substituting the word grits *for* heaven. *Rich, creamy grits are one of the simplest and most glorious foods, especially when made even richer and creamier with some melted cheese.*

For some reason, grits have never caught on in the rest of the country like they have in Dixie. In fact, when I asked for a quick show of hands from our studio audience, there were only two members who admitted openly to grits eating.

This recipe will change your mind and it's totally simple. You make some grits, you add some cheese, and then you bake your eggs in them.

Very easy. Very delicious. So y'all get in the kitchen and start cooking.

1½ cups water

1 cup whole milk

1 teaspoon salt

1 cup stone-ground hominy grits or quick grits

4 tablespoons butter

½ cup Cheddar cheese, shredded

¼ cup parsley

Vegetable oil spray

6 eggs

Black pepper, to taste

1 ham steak, grilled, to serve

1. Preheat the oven to 350 °F.

2. In a 3-quart heavy-bottomed pot, bring water, milk, and salt to a boil. Gradually stir in the grits and reduce heat. Simmer for 20–25 minutes, or until thick. Whisk often to prevent lumps.

3. Stir in the butter and cheese. Pour the grits into an 11-by-7-inch glass baking dish.

4. Make 6 depressions in the grits mixture about 2 inches apart with the back of a spoon sprayed with oil spray. Carefully break one egg into each depression. Sprinkle with freshly ground black pepper.

5. Bake uncovered for 10–15 minutes, or until eggs are at desired doneness. Garnish with chopped parsley. Serve hot with a grilled ham steak.

Quick is good, too quick isn't

Depending on how your grits are milled, they can take up to 40 minutes to make. Quick grits often claim they can be ready in 5 minutes. As far as I am concerned, there is nothing quick about grits. They need a good 20 minutes cooking in half milk and half water, with some butter and salt at the end. That's the only way to get them good and creamy and thick. Soupy grits are just no fun.

SLOW COOKER PEACHY CHICKEN

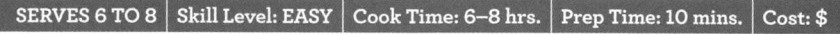

SERVES 6 TO 8 | Skill Level: **EASY** | Cook Time: **6–8 hrs.** | Prep Time: **10 mins.** | Cost: **$**

If I had to pick my favorite type of cuisine, it would either be Mexican, Persian, or Moroccan food, because I love adding sweetness and spice to the same meal. It awakens the palate in a totally different way. This dish always makes me think of a Moroccan tagine, the way it mixes chicken, peaches, and even a little apricot jam, plus a whole lot of vegetables. You put all the fruits and veggies and seasonings in your slow cooker, then place the chicken on top with a little broth or apple cider. Turn on the cooker. Go to work. Come home at the end of the day, and you have this succulent, sweet, hot, aromatic chicken that has been slowly burbling and steaming all day. If you are looking for minimal work, minimal calories, and super high flavor, these kinds of slow cooker dishes fit the bill.

FOR THE CHICKEN:

8 boneless, skinless chicken thighs

Salt

Pepper

3 sweet potatoes, cut into 1-inch cubes

1 onion, diced

1 tablespoon low-sodium soy sauce

3 tablespoons apple cider vinegar

3 cups chicken stock

1 cup peach preserves

1 tablespoon ginger, freshly grated

1 teaspoon curry powder

1 teaspoon paprika

1 teaspoon cayenne pepper

FOR THE SPINACH:

2 tablespoons extra virgin olive oil

1 clove garlic, sliced

1 bunch baby spinach, washed and trimmed

Salt

1 teaspoon sesame seeds

TO MAKE THE CHICKEN:

1. Season the chicken with salt and pepper.

2. Put the cubed sweet potatoes and onions into the slow cooker and top with the seasoned chicken.

3. Mix together the soy sauce, apple cider vinegar, chicken stock, and peach preserves, then pour over the chicken.

4. Sprinkle the chicken with salt, ginger, curry powder, paprika, and cayenne pepper.

5. Cook on low for 6–8 hours, until chicken is cooked through and potatoes are fork-tender.

TO MAKE THE SPINACH:

6. Meanwhile, in a large nonstick skillet, add the olive oil and bring to medium heat. Add the garlic. Once the garlic is fragrant, add the spinach, season with salt, and cook until wilted. Fold in the sesame seeds and transfer to a platter. Serve with the chicken.

Less than you think

When you are translating one of your favorite recipes into a slow cooker version, remember it takes less liquid because no steam escapes and any fruits or vegetables will also give up their water. My rule of thumb is about a third less liquid.

WINTER

GRILLED CHICKEN AND FENNEL SALAD

SERVES 6	Skill Level: MODERATE	Cook Time: 15–30 mins.	Prep Time: 15 mins.	Cost: $$

One of my family's faves is this chicken, soaked in a super flavorful marinade and then grilled pressed down under a brick. My update is to use boneless dark meat, because it stays succulent and juicy and has better deliciousness. White meat is a more temperamental meat. Add to that the fact that this costs $3.50 per serving, and the check balancer in the family has got to like that.

As for fennel, fennel needs more cheerleaders in its corner. Fennel is almost like celery meets licorice in a magnificent marriage of delicious beauty. I love it, but if you don't then you can definitely substitute with Savoy cabbage or celery or green apple. The big point here is we have a grill dish and salad that you can make in the winter with fresh, crunchy vegetables. Never underestimate the joy of a fresh vegetable when it's slushy and snowy outside.

FOR THE TAPENADE:

6 anchovy fillets, soaked in milk overnight

2 tablespoons anchovy paste

1 cup pitted black olives

¼ cup capers, roughly chopped

3 tablespoons Dijon mustard

3 tablespoons red wine vinegar

5 tablespoons extra virgin olive oil

FOR THE SALAD:

½ bulb fennel, thinly sliced

Zest and segments of 1 orange

1 pound arugula leaves

3 tablespoons white or red wine vinegar

4 tablespoons extra virgin olive oil

Salt, to taste

Pepper, to taste

TO MAKE THE TAPENADE:

1. Combine all the ingredients in a food processor and blend until a smooth paste is formed, about 2 minutes. Transfer to a jar, cover tightly, and store in the refrigerator up to 6 weeks.

TO MAKE THE SALAD:

2. Mix all the ingredients together, and set aside.

TO MAKE THE CHICKEN:

3. In a large mixing bowl, mix ½ cup of tapenade and the olive oil, thyme, pepper, and red pepper flakes until well blended.

The marvelous afterlife of marinade

Once you have made a delicious marinade, don't toss it. If you put it on the grill pan, it bubbles and steams and infuses the chicken with beautiful flavor.

FOR THE CHICKEN:

¾ cup olive oil

2 teaspoons fresh thyme
leaves, chopped

2 teaspoons freshly ground
black pepper

1 teaspoon red pepper flakes

6 boneless chicken thighs

SPECIAL EQUIPMENT:

Brick wrapped in foil

4. Add the chicken and toss to coat.

5. Place the chicken skin side down on the grill, 8–10 inches from the coals, and place a brick wrapped in foil on top. Cook slowly, about 6 minutes per side, until skin is crisp and brown and juices run clear when the chicken is pricked with a sharp knife at the thickest part of the thigh. Set aside and keep warm.

6. Place each chicken thigh over the fennel salad on each plate. Spoon 1 tablespoon tapenade over each half and serve immediately.

Tapenade is tops, anchovy is aces

This wonderful traditional mix of olives, anchovies, and herbs is a go-to flavor bomb and super all by itself on a crostini. Many people get a little finicky about anchovies. I'm here to tell you, please give them another try. They bring a mystical salinity, a backbone bass note to anything you cook them in. I tame mine a bit by soaking them in milk, which tones down the saltiness and does away with what I call the "pizzeria" anchovy flavor.

Let the pan do the work

If you watch enough cooking shows, you can be forgiven for thinking that the mark of a good chef is flipping things in pans as fast as you can. In fact, nothing could be further from the truth. As you can see in this recipe, I put the pork medallions in some oil and butter and leave them without moving. After they are about 75 percent cooked, I turn the meat and add liquid, which finishes the cooking with a gentle braise. That way you get a beautiful, full-flavored, crunchy crust and tender pork on the inside.

PORK AU POIVRE

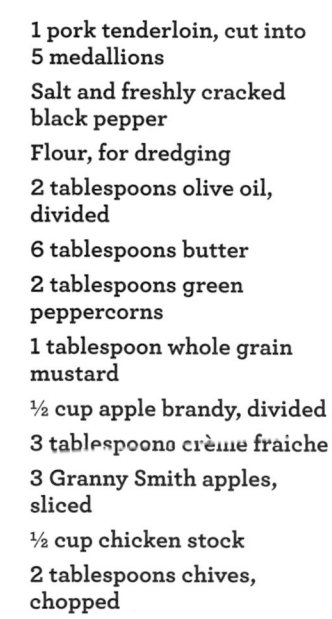

SERVES 5 | **Skill Level: MODERATE** | **Cook Time: 10–15 mins.** | **Prep Time: 10 mins.** | **COST: $$**

I loved the movie Midnight in Paris. *Why? Two reasons: I love Woody Allen and I love Paris. So in honor of it winning an Oscar, we made this French bistro classic. All that was missing on the set of* The Chew *was a guy wearing a beret with a cigarette hanging out of his mouth. Michael was originally cast for the role, but then he went and quit smoking on us. It's a very basic bistro dish—the combination of pork, peppercorns, apples, apple brandy (calvados), and—mais oui—butter. I can't guarantee Hemingway and Toulouse-Lautrec will show up at your dinner party, like they did in the movie, but it's worth a try. As someone must have said in apple brandy country, "With enough calvados, anything is possible."*

1 pork tenderloin, cut into 5 medallions

Salt and freshly cracked black pepper

Flour, for dredging

2 tablespoons olive oil, divided

6 tablespoons butter

2 tablespoons green peppercorns

1 tablespoon whole grain mustard

½ cup apple brandy, divided

3 tablespoons crème fraîche

3 Granny Smith apples, sliced

½ cup chicken stock

2 tablespoons chives, chopped

1. Lightly pound each of the pork medallions and season on both sides with salt and pepper. Dredge each medallion in flour.

2. Heat a sauté pan over medium-high heat. Add 1 tablespoon olive oil and 2 tablespoons butter to pan. Add pork medallions and sear about 2 minutes per side. Add the green peppercorns, grainy mustard, and ¼ cup of the brandy. Cook for about 3 minutes. Flip the medallions and add crème fraîche, stirring into the juices to begin making the sauce. Cook for another 1–2 minutes.

3. Meanwhile, in a separate sauté pan over medium-high heat add remaining tablespoon of olive oil and 2 tablespoons of butter. Add sliced apples and cook for 1–2 minutes. Deglaze pan with remaining ¼ cup of brandy. If desired you can flambé the apples by igniting the brandy with a far-reaching flame. Add chicken stock, remaining butter, and salt to taste. Cook for another 2–3 minutes until apples are slightly softened.

4. To serve, plate some of the apple mixture and top with one of the medallions and some of the sauce. Garnish with chopped chives and serve.

The Champagne gambit

A real visual crowd pleaser is to bring the pork—with the crown still intact—to the table and, while it is still hot, place a semi-chilled bottle of Champagne in the center. Carefully pop the cork and watch the contents overflow in a fountain of Champagne suds that bathes the pork and mixes in the cabbage braise. A word of caution here: This usually works and impresses people no end. But sometimes (like when I tried it on *The Chew* in front of millions of viewers) nothing happens when I pop the cork. At that point, you just say, "Oh well . . . ," pick up the bottle, and pour Champagne over the pork. It's still delightful to watch, and the fact that you are not bummered usually gets a round of cheers from the folks at your table.

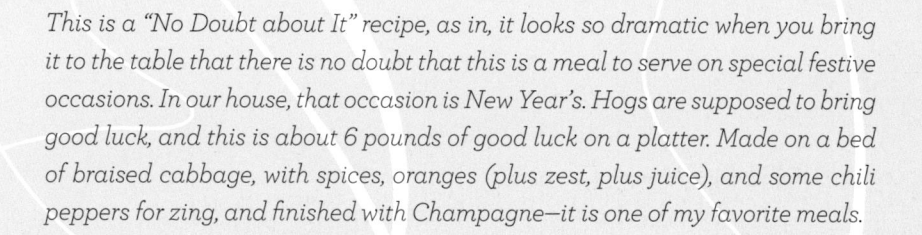

CHAMPAGNE CROWN ROAST

SERVES 10 | Skill Level: MODERATE | Cook Time: 45 mins. – 1 hr. | Prep Time: 20 mins.
Cost: $$ | Inactive Prep time: 12 hrs.

This is a "No Doubt about It" recipe, as in, it looks so dramatic when you bring it to the table that there is no doubt that this is a meal to serve on special festive occasions. In our house, that occasion is New Year's. Hogs are supposed to bring good luck, and this is about 6 pounds of good luck on a platter. Made on a bed of braised cabbage, with spices, oranges (plus zest, plus juice), and some chili peppers for zing, and finished with Champagne—it is one of my favorite meals.

1 6-pound bone-in pork loin roast

Kosher salt, to taste

Freshly ground black pepper, to taste

2 tablespoons olive oil

1 red cabbage, cored and sliced

3 red onions, sliced

2 Fresno chilies, thinly sliced into rounds

2 tablespoons caraway seeds, toasted

1 New Mexican chili, toasted to release oils

2 cups chicken stock, hot

Juice of 4 oranges, plus zest of ½ orange

2 tablespoons whole grain mustard

Splash sherry vinegar

1 bottle Champagne (semi-chilled)

½ bunch fresh cilantro, leaves picked, for garnish

1. Preheat the oven to 375 °F.

2. Generously season the pork all over with kosher salt and freshly ground black pepper. If possible, let it sit in the refrigerator overnight and bring to room temperature prior to cooking.

3. In a large roasting pan, add the olive oil and heat over medium heat. Add the cabbage, onions, Fresnos, toasted caraway seeds, New Mexican chili, salt, chicken stock, and orange juice. Top the vegetables with the pork roast.

4. Leave uncovered and place into the oven for about 45 minutes to 1 hour, or until the internal temperature on an instant-read thermometer reads between 140–145 °F.

5. When ready, remove the pork from the oven and place onto the stovetop or heatproof surface. Remove the pork from the pan and set aside. Add mustard, orange zest, and vinegar to the cabbage mixture, and stir to combine. Taste and season with salt. Return the pork to the pan. Lean the pork against the side of the pan. Place the semi-chilled Champagne bottle into the pan and take the cage off the top. You can let the top pop on its own or loosen it slowly with a kitchen towel. Allow some of the Champagne, about 2 cups, to spill into the pan.

6. Remove the pork from the pan and allow it to rest briefly on a cutting board. Remove the pork loin from the bone and slice. Place the cabbage onto a family-style platter. Fan the pork slices around the cabbage. Carve between the bones and add the bones to the platter. Garnish with cilantro leaves and spoon the pan sauce around the pork.

WINTER

89

HOLIDAY MAC 'N' CHEESE CASSEROLE

SERVES 8 | **Skill Level: EASY** | **Cook Time: 30 mins.** | **Prep Time: 15 mins.** | **Cost: $**

One of the great joys of being a parent is reconnecting with mac 'n' cheese. If you have been away from it for a few years, I guarantee that as soon as the kids are ready to eat solid food, mac 'n' cheese becomes a go-to kid pleaser. Pretty soon, you'll find yourself making a little extra and then, when your child doesn't finish the whole serving, grabbing a spoon and polishing it off, straight from the casserole dish.

My approach to mac 'n' cheese reflects my belief in what I call the "Go Big or Go Home Theory." I want a good mix of cheese and lots of it. Gruyère is terrific because it has a slight sharp bite, some aged stinkiness, and I swear a little bit of happiness in it. Must be the contented cows. And then there's creamy, sweet mascarpone that melts into a wonderful consistency. If you don't have Gruyère, Swiss is nice, and cream cheese is fine in place of mascarpone. The basic idea is a full-flavored hard cheese and a sweeter, creamier cheese. The result is a creamy center and a really crunchy crust.

6 quarts water

2 tablespoons salt

1 pound rigatoni

1 pound bacon, diced

1 onion, diced

1 butternut squash, peeled and diced

2 cloves garlic, minced

3 tablespoons all-purpose flour

1 quart plus 3 cups half-and-half

1 cup Gruyère

Pinch of nutmeg

1 cup mascarpone

2 cups bread crumbs

1 bunch parsley, chopped

1. Preheat the oven to 375 °F.

2. Bring the water to a boil in a large pot. Add the salt. Cook the rigatoni in boiling water until tender but a little less cooked than the package instructions suggest. Drain, then set aside.

Less is more

There are few things worse than mac 'n' cheese where the pasta has cooked so long it just about disintegrates. Mario often says to cook your pasta for a minute less than it recommends on the box, and that's good advice for a pot-to-plate pasta dish, but in this casserole, the pasta is going to keep cooking, so I precook my pasta for 4 minutes less than recommended on the box before putting it in with the cheese and baking.

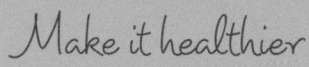

Make it healthier

Butternut squash or pumpkin baked into a mac 'n' cheese casserole adds sweetness, nutrients, and enough vegetables to make it a healthier one-course meal.

3. Cook the bacon until crisp. Sweat the onion, butternut squash, and garlic in a pan until translucent, then add flour to the pan to make roux. Slowly pour in the half-and-half while mixing, and bring mixture to simmer. Add in ½ cup of the Gruyère and nutmeg, and constantly stir until all the cheese is melted. Add the mascarpone, and mix until melted and combined. Add the cooked rigatoni and toss pasta until it's well mixed in the cheese mixture. Transfer to a 9 x 13 casserole dish.

4. In a medium mixing bowl, toss the bread crumbs, remaining Gruyère, and parsley. Sprinkle the bread crumb mixture over the casserole, and bake at 375 °F for 5–8 minutes, until the top is golden brown.

Travels well

There are few recipes more suited to a potluck dinner than mac 'n' cheese. Apart from the fact that everyone loves it, it is really easy to make at home and bring to a social gathering. Just cover it with plastic wrap and a rubber band to secure it, and it's ready to go. All that's needed to serve is reheating it in the oven when you reach your destination. And if the oven is too crowded, serve it as is. People will eat it. I promise.

Clinton gets the greatest Christmas present of his life: JoBeth Williams!

THE CHEW **FACE OFF**

CHILI CHAMPION

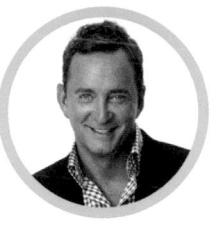

Clinton: When football season rolls around, there are somewhere between two and three million people cooking in parking lots outside of America's football stadiums: braising brats (that's bratwurst to you non-fans), slurping suds, killing kegs, roasting ribs, and making chili. If you can cook it for a long time with chili peppers, I guarantee you, somewhere in this great land of ours, some football fan is doing it. And since football brings out the competitive spirit, it is true that where there is chili, there are chili cook-offs, especially at Super Bowl time. So if you were asking yourself what kind of all-American cookbook would not have a chili cook-off, the answer is not this one.

Ladies and gentlemen, I give you a stalwart of the Seattle Seahawks, Mario Batali, and a son of the heartland and a bulwark of the Cleveland Browns, Michael Symon.

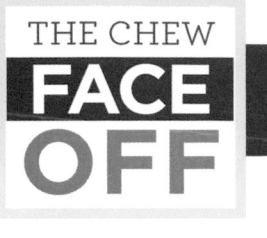

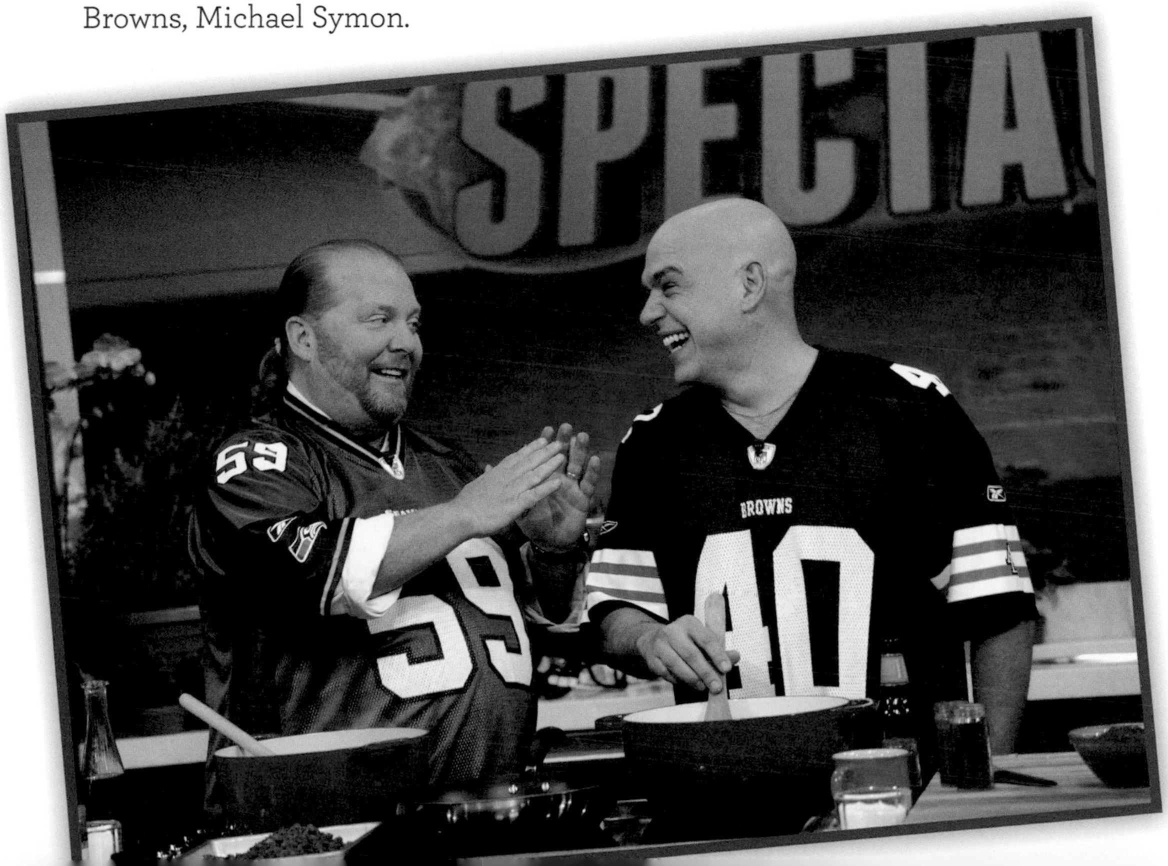

Michael: It's a duel of the chilies. Looking to score some easy points, I figure Daphne is going to go for my chili because it's made with chicken so it's a little lighter.

Mario: I'm coming out all guns blazing with my Restrictor Plate Chili.

Michael: Sounds like something out of *The Terminator*. What's a restrictor plate?

Mario: It's something they put on really hot cars to slow them down on a small track. Likewise, my chili is so full of power, I need to contain it before it blows you away.

We both start with onions, because everything starts with onions, doesn't it?, and I throw in some bacon notably missing in Michael's recipe.

Michael: Hey, somebody stole my bacon!

Mario: You said you were going for a lighter chili, so I was only helping.

Michael: You know, one day I give up smoking and the next thing you know I'm making chicken chili and cutting down on the bacon. Am I on the road to becoming a vegan? But I am not cutting back on flavor, so I toss in coriander, cumin, cocoa, and then chipotle and smoked paprika.

The hot oil in the pan really makes those spices bloom. Great smell.

Mario: And the moment of truth as we add chilies to our chili. Michael . . . you first.

Michael: Chipotles and fresh serranos . . . good overall mouth heat, but not thermonuclear. And Mario, pride of the Northwest, what kind of chilies for you?

Mario: Well, I like hot, but I also like bright tanginess, so I'm going with pickled jalapeños.

Michael: Okay, Chef, now for the tomatoes and meat.

Mario: You mean chicken, don't you? Good red meat for me and chicken for you.

Michael: To amp up my guy points, I'm cooking in beer.

Mario: Back into your man cave, Cleveland Browns fan: I've got manliness to spare, enough so that I have the self-confidence to braise my chili in fresh pure water!

MICHAEL'S CHICKEN CHILI

SERVES 6 | Skill Level: EASY | Cook Time: 2–2 ½ hrs. | Prep Time: 15 mins. | Cost: $

5 tablespoons olive oil

2 pounds ground chicken

Salt, to taste

2 cups onion, diced small

3 cloves garlic, minced

2 serrano chilies, sliced into thin rings

1 tablespoon smoked paprika

2 tablespoons chili powder

2 tablespoons coriander, toasted and ground

1 tablespoon cumin, toasted and ground

1 teaspoon cayenne

1 12-ounce bottle beer (an IPA if possible)

1 14½-ounce can petite diced tomatoes

1 15-ounce can cannellini beans, drained and rinsed

1 15-ounce can red kidney beans, drained and rinsed

2 tablespoons brown sugar

2 teaspoons cocoa powder

2 cups water, plus 2 tablespoons

Chipotle hot sauce, to taste

7 ounces Greek yogurt

½ cup cilantro leaves, chopped

1. Heat a large Dutch oven over medium-high heat and add 3 tablespoons of the olive oil. When the oil is hot, add the ground chicken with a large pinch of salt and brown on all sides, breaking up the meat into smaller pieces as it cooks. Remove with a slotted spoon to a plate and set aside.

2. Drain the fat from the pot, then place back over the heat and add 2 tablespoons of olive oil. Reduce the heat to medium, and add the onion, garlic, and serranos with a small pinch of salt. Let the vegetables sweat for a few minutes, then add all of your spices. Toast them for about 30 seconds, being careful not to burn them.

3. Next, add the bottle of beer, making sure to scrape the bottom of the pot well. Add the meat back in along with the tomatoes and both beans.

4. Stir in the brown sugar, cocoa powder, and 2 cups of water, and reduce the heat to low. Season with some more salt and hot sauce to taste, and simmer, stirring occasionally, for 2 hours.

5. In the meantime, make the garnish by mixing together the yogurt and cilantro with a pinch of salt. Refrigerate until ready to use.

6. To serve, ladle some of the chili into bowls, garnishing with a big dollop of the yogurt.

MARIO'S RESTRICTOR PLATE CHILI

SERVES 8 | **Skill Level: EASY** | **Cook Time: 1 hr.** | **Prep Time: 20 mins.** | **Cost: $**

6 slices bacon, cut into 1-inch pieces

2 onions, finely chopped

2 red bell peppers, stemmed, seeded, and finely chopped

6 cloves garlic, finely chopped

2 pounds ground sirloin

1 6-ounce can of tomato paste

¼ cup chili powder

2 tablespoons ground cumin

1 8-ounce can diced green chilies, drained

1 4-ounce can diced jalapeño chilies

4 cups water

1 28-ounce can crushed tomatoes

1 cup pitted green olives, coarsely chopped

1 teaspoon ground cinnamon

2 tablespoons dried oregano

1 12-ounce can pinto beans, drained

¾ cup fresh or frozen corn

8 8-inch flour tortillas

2 tablespoons olive oil

½ cup Cheddar cheese

¼ cup scallions, finely chopped

2 teaspoons cilantro

8 quail eggs

1. Place a large pot over medium-high heat and add the bacon pieces. When the bacon is cooked through, about 6 minutes, pour out some of the fat, add the onions and red bell peppers, and cook until the vegetables soften, about 6 minutes more. Add the garlic and cook for 1 minute more.

2. Add the ground sirloin and cook, breaking up the sirloin, until all the pink is gone, about 6 minutes more.

3. Add the tomato paste, chili powder, and ground cumin, and cook for 1 minute, stirring often.

4. Add the green chilies, jalapeños, water, tomatoes, olives, cinnamon, and oregano, and bring the liquid to a boil. Reduce the heat to medium-low, cover, and simmer the chili for 1 hour, stirring every 20 minutes or so to keep the bottom from scorching.

5. Add the pinto beans and corn, and simmer for 10 minutes more, stirring often. Remove from heat and serve, or let cool and keep cold in a refrigerator or ice-filled cooler for up to 3 days.

6. Brush the tortillas with olive oil. Fill with Cheddar, scallions, and cilantro, and grill until crispy on both sides, about 3–5 minutes.

7. Fry the quail eggs sunny-side up with a drizzle of olive oil in a pan.

8. Serve the chili with the quesadilla and quail egg.

WINTER

95

Clinton: And now, in a less macho moment, it's the women's turn. First Carla:

Carla: I'm from Tennessee, which begins with *T* as in *Texas*, where they are the masters of cooking brisket. So I'll leave it to the boys as to who is more macho and simply point out that mine has a lot of hearty, manly—and, for that matter, me-big-strong-girl—beef.

My chili cooks for a long, long time in a low oven. For liquid, since I don't drink, I eat my alcohol and cook it off with beer. Ancho chilies give it beautiful heat, with a touch of sweetness. And finally, you know how in Mexico their most famous mole is made with chocolate? I figured, why not with chili? When you taste it, you'll see—no reason why not. Yum!!

CHILI CON CARLA

SERVES 8 | Skill Level: EASY | Cook Time: 3½ –4 hrs. | Prep Time: 15 mins. | Cost: $

6 large dried ancho chilies

2 tablespoons canola oil

1¼ pounds onions, chopped

1 5-pound flat-cut beef brisket, cut into 2½- to 3-inch cubes

Coarse kosher salt, to taste, plus 1½ teaspoons

Pepper, to taste

6 large cloves garlic, peeled

2 teaspoons cumin seeds

1 teaspoon ground coriander

1¾ cups fire-roasted diced tomatoes with green chilies

1 12-ounce bottle Mexican beer

1 7-ounce can roasted green chilies, diced

2 tablespoons chili powder

4 ounces dark chocolate, chopped

Red onion, sliced, to garnish

Avocado, diced, to garnish

Monterey Jack cheese, grated, to garnish

Tortillas, to garnish

Cilantro, to garnish

Sour cream, to garnish

1. Place the ancho chilies in a medium bowl. Pour enough boiling water to cover them and soak the chilies for about 4 hours, or until they are soft.

2. Preheat the oven to 350 °F.

3. In a large, ovenproof Dutch oven over medium-high heat, add 2 tablespoons canola oil and the onion and cook until translucent. Season the brisket liberally with salt and pepper. Add this to the pot and toss to coat with fat.

4. Drain the chilies, reserving the soaking liquid. Pour 1 cup of the soaking liquid, along with the chilies, into a blender with the garlic, cumin seeds, coriander, and salt. Blend until pureed, then add to the Dutch oven, along with the tomatoes, beer, green chilies, chili powder, and chocolate.

5. Stir and bring to a simmer, cover, and transfer to the oven. Cook for 2 hours, and then remove the lid and continue to cook for 45 minutes, until the brisket is almost tender. Skim the fat from the surface and add water, if necessary, to keep the brisket submerged. Cook an additional 45 minutes, until meat is tender.

6. To serve, spoon into bowls and top with desired garnishes.

Daphne: Mine is a total vegetarian chili, and it also happens to be a longtime favorite of the Oz family. I like to make it on Friday and let the flavors mingle and multiply until Sunday. It's always better when you let it sit and work its alchemy.

Carla has beer as her secret ingredient. So does Michael. When you think about it for a second, beer is probably the most common drink at tailgates, so why not go with the flow and toss it in your chili? Well, my extra-special super flavor-enhancing ingredient is tangy, smoky, hot chipotles in adobo. Don't let me forget the beans, as my cohost sister seems to have done. Whenever you order chili in a restaurant, it has beans, doesn't it? Full of protein, creaminess, and rib sticking enough to take the place of meat. There is so much power and flavor in this chili that I have seen 280-pound fullbacks eat it and smile with satisfaction.

DeMarcus Ware adds a little spice like a true champion!

DAPHNE'S VEGGIE CHILI

SERVES 8 | Skill Level: EASY | Cook Time: 45 mins. | Prep Time: 10 mins. | Cost: $

2 tablespoons canola oil

1 large yellow onion, chopped

4 cloves garlic, smashed

2 medium zucchinis, sliced and diced

1 bag corn, frozen or fresh

2 tablespoons tomato paste

1 16-ounce can of roasted tomatoes, chopped, with juice

Salt

Pepper

2–3 bay leaves

2 tablespoons oregano

¼ cup chili powder

2–3 tablespoons cumin

1–2 chipotle peppers in adobo sauce, chopped

2 15-ounce cans kidney beans (drained and rinsed)

1 15-ounce can black beans (drained and rinsed)

1 12-ounce bottle beer

1 cup vegetable stock

Cheddar cheese, shredded, to serve

Avocado, chopped, to serve

Juice of 2 limes, to serve

Sour cream, to serve

1. In a large, heavy pot, heat the oil over medium-high heat.

2. Add the onion and garlic, and sauté until translucent.

3. Add the zucchini and corn, and sauté for 5 minutes, stirring occasionally.

4. Add the tomato paste and chopped tomatoes with their juice from the can. Then add the salt, pepper, herbs, and spices.

5. Add 1–2 chopped chipotle peppers and the beans. Stir well.

6. Add the beer and vegetable stock until liquid covers all ingredients in the pot.

7. Bring to a boil, and then reduce heat to medium-low. Simmer for a half hour, stirring occasionally. Remove from heat, and adjust seasonings to taste.

8. Serve with shredded Cheddar, chopped avocado, fresh lime juice, and sour cream.

Clinton: Before our cook-off chefs take off the pads and go at it bare knuckles, we'll leave this battle for the Champion of Chili and leave it to you to try to make your own call. If your Super Bowl party is big enough, make all four. You'll know who the winner is pretty easily. It's the pot that's empty at the end of the game.

DEEP-DISH PIZZA CASSEROLE

| SERVES 10 | Skill Level: EASY | Cook Time: 40 mins. | Prep Time: 30 mins. | Cost: $ |

Inactive Prep Time: 12 hrs.

First an apology. "Chicago, I'm sorry." You see, when I think of pizza, the only thing that comes to mind is thin-crust pizza like they make in New York (and Naples, and Rome). The delicious food that they call deep-dish pizza is, to me, a casserole. Why? Because to my way of thinking, anything that you bake for more than 30 minutes crosses the line from pizza to casserole.

Glad I got that off my chest!

Mario suggested that I take full responsibility and call it– after my home-town—"Cleveland pizza."

Not going there. That would really get Chicago on my case. Basically, you take my pizza dough, line a casserole dish with it, and fill it with pureed San Marzano tomatoes, onions, ham, bacon, maybe a little sausage if you are feel-ing extra carnivorous, and lots of provolone and Parmigiano cheese. Or you could go vegetarian, leave out the meat and put in mushrooms, broccoli, or whatever strikes your fancy. Then call it whatever you want. I'm sure you'll be back for seconds.

FOR THE DOUGH:

1¼ teaspoons fresh yeast

3½ cups warm water

10 cups all-purpose flour

2¼ tablespoons kosher salt

Oil, for the bowl

FOR THE SAUCE:

1 15-ounce can San Marzano tomatoes, drained

2 cloves garlic

1 tablespoon dried oregano

1 tablespoon dried basil

Salt

Freshly ground black pepper

TO MAKE THE DOUGH:

1. In the bowl of your mixer, bloom the yeast in the wa-ter by mixing it in, breaking up any lumps, then letting it sit until it becomes slightly foamy and the water is cloudy, about 5 minutes.

2. Combine the flour and salt, then add to the bloomed yeast mixture. With the dough hook attachment for your mixer, mix on medium speed for 11 minutes. The dough should come together as one mass and begin climbing the hook.

3. After the dough has been mixed, turn it out into a light-ly oiled mixing bowl, and let it proof until it is doubled in size. This should take a few hours, depending on how warm the air is. You should also cover the bowl with a damp cloth or plastic wrap during this process so it doesn't dry out.

FOR THE PIZZA:

2 tablespoons olive oil

4 pieces bacon, chopped

1 tablespoon butter

1 onion, chopped

¼ pound provolone, cut into thin slices

4 pieces good-quality ham, cut into strips

Freshly grated Parmigiano

Basil, to serve

4. After the dough has risen, portion it into 7–8 9-ounce balls. Place the portioned dough on a sheet tray with a piece of parchment paper that has been lightly oiled. Cover the sheet tray really well with plastic wrap and refrigerate overnight. The dough will be rested and ready to use the next day.

TO MAKE THE SAUCE:

5. Combine the drained tomatoes, garlic, and dried herbs in a blender or food processor. Pulse until the desired consistency. Pour into a bowl and season with salt and pepper.

TO MAKE THE PIZZA:

6. In a large sauté pan, heat the olive oil over medium-high heat. Add the bacon, and cook until crisp. Remove the bacon, leaving some of the fat behind. Add the butter and the onion, and cook until softened. Remove from heat and set aside.

7. On a floured work surface, roll out the dough into a ¼-inch-thick circle. In a 14-inch oiled cast-iron skillet, fit the dough inside and pinch around the top.

8. Add onions to the skillet. Next, add some of the bacon as a layer. Add a layer of provolone. Add a layer of ham, then pour the sauce over and sprinkle the Parmigiano over the sauce. Repeat the layers until the skillet is full. Bake for 25–30 minutes, until the crust is golden brown and cheese begins to bubble through the sauce. Let cool for about 10 minutes before serving. Garnish with basil.

MEATLOAF ALLA MARIO

SERVES 8 | **Skill Level: EASY** | **Cook Time: 1 hr. 30 mins.** | **Prep Time: 20 mins.** | **COST: $$**

Everyone has a favorite meatloaf recipe that their mom made. That kind of leaves me out because my mom wasn't a big meatloaf maker. But Grandma was a Meatloaf Mama from the get-go. Being of good Italian blood, she wasn't content with just throwing together some chopped meat, ketchup, and onions and calling it a recipe. She stuffed her meatloaf with wonderful vegetables and some mortadella and cheese. When I made this on the show, Carla pointed out—no doubt with her sense of the surreal—that this recipe will feed a group of 375 people. All I can say to Carla is, this is so delicious that a family of eight can work through it quite nicely.

2 pounds sweet Italian sausage, casings removed

2 pounds lean ground beef

4¼ cups fresh bread crumbs

2 cups freshly grated Pecorino Romano

3 eggs, lightly beaten

1 cup whole milk

Salt

Freshly ground black pepper

8 quarts plus 1 cup water

1 pound baby spinach, trimmed

4 carrots, peeled and cut lengthwise into strips

12 scallions, trimmed

¼ cup all-purpose flour, plus extra for dusting

10 pieces mortadella, sliced thin

6 slices Cacio di Roma

2 sprigs fresh rosemary

¾ cup extra virgin olive oil

1. Preheat the oven to 375 °F.

2. In a large bowl, combine the sausage, beef, 4 cups of the bread crumbs, the Pecorino Romano, eggs, milk, salt, and pepper. Mix gently but thoroughly with your hands. Cover and refrigerate.

3. Bring 8 quarts of water to a boil in a large pasta pot. Set up an ice bath nearby.

4. Add 2 tablespoons of salt to the boiling water. Dip the spinach leaves in the water just to wilt them, and immediately transfer them to the ice bath; then drain them in a colander. Add the carrots to the boiling water and cook for 10 minutes; then remove with a spider or slotted spoon and set aside. Drop the scallions in the boiling water and cook for 1 minute; then plunge them in the ice bath and let them cool for 1 minute. Drain and set on a towel-lined plate.

5. Combine the flour with the remaining ¼ cup bread crumbs, and heavily dust a wooden board or other work surface with the mixture. On the dusted board, pat the meat mixture into a 1½-inch-thick rectangle, about 6 by 16 inches. Place the spinach leaves between two plates and press them together to remove any remaining water, and then lay the spinach over the meat, leaving a 1-inch border on the short sides. Lay the carrot pieces and then the scallions over the spinach, arranging them lengthwise down the rectangle. Lay the mortadella and Cacio di Roma over the

scallions. Starting from a long side, roll the meat up like a jelly roll, making it as compact as possible; patch any holes like modeling clay. The roll should be about 16 inches long. Dust the outside with flour.

6. Place the loaf on a rimmed baking sheet. Press a sprig of rosemary into each side of the meatloaf, and pour 1 cup of water into the pan. Drizzle ½ cup of the olive oil down the length of the loaf. Bake the meatloaf for 1 hour 20 minutes, or until it reaches an internal temperature of 165 °F.

7. Carefully transfer the load to a cutting board and allow it to rest for 15 minutes.

8. Strain the pan juices into a saucepan and bring to a boil. Season with salt and pepper to taste, add the remaining ¼ cup oil, and whisk to form a loose sauce.

9. Slice the meatloaf into 1-inch-thick slices and arrange them on warmed plates. Drizzle with the sauce and serve.

CHOCAHOLIC WHOOPIE PIES

MAKES 36 | **Skill Level: EASY** | **Cook Time: 30 mins.** | **Prep Time: 20 mins.** | **Cost: $**

Spurred on by the nationwide cupcake craze, I wanted to do something a little different but just as easy—in fact easier. For those of you not from the Northeast, a whoopie pie is two chocolate cakes sandwiched around a layer of white filling. For the longest time, I have wondered why it's called whoopie pie. In Pennsylvania, they say it's an Amish invention, and that when Amish women would serve this, their menfolk would go, "Whoopie!" I think that's the PG version. I tend to side with Michael that whenever they ate this, they were ready to make whoopie. Michael got a little carried away, though, because when he learned that they take only a few minutes to make, he said, "Just like making whoopie!"

TMI, Michael.

FOR THE CAKES:

2 cups unbleached all-purpose flour

½ cup unsweetened cocoa (such as Droste)

½ teaspoon baking soda

½ teaspoon fine salt

Cinnamon, optional

1 stick unsalted butter at room temperature

1 cup granulated sugar

1 large egg

1 cup milk

FOR THE FILLING:

1 stick unsalted butter, softened

2 cups powdered sugar

½ teaspoon vanilla extract

1 cup mascarpone

½ cup white chocolate, melted

TO MAKE THE CAKES:

1. Arrange the oven racks in the upper and lower thirds of the oven, and preheat the oven to 425 °F. Line 2 large baking sheets with parchment paper.

2. Whisk together the flour, cocoa, baking soda, and salt in a medium bowl. You can add additional spices, like cinnamon, if you wish.

3. Cream the butter and sugar in the bowl of an electric mixer at high speed until fluffy, about 4 minutes. Add the egg, and beat at medium speed until incorporated. At low

speed, add the flour mixture in 2 batches, alternating with the milk, mixing until just blended.

4. Using a ½ tablespoon measure, drop 18 generous teaspoons of batter onto each sheet, leaving about 2 inches between cakes. Bake the 2 sheets at the same time, 5–7 minutes, until springy to touch. Let cool on the sheets for 5 minutes, and transfer to racks to cool completely. Change the parchment and repeat using the remaining batter (72 cakes in total).

TO MAKE THE FILLING:

5. Beat the butter and powdered sugar at low speed until blended, and then beat at high speed until fluffy, about 5 minutes. Add the vanilla and mascarpone, and mix at low speed until blended, about 1 minute. Slowly mix in the cooled melted white chocolate.

TO MAKE THE WHOOPIE PIES:

6. Match pairs of cake with the same shapes and spread the bottom side of 1 cake with filling (or use a piping bag), and sandwich together with the other cake. Store the finished whoopie pies in a covered plastic container and chill for up to 3 days.

GRILLED BACON, CHOCOLATE-HAZELNUT SANDWICH

MAKES 3 Sandwiches | Skill Level: EASY | Cook Time: 15 mins. | Prep Time: 5 mins. | Cost: $

I don't know what to call this: a dessert, a snack, or Falling Off the Dieting Wagon. It's one of my favorite midnight munchies. I got addicted to them when I was in high school. The combinations of salty and sweet, smooth and crispy . . . are the ones that most human beings find irresistible. I don't recommend it as part of any diet plan. On the other hand, a diet that doesn't take account of a very occasional indulgence is one that will soon be thrown in the dustbin of dining history. How about we make a deal? Have it every other weekend. Beware, though: once you buy a jar of the chocolate-hazelnut spread that I use for this, it will call to you in the middle of the night. Don't answer it.

½ pound bacon

½ loaf Pullman bread or pain de mie

½ cup chocolate-hazelnut spread

3 bananas

6 tablespoons butter

1. Preheat a skillet, and fry the bacon until crisp. When ready, transfer the bacon to a paper towel–lined plate to cool.

2. Slice the Pullman loaf into 6 ½-inch slices, and spread a tablespoon, give or take, of the chocolate-hazelnut spread onto each of the slices. Slice the bananas lengthwise and then in half, and add 4 slices to each sandwich. Arrange 3 slices of bacon onto the banana slices, and make a sandwich. Generously butter both sides of each sandwich.

3. In a preheated nonstick skillet over medium heat, grill the sandwiches on either side, until golden brown, and serve.

Valentine's at Our House

Clinton

Today is the day for lovers and, if you make the right meal, the night for loving. We asked our Chewster Board of Romantic Knowledge about food and love on the same day.

Mario

The way to impress someone is to make something that is delicious and kind of erotic and sexy yet very simple, so you look good when you make it, it's delicious, and the payoff is immense.

Carla

Tell you the truth, I pretty much always worked on Valentine's Day, so whatever I do, I do just for my husband. I make something that is nice and light so that when you wanna get busy later, you still have the energy to do it! This year, I think I'm gonna do something really special, like put on an old-fashioned Pan Am stewardess outfit. I'll put that on . . . and . . .

Clinton

TMI, Carla.

Mario

Word, Carla! With Valentine's dinner, make sure you leave some of the food on the plate. The "Clean Plate Club" never needs to exist on Valentine's Day. Because you should be focused on other things!

Michael

In Cleveland, because Hallmark and American Greeting cards are there, we have a lot of those Hallmark holidays. We go out with our kids. Because we all love each other so much, we think it's a family date, not a man/woman or a spouse/spouse date. We traditionally get cheese fondue and then chocolate fondue.

Daphne

I make a meal that's all red things. I do a red main course, a red salad with beets. I do a red dessert with strawberries and a red velvet cake, so it's all red! Maybe I'll cheat a little with some pink Champagne.

Mario presents a Valentine's Day rose to Jewel.

Clinton

You're all so thoughtful! We don't do anything at my house because each day is Valentine's Day!

HOT MUTTERED BUM

SERVES 4 | **Skill Level: EASY** | **Inactive Cook Time: 5 hrs.** | **Prep Time: 5 mins.** | **Cost: $**

There may not be a cure for the common cold, but this drink is a killer of the winter blues. What makes it different from the classic hot buttered rum is that I put all the ingredients, except for the rum, in a slow cooker for 4-6 hours. You have to add the rum at the end, otherwise the alcohol cooks away and your cocktail becomes a mocktail. This was so good that Mario growled like a lion (although he was about as convincing as Bert Lahr in The Wizard of Oz).

2 cups dark brown sugar

½ cup butter

1 teaspoon salt

1 teaspoon vanilla extract

2 quarts hot water

3 cinnamon sticks

6 whole cloves

2 cups spiced rum

1 cup sweetened whipped cream

¼ teaspoon ground nutmeg

1. Combine the dark brown sugar, butter, salt, vanilla extract, and hot water in a slow cooker. Add the cinnamon sticks and cloves. Cover and cook on low for 5 hours. Stir in the rum.

2. Ladle from the slow cooker into mugs, and top with whipped cream and a dusting of nutmeg.

ROLES ROYCE

SERVES 10 | **Skill Level: EASY** | **Prep Time: 5 mins.** | **Cost: $**

I made this in honor of Cheryl Hines for her character on Suburgatory, Dallas Royce. (Get it? Her role is Royce.) It is a super holiday punch: deep red cranberry juice swirling in a sea of black currant-rich cassis and luxurious Champagne. The great thing about this punch—make that all punches—is if you are the host, you are not stuck playing bartender to a roomful of demanding guests who want their drinks just so.

8 cups cranberry juice

2 bottles dry Champagne or sparkling wine

3 cups crème de cassis (black currant–flavored liqueur)

4 cups seltzer

Lemon peel for garnish

1. Combine ingredients in a punch bowl. Garnish each glass with a lemon peel and serve.

113

POTATO LEEK SOUP

SERVES 4 | **Skill Level: EASY** | **Cook Time: 30 mins.** | **Prep Time: 10 mins.** | **COST: $**

I made this for our St. Patrick's Day show and, as I told the audience, "It's so good you are going to want to kiss the Blarney Stone!" Usually by the time St. Paddy's Day rolls around, I've had it up to my eyeballs with Old Man Winter. There are few things that fight off the chill like a spud-based soup. Top it with some good Irish Cheddar and crumbled bacon.

FOR THE SOUP:

Extra virgin olive oil

1 onion, diced

2 leeks, washed and sliced

2 stalks celery, chopped

1 clove garlic, minced

4 cups chicken stock

2 cups milk

1 bay leaf

4 Yukon gold potatoes, peeled and cubed

Salt

Freshly ground pepper

2 tablespoons fresh parsley, chopped

½ cup half-and-half

1 cup bacon, fried crisp and chopped into small pieces, for garnish

FOR THE IRISH CHEDDAR CROUTONS:

4 thin slices Irish Cheddar cheese

4 slices country bread, toasted golden brown

1. In a large stockpot, heat the oil over medium-high heat. Add the onion, leeks, celery, and garlic, and cook until all have softened and become fragrant, about 5 minutes. Add the stock, milk, bay leaf, and potatoes, and season with salt and pepper. Bring to a simmer. Cook until the potatoes are tender, about 25 minutes. Stir in the parsley and half-and-half. Allow to cool slightly. In batches, puree in a blender.

2. Serve with the Irish Cheddar croutons and sprinkle with bacon.

TO MAKE THE IRISH CHEDDAR CROUTONS:

3. Preheat the broiler and place the cheese slices on the toasted bread. Broil until the cheese is melted and browned in spots, about 2–3 minutes.

Grit ain't great

Because of the kind of soil they are grown in, leeks can be quite sandy and gritty. That's no fun. To get rid of grittiness, I recommend slicing leeks and putting them in a bowl filled with cold water. Slosh the sliced leeks around and the grit will fall to the bottom.

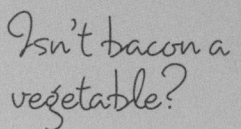

Gordon Elliott brings a dramatic flair to the stage.

Isn't bacon a vegetable?

Instead of using chicken stock, use vegetable stock to make this a vegetarian recipe. I guess you'll have to skip the bacon, although I kind of think bacon always gets a free pass. I think we should make it an honorary vegetable.

WINTER

115

IRISH SODA BREAD

SERVES 8 | **Skill Level: EASY** | **Cook Time: 1 hr. 10 mins.** | **Prep Time: 15 mins.** | **Cost: $**

St. Paddy's Day without soda bread is like the Fourth of July without fireworks. So dipping down into the Irish part of my soul—and on St. Patrick's Day, we're all a little Irish—I offer you this quick bread. I say quick because there is no yeast, no waiting hours for the bread to rise, and no kneading. Buttermilk gives it extra depth and the mouth-fillingness of the best southern biscuits. Serve warm and slather with Irish butter or melted Irish Cheddar. Then make a wish on a shamrock!

½ cup unsalted butter, cut into cubes, plus 1 tablespoon and to serve

5 cups all-purpose flour

1 cup sugar

1 tablespoon baking powder

½ teaspoon baking soda

1½ teaspoons salt

2½ cups golden raisins

Zest of 1 orange

2½ cups buttermilk

1 large egg

1. Preheat the oven to 350 °F.

2. Butter a 10-inch cast-iron skillet with 1 tablespoon of butter and set aside.

3. In a large bowl combine the all-purpose flour, sugar, baking powder, baking soda, and salt. Add remaining butter and the orange zest. Using your fingertips, combine until the mixture resembles wet sand. Stir in the raisins.

4. In a separate bowl, whisk together the buttermilk and egg, and fold into the flour mixture using a wooden spoon.

5. Transfer the dough to the prepared skillet. Smooth the top, mounding slightly in center. Dip a knife in flour and mark an X on the top of the batter.

6. Bake until bread is cooked through and a toothpick inserted into the center comes out clean, about 1 hour 10 minutes. Cool bread in skillet for 10 minutes.

7. Serve with butter or melted Irish Cheddar.

SUPER BOWL PUNCH

SERVES 8 | **Skill Level: EASY** | **Prep Time: 10 mins.** | **Cost: $**

For our Super Bowl show, our tasting panel included some NFL greats: Dwight Freeney, DeMarcus Ware, and a member of my NFL Hall of Fame, the great Joe Theismann. We did some world championship cocktail tasting and ended up with my trademark Super Bowl Punch. It's a super easy recipe to remember because basically it's one cup of everything. I don't know if it's because we were so buzzed by the time we drank it, but when we all voted on our fave cocktail at the end of the show, the Super Bowl Punch came out on top.

1 cup vodka

1 cup tequila

1 cup rum

1 cup gin

1 cup triple sec

1 cup fresh lime juice

2 cups cranberry juice

4¼ cups ginger ale

2 cups blueberries

2 cups sliced strawberries

1. Combine alcohol and juice in a large punch bowl. Top with the ginger ale, and stir in the blueberries and strawberries.

2. When ladling out to guests, top glasses with a touch more fizz on top.

THE WARM AND TOASTY

| SERVES 1 | Skill Level: EASY | Prep Time: 15 mins. | Cook Time: 5 mins. | Cost: $ |

I suppose if you drink enough of my version of Irish coffee, you could call yourself "warm and toasty" or "hot and plastered." Since people really like hazelnut coffee these days, I put in some hazelnut liqueur (think of it as liquid Nutella). Of course you need Irish cream and—to give you a little jolt—some nice, strong coffee. After three of these, I guarantee you'll be having a nice chat with a leprechaun who strolled into your cocktail party.

¾ cup brewed coffee

1 ounce hazelnut liqueur

1 ounce Irish cream

1½ ounces whipped cream

Chocolate shavings, to garnish

1. Pour coffee into a mug. Add the hazelnut liqueur. Finally add the Irish cream and stir.

2. Top with the whipped cream and chocolate shavings.

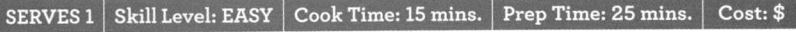

SPICY GRAPEFRUIT MARGARITA, AKA "THE CLINTON CALIENTE"

| SERVES 1 | Skill Level: EASY | Cook Time: 15 mins. | Prep Time: 25 mins. | Cost: $ |

Inactive Prep Time: 12 hrs.

There is an old saying: "If it ain't broke, don't fix it." True enough, but if the classic margarita is great, then so is the idea of seeing what else you can do with it that is equally delicious. My solution is to add some habañero peppers in the salt that rims the glass and in the ice cubes. I guarantee they'll be the hottest cubes you ever taste. Also, some grapefruit juice in the cubes, when mixed with your tequila, gives it some fruitiness and a dash of bitter taste that balances the sweetness of the simple syrup and orange liqueur in the classic margarita. I'm sure the Mayor of Margaritaville, Jimmy Buffett, would approve.

FOR THE SPICY SALT:

Kosher salt

1 habañero, sliced

FOR THE SIMPLE SYRUP:

1 cup sugar

1 cup water

1 habañero, sliced

FOR THE ICE CUBES:

Habañero slices (from the simple syrup recipe)

1 grapefruit, sliced into small wedges or quarters

Water

FOR THE MARGARITA:

2 ounces tequila

2 ounces fresh pink grapefruit juice

1 ounce orange liqueur

½–1 ounce spicy simple syrup

2 ice cubes

FOR THE SPICY SALT:

1. Combine salt and habañero in a food processor. Grind together and set aside.

FOR THE SIMPLE SYRUP:

2. In a small sauce pot add sugar and water. Cook over medium heat until sugar has dissolved into the water. Add the habañero and steep for a few minutes. Strain out the habañero slices and reserve on a separate plate. Set the simple syrup aside to cool.

FOR THE ICE CUBES:

3. In each cavity of an ice cube tray add a slice of grapefruit and a slice of habañero pepper (reserved from making the simple syrup). Fill tray with water and freeze overnight.

FOR MARGARITA:

4. Dip glass in salt to cover the rim. Combine the tequila, grapefruit juice, orange liqueur, and simple syrup in a cocktail shaker. Shake to combine and strain into a salted rocks glass. Add ice cubes and serve.

THE CHEW

SPRING

Daphne

Q: **In a sense . . . you're the voice of the viewer who looks at food in terms of their family experience, usually with Mom.**

Daphne: One of the things I loved about how my mom cooked is we would look through a cookbook together and then we'd go food shopping and get a bunch of ingredients and then we'd never look at the recipe again! She'd add this spice and that, she'd go by her tongue, she'd teach me how to find the flavor pairings that made sense, even if they aren't traditional. Now when I am on the show presenting recipes that I grew up on, I am literally sharing a piece of my home and family.

Q: **How does it feel to be cooking alongside famous TV and restaurant chefs?**

Daphne: I am especially grateful for the way they won't ever let you mess up. Before we do a segment together, Mario always tells me, "I've got your back." Literally, every single time. And he does! He makes sure the recipe

is the way it should be. If I miss something or if the way that I make it isn't right, he adds those pointers in, and it's great to learn from someone who's had that level of mastery in his career.

Q: **What do you take away from your experience on the show?**

Daphne: What I love being reminded of daily is that it's okay to mess up. Even the professionals who have been doing it for thirty years mess up, as when Michael messed up his omelet and Mario's burnt things and Carla's burnt things and Clinton's burnt things. It happens, and there are ways you can recover. I learn something, a kernel of truth about cooking, every single day; things like "don't overwork your biscuits" or "don't load the pan with too many mushrooms or they'll steam and they won't come out with the best texture." It's those little things that you want people to take away, because it'll make home cooking different and better.

Q: **How about yourself as the health expert on the show?**

Daphne: Having struggled with my weight all throughout childhood and in a fairly health-conscious family, I came with a commitment to make health a priority and not simply losing weight and fad dieting.

I'm always looking for those ways to strip down calories and fat, always asking, "How are we going to enjoy our food and put a priority on health?" But I would never recommend artificial sweeteners or lower-grade oils just to save calories, because at the end of the day, we are trying to send a message about enjoying food.

If there is one thing I would like viewers to remember is the less processed it is, the better it is for you no matter what. Even if it's very high fat, high calorie, very calorie dense. I would always have whole milk instead of skim, and I'll have less of it. I would always have real sugar or real honey or maple syrup or whatever, rather than some no-cal sweetener that may or may not be a carcinogen. What we try to point you toward is things you're going to find in your supermarket, if not already in your refrigerator, and then some creative ways to put them together that will bring more pleasure to your table in a healthy way.

SPICY SHRIMP COCKTAIL

SERVES 4 | Skill Level: EASY | Cook Time: 15 mins. | Prep Time: 15 mins. | Cost: $$

I've been making this shrimp cocktail this way since the 1980s. It's probably as much a part of my identity as my orange Crocs. My humble addition to the noble traditions of shrimp cocktail-dom is a lot of peppercorns in the poaching liquids and the bite of serrano chili and scallions in the sauce. Just writing these words makes me want a glass of cold beer, so I guess it goes well with beer.

FOR THE SHRIMP:

2 tablespoons whole black peppercorns

5 sprigs fresh thyme

½ bunch parsley (leaves and stems)

1 lemon, halved

2 bay leaves

3 tablespoons kosher salt

3 quarts water

12 colossal shrimp, heads removed

FOR THE COCKTAIL SAUCE:

½ cup ketchup

¼ cup fresh horseradish (or 2 tablespoons prepared)

Juice and zest of 1 lemon

1 tablespoon Worcestershire sauce

1 serrano chili, seeded and finely minced

2 scallions, minced

1 teaspoon kosher salt

TO MAKE THE SHRIMP:

1. Combine the peppercorns, thyme, parsley, lemon, bay leaves, and salt in a large pot filled with 3 quarts of water. Bring to a boil.

2. Drop the shrimp into the water and lower the heat to a simmer, stirring occasionally. Simmer until the shrimp turn pink and curl slightly, about 4–6 minutes. Remove the shrimp from the cooking liquid and cool to room temperature. Once cool enough to handle, remove the shells from the shrimp, leaving the tails intact. Refrigerate until ready to serve.

TO MAKE THE COCKTAIL SAUCE:

3. Whisk together the ketchup, horseradish, lemon juice and zest, and Worcestershire sauce. Fold in the serrano and the scallions. Season with salt, and serve alongside the shrimp.

RICOTTA, MINT, AND SPRING PEA BRUSCHETTA

SERVES 6 | Skill Level: EASY | Cook Time: 5 mins. | Prep Time: 10 mins. | Cost: $

Bruschetta: that's Italian for something delicious on toast. Actually, I don't know what it literally means in Italian, but every bruschetta I have ever seen is something great on toast. This recipe is my way to welcome spring. It also revealed another side to the ever-fascinating Carla. That woman loves her peas! When we made this on the show, she snatched the whole bowl of peas and stuffed about a hundred in her mouth before I could rescue enough to make this recipe.

4 cups shelled English peas

1–2 teaspoons kosher salt

2 cups fresh sheep's milk ricotta cheese

Zest of 1 lemon

3 tablespoons grated Parmesan

¼ cup fresh mint leaves

Freshly ground black pepper

½ teaspoon red pepper flakes

¼ cup extra virgin olive oil

1 baguette, cut into ½-inch slices at a bias

1. Bring 1 gallon of water to a boil and add a large pinch of salt. Add the peas and blanch for about 30 seconds. Remove the peas to an ice bath.

2. To a food processor, add the ricotta, lemon zest, Parmesan, and mint. Drain the peas and add them to the food processor. Pulse just until the mixture becomes smooth, scraping down the sides from time to time.

3. Spoon the mixture into a serving bowl, crack some black pepper over the top, sprinkle with the red pepper flakes, and drizzle with extra virgin olive oil.

4. Heat a grill pan to medium-high. Brush the pieces of bread with olive oil and season with salt and pepper. Grill on each side until crisp and grill marks appear, about 1–2 minutes per side.

5. Serve each crostini topped with the pea mixture.

Stay seasonal

Eating seasonally and locally is always a good idea with fruits and vegetables. More flavor, better texture. With peas it's really important, because fresh green peas are super sweet. Leave them a few days and they get starchy.

Blanching is better

Blanching is a time-honored method for boosting green in fresh vegetables. With peas it also changes starchiness to sweetness. Spring peas are so tender and green, you really want to accent their sweetness.

CARROTS WITH FETA AND MINT

SERVES 4 | Skill Level: EASY | Cook Time: 20–30 mins. | Prep Time: 5 mins. | Cost: $

This dish is inspired by my mom, who was no doubt inspired by her mom: in other words, it's Greek. Feta cheese and mint are a classic combination with charred pan-roasted carrots. Cumin is a traditional partner for carrots as well, and so is the orange juice that I add to my vinaigrette. I leave the skins on the carrots because they really pick up the char well when the sugar in the carrots superheats in the pan. Dressing the carrots when they are hot allows them to soak up some of the vinaigrette. The flavors are so big that this recipe works as an appetizer all on its own, or as a side to roasted lamb or fish grilled over a wood fire.

1½ pounds carrots, cut into 2-inch chunks at a bias

1 teaspoon honey

2 tablespoons sherry vinegar

1 tablespoon whole cumin seeds, toasted

3 tablespoons extra virgin olive oil

Kosher salt

Freshly ground black pepper

FOR THE DRESSING:

¼ cup extra virgin olive oil

Zest and juice of 1 orange

1 tablespoon honey

1 tablespoon sherry vinegar

¼ cup mint (leaves only)

1 shallot, thinly sliced

¼ cup slivered almonds

Pinch of kosher salt

1 cup feta, crumbled, to serve

1 teaspoon orange zest, to serve

Olive oil, to serve

1. Preheat the oven to 450 °F.

2. In a mixing bowl, add the carrots and toss with the honey, vinegar, cumin seeds, and 1 tablespoon of olive oil.

3. In an oven-safe skillet over medium-high heat, heat the remaining olive oil, then add the carrots. Season generously with salt and pepper, and then toss to coat. Transfer to the oven and roast for 20 minutes, or until the carrots have caramelized and browned in spots.

4. Meanwhile, make the dressing by whisking together the extra virgin olive oil, orange juice and zest, honey, vinegar, mint leaves, shallot, and almonds. Add a pinch of salt and set aside.

5. Once the carrots have finished and cooled slightly, toss them in a large bowl with the dressing. To serve, garnish carrots with feta, orange zest, and a drizzle of olive oil.

Wonderful water

I always put a little pasta water in my pan sauce when it gets to the finishing stages. The starch in the water thickens the pan sauce so that it clings to the pasta.

Favas: to peel or not to peel?

If I'm making them on TV or in a restaurant, I peel them. At home, it's purely a question of how ambitious I feel. Most of the time I shuck the favas but don't peel each individual bean. I guess it also depends what's on TV. Peeling beans while you're watching something isn't a big deal.

SPRING VEGETABLE PASTA WITH CHIVE BREAD CRUMBS

SERVES 4 | Skill Level: EASY | Cook Time: 15 mins. | Prep Time: 10 mins. | Cost: $

Spring can't come fast enough in the Midwest. That's probably true everywhere, but all I know is that when I start to see asparagus and favas and peas in the markets in Cleveland, my spirits improve. The flowers are starting to pop. The pretty girls aren't so covered up. I can't get enough of spring or spring vegetables, so why not use them all at once? This pasta with a quick pan sauce is my version of spring training. It gets me back into cooking fresh green things. When I made this on the show, we nearly had to physically restrain Carla from rushing the serving bowl and devouring the whole thing. For sure, it's a lot for one person to eat, but Carla is a dedicated diner.

FOR THE CHIVE BREAD CRUMBS:

1 tablespoon olive oil

1 cup bread crumbs

¼ cup minced chives

Zest of 1 lemon

2 tablespoons Parmesan cheese

Salt

FOR THE SPRING PASTA:

1 pound fresh linguini pasta

Salt

2 tablespoons olive oil, plus extra to drizzle

2 cloves garlic, minced

1 bunch asparagus, chopped

½ pound fava beans, shelled and blanched

½ pound English peas, blanched

Parmesan cheese, to taste

2 tablespoons butter

1. Place a saucepan over medium-high heat and add the olive oil. Toss in the bread crumbs and cook until golden brown, about 3 minutes, stirring constantly. Remove from the heat and, in a mixing bowl, stir in the chives, zest, and the cheese. Season with salt and set aside.

2. Bring a large pot of water to a boil and add a generous pinch of salt. Cook the pasta 1 or 2 minutes less than the package instructions suggest.

3. Heat a large sauté pan over medium-high heat and add the olive oil. Once hot, add the garlic and the asparagus and season with salt.

4. Add in the fava beans and peas. Add a ladle of pasta water to the pot along with the cooked pasta. Toss to coat, and season again with salt, add some freshly grated Parmesan, the butter, and a drizzle of olive oil. Top with the chive bread crumbs and serve.

Extra virgin sometimes equals extra flavor

I use extra virgin olive oil to sauté my vegetables. Usually I don't recommend this because extra virgin (or EVOO, as cookbooks usually abbreviate it) smokes easily. But by cooking over medium heat for a short while, which is all that tender spring vegetables need, you get that extra floral whiff that only EVOO can give.

BACON, EGG, AND CHEESE CASSEROLE

SERVES 8 | Skill Level: EASY | Cook Time: 50 mins. | Prep Time: 30 mins. | Cost: $

Bacon, egg, and cheese on a biscuit always calls my name when I'm at a drive-through. That thought gave birth to this casserole. It's really perfect to serve for Sunday breakfast when you have people staying over. I start with your basic biscuit with some chives and cheese baked in. They need to be small, about the diameter of a golf ball. Then you layer in lots of bacon and lots of cheese and top with more biscuits. Finally, add the eggs and let it sit awhile so all the ingredients can get to know one another.

CHEDDAR CHIVE BISCUITS:

2 cups all-purpose flour

1 tablespoon baking powder

1 teaspoon sugar

¼ teaspoon baking soda

½ teaspoon salt

6 tablespoons unsalted butter, chilled and cut into cubes

¾ cup buttermilk

½ cup chives, chopped

¾ cup Cheddar cheese, shredded

CASSEROLE:

1 batch Cheddar Chive Biscuits

1 pound bacon, cooked and chopped

½ cup Cheddar cheese, grated

6 large eggs

1½ cups milk

½ cup chives, chopped

Salt and pepper to taste

FOR THE CHEDDAR CHIVE BISCUITS

1. Preheat the oven to 425 °F. In a large bowl, combine flour, baking powder, sugar, baking soda, and salt. Whisk until well combined. Into the dry mixture, cut in chilled cubes of butter. Texture should resemble small pebbles. Pour buttermilk over mixture, fold in chives, and gently stir to combine. Pour mixture out onto a lightly floured surface. Knead mixture just until dough comes together. Roll out dough to ⅓-inch thickness. Using a 1½-inch ring mold, cut out biscuits. Repeat process; be careful not to over-knead dough. Top each biscuit with Cheddar cheese. Place on a prepared baking sheet, bake for 8 minutes or until golden brown.

Cover up

I bake this in a medium oven and always cover my casserole with tin foil so that the eggs don't get too brown on top. You want a nice custardy interior.

FOR THE CASSEROLE

2. Lower the oven to 350 °F. Butter a 9 x 13-inch casserole dish. Halve all biscuits. Place a single layer of Cheddar Chive Biscuit halves (the bottoms) into the casserole dish. Cover the biscuits with cooked and chopped bacon. Sprinkle Cheddar cheese over the bacon layer. Place biscuit tops over the cheese. In a large bowl, whisk together eggs, milk, chives, salt, and pepper. Pour egg mixture over biscuits. Cover and refrigerate for 30 minutes, allowing the egg custard to absorb into the biscuits. Bake, covered in foil, for 35–45 minutes until set.

SPRING

135

ASPARAGUS AND GOAT CHEESE FRITTATA

| SERVES 8 TO 10 | Skill Level: EASY | Cook Time: 20 mins. | Prep Time: 10 mins. | Cost: $ |

I'm pretty religious about making a frittata every Sunday that I'm home. If you ask me what I put in a frittata, my answer is (like it is for so much in cooking): "Whatever looks good in the market." I always celebrate the arrival of spring with asparagus in my frittata. Around that time, on the banks of rivers and streams around Cleveland, you can pick wild ramps. And soon after the ramps sprout, if we are very lucky and if the weather gods have treated us right, there might even be some wild morels. I'm going to figure that you aren't planning on a foraged frittata, so stick with the asparagus.

1 dozen eggs

½ cup heavy cream

2 tablespoons unsalted butter

1 shallot, minced

1½ pounds asparagus, trimmed and cut into 2-inch pieces

2 teaspoons kosher salt

½ teaspoon coarse ground black pepper

8 ounces soft goat cheese at room temperature

2 tablespoons tarragon, chopped

1. Preheat the oven to 375 °F.

2. In a large bowl, whisk together the eggs and the heavy cream, and set aside.

3. Melt the butter in a 10-inch cast-iron skillet or a non-stick oven-safe pan over medium heat. Add the shallot to the pan and sauté for 2 minutes, then add the asparagus. Season with the salt and pepper, and cook for 3 more minutes, until the asparagus has turned bright green but has not browned.

4. Add the egg and cream mixture, and pull a rubber spatula along the bottom of the pan until the eggs begin to scramble, about 3 minutes. Once the eggs begin to set, remove the pan from the heat and sprinkle in chunks of the goat cheese and the chopped tarragon. Place the pan in the oven and cook for about 15 minutes, or until the center is set but still jiggles slightly when you shake the pan.

5. Cut the frittata into 8-10 pieces and serve.

ROMAN-STYLE ARTICHOKES

| SERVES 6 | Skill Level: EASY | Cook Time: 45 mins. | Prep Time: 20 mins. | Cost: $ |

There's nothing more Roman than artichokes braised in wine, olive oil, and seasonings, especially when you buy them all peeled and trimmed the way they do it for you in Rome. No such luck here in the States. You have to be your own artichoke trimmer. But it's really not that hard. Then pop them in the pot, toss in seasonings, some onion, garlic, fresh herbs—whatever you like—bring it to a boil, and then simmer for 15 minutes. The result: succulent, slithery, smoothness that boldly declares, "Arrivederci, Winter, Spring has finally sprung."

6 young artichokes
Juice of 2 lemons
¾ cup dry white wine
¾ cup boiling water
¾ cup extra virgin olive oil
Pinch of kosher salt
¼ bunch fresh parsley leaves
¼ bunch fresh mint leaves
2 cloves garlic, finely chopped
½ red onion, sliced
1 teaspoon chili flakes

1. Trim the artichokes of their tough outer leaves and cut in half. Remove the fuzzy choke with a spoon and place immediately in a bowl filled with water and the juice of one of the lemons.

2. Arrange all the chokes in a deep pan that keeps them close together.

3. Add the wine, boiling water, oil, and a pinch of salt.

4. Sprinkle the parsley, mint, garlic, red onion, and chili flakes over the top.

5. Squeeze the other lemon over the top, cover, and simmer on the stovetop for 25-30 minutes. Serve hot or at room temperature.

Tip

The braising liquid picks up wonderful flavor from the artichokes. Don't toss it. Use it to braise fennel, carrots, onions, string beans—whatever vegetable strikes your fancy.

Staying green: the acid test

To keep your nicely trimmed artichokes from turning gray, put them in an ice water bath with lemon juice or vinegar.

SPRING

137

GRILLED SALMON WITH SHAVED CARROTS AND PEANUT SALAD

SERVES 4 | **Skill Level: EASY** | **Cook Time: 5 mins.** | **Prep Time: 5 mins.** | **Cost: $**

I made this when Hugh Jackman visited The Chew. *He said this combination of fresh salmon, fresh vegetables, and nuts is something his coach recommends when he's training for the role of Wolverine. That's some serious training! Cooking salmon to rare or medium rare is perfect for people who don't love "fishy fish." It's a lot milder and more buttery. Serving up raw vegetables with fish, poultry, or meat, is one of my favorite things and it definitely keeps the prep time down.*

4 6-ounce fillets of salmon, skin on

2 teaspoons salt

½ teaspoon fresh ground black pepper

¼ cup, plus 2 tablespoons extra virgin olive oil

3 medium organic carrots, peeled

1 tablespoon cumin seeds, toasted

1 bunch scallions, thinly sliced

1 cup mint leaves

½ cup toasted peanuts

2 tablespoons red wine vinegar

1. Season the salmon with 1 teaspoon salt and ½ teaspoon pepper, then brush with 2 tablespoons olive oil and grill for 2 minutes per side.

2. While the salmon is grilling, shave the carrots with a peeler or mandolin and add to a large bowl. Add the cumin seeds, scallions, mint, and peanuts.

3. In a separate bowl, whisk together the remaining olive oil and red wine vinegar, and add to the shaved vegetables.

4. Season liberally with salt and pepper. Place the salmon on a platter and top with the shaved carrot salad.

Don't flip out over flipping

The key to making fish on the grill is not to flip it too quickly or it will stick. For a piece of fish like this salmon, about 1½ inches thick, if you leave it for 2 minutes, it will crisp up nicely and not stick or tear when you flip it.

Roast and toast your spices

This recipe calls for cumin. With all aromatic spices, you'll find if you pan roast just before you use them, you release all the delicious, flavorful, fragrant oils that create intense flavor.

Sliced fingers not recommended!

All of us on *The Chew* love to use the Japanese vegetable slicer known as a mandolin (or Benriner). It makes beautiful, even slices. One word of caution: They're sharp! Definitely use the hand guard that comes with it. After a while, you may feel you are okay without extra precautions. If you do . . . concentrate and never take your eyes off what you're doing. I'm speaking from experience, and I have the cuts to prove it.

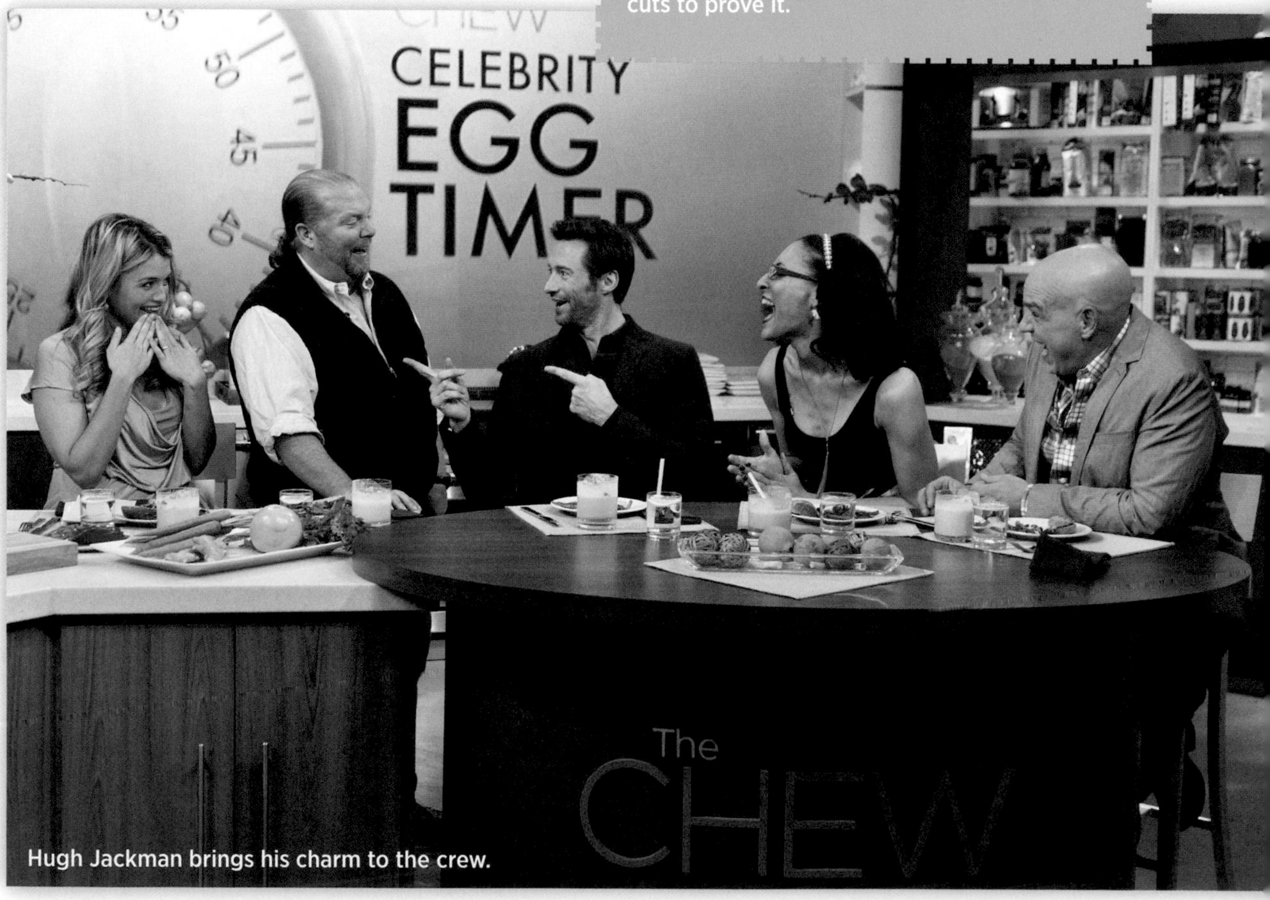
CELEBRITY
EGG
TIMER
The
CHEW

Hugh Jackman brings his charm to the crew.

BEER-BATTERED FISH AND CHIPS

SERVES 4 | **Skill Level: EASY** | **Cook Time: 8–10 mins.** | **Prep Time: 20 mins.** | **Cost: $**

Fish and chips are about the most favorite foods in England, Scotland, and Ireland. America sure has millions of people with that heritage. Still, many people have a fear of frying. There's no reason. If you make your batter right, get the oil to the correct temperature (about 360 °F), and don't over fry, you will have a crunchy crust and succulent fish. Just follow these instructions and I give you my triple money-back guarantee that it will turn out great. Wait . . . there's more! As a bonus, I'll toss in my secret to waking up the flavor in your batter: grate in some orange zest.

4 cups Wondra flour, plus 1 cup for dredging

1 tablespoon baking powder

½ teaspoon baking soda

2 tablespoons cornstarch

3 eggs

1½ cups milk

¾ cup wheat beer

Kosher salt, to taste

1 tablespoon chives, minced

Zest of 1 orange

2 quarts vegetable oil, for frying

1½ pounds cod, cut into small pieces for kids and larger ones for adults

Lemon wedges, to serve

Malt vinegar, to serve

Potato chips, to serve

1. In a medium bowl, stir together the flour, baking powder, baking soda, and cornstarch.

2. In a large bowl, beat together the eggs and milk. Whisk in the beer. Stir this wet mixture into the flour mixture. Season with salt and add the chives and orange zest.

3. In an electric deep fryer or a heavy saucepan, heat the oil to 360 °F.

4. Season the fish liberally with salt and dust with flour. Coat the fish in batter, and submerge in the hot oil. Fry in batches until golden brown, about 4–5 minutes.

5. Remove the fish to a paper towel–lined plate and season with a little more salt. Serve with lemon wedges, malt vinegar, and potato chips

Dry and wet

For smooth, lumpless batter, mix your wet ingredients first and then add to the dry ingredients. This works for all batters, including pancakes. And speaking of dry, make sure to pat the fish dry before battering.

Frying: the golden rule

Fry only until the crust turns light golden, not dark brown. When it does, immediately drain on paper towels and season with salt.

Size matters

For kids and other picky eaters, I recommend making the fillet pieces small enough to pick up with a toothpick (although you are allowed to use a fork if you like). The point is, if it's just a mouthful, people are more willing to try it, and once they've had that first moist, crunchy, flaky piece, the sale is made. They'll be back for more. Count on it.

MOM'S CHICKEN WITH SAFFRON, OLIVES, AND ONIONS

SERVES 6 | **Skill Level: EASY** | **Cook Time: 40–45 mins.** | **Prep Time: 15 mins.** | **Cost: $$**

"My mom used to make . . ." That's a phrase we all use, and for each of us it brings up the strongest and often the most pleasant memories. You may forget who was the king of England in 1602, or where Columbus set sail from, but no one forgets their mom's pancakes, or meatloaf, or, in the case of this recipe, my mother's chicken with saffron. She made it all the time when we were in junior high and high school. I can literally taste and smell that dish just by saying the words. It's not very demanding. It just requires patience. Let your onions caramelize over low heat for a good long while. Then when you add liquid, it's just a little at a time. You want a good thick broth, not a thin soupy gravy.

8 chicken thighs

Kosher salt, to taste

Cayenne pepper, to taste

2 tablespoons extra virgin olive oil

4 yellow onions, thinly sliced

1 tablespoon all-purpose flour

½ cup chicken stock

1 teaspoon saffron

2 bay leaves

½ cup pitted Moroccan olives

3 tablespoons cilantro, minced, for garnish

1 scallion, chopped, for garnish

1 pomegranate, separated into seeds, for garnish

1. Season the chicken pieces with salt and cayenne.

2. Heat a large Dutch oven over medium-high heat and add the oil. When the oil is hot, add the chicken and brown, cooking for 4–6 minutes on each side. Remove the chicken to a plate and set aside.

3. Add the onions and cook for another 8–10 minutes, until soft and browned. Stir in the flour and season again with salt and cayenne, depending on how hot you like it.

4. Stir in the chicken stock, and add the chicken pieces back to the pan. Top with the saffron, bay leaves, and olives.

5. Bring to a simmer, cover, and reduce the heat to medium. Stir occasionally and cook for about 20–25 minutes, or until the chicken is tender.

6. Serve on a large platter and finish with chopped cilantro and scallions, and sprinkle with pomegranate seeds.

BIG TURKEY MEATBALL SUBS

SERVES 6 | Skill Level: EASY | Cook Time: 35 mins. | Prep Time: 25 mins. | Cost: $

The secret to making great meatballs isn't necessarily the meat. Let's take it for granted that you start with a mound of beautiful ground meat, not too lean (or you will end up with something that's chewy, rubbery, and no fun). It's what you mix it with that makes all the difference. In this case, I start with a mix of turkey and sausage and then I add in some freshly grated Pecorino cheese, eggs, crunchy bread crumbs, and milk. Then—very important—mix thoroughly. What does thoroughly mean? When you think it is mixed enough, give it another 10 seconds. The result is a meatball that holds its shape but is tender and moist. This is one of those recipes that's ideal for a potluck meal because all that needs to be done is reheat. No on-site fussing required.

2 cups panko bread crumbs

1½–2 cups milk

2 pounds ground turkey

4 ounces prosciutto di Parma, cut into ⅛-inch dice

8 ounces sweet Italian sausage, casings removed

3 large eggs

½ cup freshly grated Pecorino Romano

¼ cup freshly grated Parmigiano-Reggiano

¾ cup Italian parsley, finely chopped

Several gratings of nutmeg

½ cup extra virgin olive oil

Salt

Freshly ground black pepper

2 cups Mario's Basic Tomato Sauce (see page 30)

6 soft Italian rolls

12 slices provolone cheese

1. Soak the bread crumbs in the milk for 5 minutes. Strain out the bread crumbs and set aside, reserving the milk.

2. In a large bowl, combine the turkey, prosciutto, sausage, bread crumbs, eggs, reserved milk, ¼ cup of the Pecorino, the Parmigiano, ½ cup of the parsley, the nutmeg, and ¼ cup of the olive oil, and mix very gently with your hands. Season with salt and pepper.

3. Form the mixture into 1 ½ -inch balls and set aside.

4. Add the tomato sauce to a pan and bring to a boil. Place the meatballs in the sauce and return to a boil, then lower the heat and simmer for 30 minutes.

5. Lay 2 slices of provolone in each roll and top with 3 or 4 meatballs. Garnish with the remaining Pecorino and parsley sprinkled over the top.

Entertaining with Pizzazz

HAVE YOU EVER DECIDED to throw a party and got that icky feeling inside like you don't want to throw this party anymore because it's going to cost too much? And that's before you buy the drinks? I've got five easy and inexpensive tabletop ideas where you save money by doing it yourself.

Who needs tablecloths?

The bummer about tablecloths is they can really be an expensive number and you've got to be satisfied with what the designers want you to have. You can express yourself and save your wallet if you go to the fabric store and buy some fabric by the yard. It ranges anywhere from five to twenty dollars per yard.

Okay, I can hear you saying, "What about those nasty frayed edges?"

And I answer, "Hey, you're getting a bargain, don't complain." Some iron-on tape makes for a fast and easy hem that will last through anything, except maybe a toga party. While you're shopping, keep an eye out for smaller remnants. They make great one-of-a-kind placemats and runners.

Color scheming

Now that you have your tablecloth, think like a designer. How will the rest of your décor pick up on the color theme? Suppose you have a checked tablecloth with a lot of blue in it. It's telling you something.

Now grab some wine bottles from the recycle bin, clean off the labels, and then spray-paint them blue. Voilà! You now have custom-colored candleholders that give a coordinated look to your room. I find that high-gloss paint gives some extra sparkle and reflects the light of the candles.

Mirror magic

The next time you go to a yard sale, keep your eyes open for antique mirrors. Clean them up and they make great trays for hors d'oeuvres, cheeses, and fruits. It adds some sparkle, shine, and romance to a table setting, especially with the candles.

Gourd-geous

I can hear your groans at my pun even as I write. I'm talking about gourds—dried squashes. People have been using them as table décor forever, and they'll get no argument from me, but if you spray-paint them a high-gloss black (again to reflect light), then you have these knobby odd-shaped weird things that look interesting on the serving table.

Make a new friend

Flowers make everyone happy. *Make friends with your local florist.* Then drop by at the end of the day and see if you can have the castaways—the blooms that might not make it through tomorrow. They'll be just fine for your party and won't cost a stem and a leg. I wouldn't worry too much about the fine points of flower arranging. I don't. The flowers themselves are beautiful to begin with, so stick them in a bunch of little vases and Mother Nature will be the best decorator's assistant you ever had.

The Chew crew celebrates Mama T's birthday.

PAELLA

SERVES 8 | Skill Level: EASY | Cook Time: 40–45 mins. | Prep Time: 15 mins. | Cost: $$

Paella is one of those words that might as well have a blinking light and sound effects coming off the page. Like a burger, or pizza, or cappuccino, it makes me feel good. When you use the best fresh seafood, succulent dark meat chicken, and savory sausage, you've got my attention. The ability of rice to suck up and marry those flavors is what makes paella so comforting and satisfying. I always caution people that making paella is not like making risotto. When you make risotto, you are looking for ultimate creaminess in the rice, constantly stirring as it cooks. With paella, although you get some creaminess, if you don't bother it too much while it's cooking and let it work its magic, you get a beautiful crunchy crust called socarrat. Flavorful crunch is always a crowd pleaser. Just watch what your kids go for when you put anything with crunch in front of them.

1 tablespoon olive oil

½ pound Spanish chorizo

8 chicken thighs

Salt, to taste

Freshly ground black pepper, to taste

1 yellow onion, chopped

2 cups short-grain rice

¼ cup white wine

1 heaping teaspoon saffron threads

1½ cups San Marzano tomatoes, drained and chopped

5 cups chicken stock

12 mussels, debearded and scrubbed

12 littleneck clams, scrubbed

1 pound large shrimp

1 cup frozen peas

¼ cup flat-leaf parsley, chopped, for garnish

1. Preheat the oven to 350 °F.

2. In a paella pan or a large high-sided skillet, heat the olive oil over medium heat. Add the chorizo and cook until it has browned and rendered some of its fat, about 3 minutes. Remove the chorizo from the pan and set aside on a plate.

3. Season the chicken with salt and pepper and add to the pan, browning for 3–4 minutes per side. Remove to the plate with the chorizo.

4. Add the onion and cook until translucent, about 5 minutes.

5. Add the rice and toast, stirring to coat the rice in the oil. Deglaze the pan with the white wine and add the saffron and the chopped tomatoes.

6. Slowly add the stock, stirring as you add. Season again with salt, and add the chicken and chorizo back to the pan. Nestle the mussels, clams, and shrimp into the rice. Sprinkle the peas all around and cover with foil and place in the oven.

7. Cook for 25–30 minutes, or until the clams and mussels have opened and the chicken has cooked through. Remove from the oven and take straight to the table. Garnish with chopped parsley and enjoy.

Saffronific

Saffron is pretty pricey. But when you realize that it takes more than 100,000 crocus blossoms to make a pound—and they are all picked by hand—then you can understand the price. Still, a little goes a very long way. A pinch of saffron only costs a couple of dollars and it makes a big difference in flavor. Go for it!

CURRIED CHICKEN AND DUMPLINGS

SERVES 6 | **Skill Level: EASY** | **Cook Time: 25–30 mins.** | **Prep Time: 20 mins.** | **Cost: $**

Look in any American recipe book from the last 150 years and you are going to find some version of curried chicken and some form of chicken and dumplings. I think they're telling us something: these are two great ways to make chicken, which I have combined here into one super chicken recipe. One of the things I love about it is that once you've bought the chicken, you probably have everything else in your pantry and your vegetable drawer. I mean, who doesn't have a can of chicken broth on the shelf? And I'm willing to bet that you have a tin of curry powder that's been hanging around your spice shelf since 1776. And if you are like me, then you probably have some coconut milk too. If you don't, get some. It's so good in so many ways.

FOR THE CHICKEN:

2 tablespoons olive oil

1 cup all-purpose flour, for dusting

Salt, to taste

Pepper, to taste

6 boneless, skinless chicken thighs

1 onion, diced

3 stalks celery, diced

3 carrots, diced

2 tablespoons curry powder

½ teaspoon cayenne pepper

4 cups chicken stock

1 12-ounce can coconut milk

1 cup cooked chickpeas

FOR THE DUMPLINGS:

1½ cups chickpea flour

¼ cup all-purpose flour

⅓ teaspoon salt

1 teaspoon baking soda

1 cup Greek yogurt

¼ cup fresh parsley, chopped

¼ cup fresh cilantro, chopped

1. Preheat the oven to 350 °F.

2. Heat the olive oil in a Dutch oven. Season the flour with salt and pepper, and dredge the chicken in the flour, shaking off any excess. Add the chicken to the pan and brown on both sides, about 2 minutes per side. Remove the chicken to a plate and set aside.

3. Add the onion, celery, and carrots to the pot, and cook for 3 minutes. Stir in the curry powder and cayenne pepper.

4. Add the chicken broth, coconut milk, chickpeas, and browned chicken, and bring to a simmer.

5. Place the dumpling ingredients in a mixing bowl and stir until combined.

6. Dollop tablespoons of the dumpling mixture into the pot.

7. Place into the oven uncovered for 15–20 minutes, or until the dumplings are golden brown and cooked through.

Dense isn't dumb

Coconut milk is what food scientists call "nutrient dense": it's full of things that are good for you, particularly protein. I love it in fish stews with poultry, and it's an interesting, flavorful base for stewing vegetables.

THE CHEW

148

GREEK EASTER LEG OF LAMB

SERVES 12 | Skill Level: **EASY** | Cook Time: 1½–2 hrs. | Prep Time: 20 mins. | Cost: $

Inactive Prep Time: 24 hrs.

A lot of our viewers Twittered and Facebooked us asking how to make lamb for Easter. Being of Greek heritage, I thought lamb on this happy and holy day was the 11th Commandment. We always made a whole lamb on a spit. We'd baste it with lemon and oregano and olive oil. It was amazing!!! It's also something that most folks aren't going to tackle at home, so here is a leg of lamb recipe that I think delivers a lot of the flavor and texture of my family's Easter lamb.

Apart from having a great piece of meat, using an herb and spice rub that sits on the lamb for 24 hours or at least overnight raises the level of flavor to the peak of Mt. Olympus.

FOR THE ROASTED LAMB:

6 shallots, minced

4 cloves garlic, minced

¼ cup fresh rosemary

¼ cup fresh oregano

2 tablespoons sugar

2 tablespoons coriander seeds, toasted and crushed

1 tablespoon crushed red pepper flakes

1½ tablespoons kosher salt

1 6-pound bone-in leg of lamb

Rosemary sprigs (optional)

3 tablespoons olive oil

TO MAKE THE ROASTED LAMB:

1. Mix together in a medium bowl the shallots, garlic, spices, and herbs. Rub the mixture all over the surface of the lamb. Place in a large glass baking dish, cover with plastic wrap, and refrigerate overnight. Remove the lamb from the baking dish, rinse off the seasonings, and pat dry. Let the lamb sit at room temperature for 1 hour. Preheat the oven to 375 °F.

2. Heat a roasting pan or large ovenproof skillet over medium heat. Add olive oil and heat until it begins to smoke and then add the lamb and brown on all sides, 7–10 minutes. Transfer the lamb, fat side up, to a roasting rack set into a roasting pan. If you have extra rosemary, lay the sprigs over the lamb with a drizzle of olive oil over the top. Roast until the lamb reaches an internal temperature of 140 °F, about 1½ hours.

3. Remove the lamb from the pan and set it aside to rest for 20 minutes.

4. Slice and serve with the tzatziki sauce and roasted potatoes.

FOR THE ROASTED POTATOES:

4 pounds unpeeled fingerling potatoes, rinsed and halved lengthwise

½ cup olive oil

Salt

Freshly ground black pepper

1 cup extra virgin olive oil

½ cup fresh lemon juice

6 tablespoons fresh dill, chopped

4 teaspoons lemon peel, finely grated

24 cloves garlic, sliced

FOR THE TZATZIKI SAUCE:

2 cups Greek yogurt

1 cucumber

Kosher salt, to taste

Juice and zest of 2 lemons

2 tablespoons fresh mint, chopped

1 tablespoon garlic, minced

1 tablespoon shallot, minced

Freshly ground black pepper, to taste

TO MAKE THE POTATOES:

5. Position a rack in the top third and a rack in the bottom third of the oven, and preheat to 375 °F. Spray two large-rimmed baking sheets with nonstick spray. Toss the potatoes with ½ cup olive oil in a large bowl. Sprinkle generously with salt and freshly ground black pepper. Spread the potatoes in a single layer on the baking sheets, dividing equally. Roast 30 minutes, tossing the potatoes halfway through.

6. Meanwhile, whisk the extra virgin olive oil, lemon juice, dill, and lemon peel in a small bowl to blend for dressing. Toss the garlic and 2 tablespoons dressing in another small bowl. Divide the garlic mixture between the baking sheets and toss with the potatoes; reverse the baking sheets and continue to roast until the potatoes are tender and brown around the edges, about 15 minutes longer.

7. Toss the roasted potatoes in a large bowl with the remaining dressing to coat and serve.

TO MAKE THE TZATZIKI SAUCE:

8. Put the yogurt in a cheesecloth-lined strainer set over a bowl and let drain for 24 hours in the refrigerator. Peel and dice the cucumber, sprinkle it with salt, and place in a strainer at room temperature for 2–3 hours to drain.

9. Stir together the yogurt, cucumber, lemon juice and zest, mint, garlic, and shallot in a medium bowl until thoroughly combined. Season to taste with salt and pepper.

Great on the grill too

Grilling the lamb on a charcoal grill is a way to get wood fire crustiness that pumps up the flavor even more. With big pieces of meat like this, you want a hot fire in one part of the grill and a very low one in the other. You start out by searing the meat all over on the hot side of the grill and then, to finish cooking, move it over to the cooler side, covering it and fiddling with the coals and the vents to keep the heat at about 350 °F.

POT ROAST WITH SHAVED CARROT SALAD

| SERVES 8 | Skill Level: EASY | Cook Time: 2–2½ hrs. | Prep Time: 20 mins. | Cost: $ |

Here we have comfort food that reflects my M&M roots—that stands for Mediterranean and Midwestern. A beautifully browned pot roast is the Mediterranean part. The crunchy, tangy carrot salad that cuts through the big, strong meaty flavor is the kind of taste and flavor matchup we love in the Midwest. Braised in beer and apple cider, and given some extra meaty oomph from bacon, it brings back memories of cool spring days when the hills are finally shaking off their winter coat and the first hints of green brighten the Ohio countryside.

FOR THE POT ROAST:

3 tablespoons extra virgin olive oil

1 3-pound brisket

Salt, to taste

Pepper, to taste

2 tablespoons coriander, toasted and crushed

½ pound bacon, diced

1 red onion, sliced

2 cloves garlic, smashed

2 carrots, peeled and roughly chopped

1 jalapeño, split

1 12-ounce bottle beer

1½–2 cups water

12 ounces apple cider

FOR THE SALAD:

4 carrots, shaved

1 bunch mint leaves

1 bunch scallions, sliced

2 tablespoons red wine vinegar

3 tablespoons olive oil

Salt, to taste

Pepper, to taste

1. Preheat the oven to 325 °F.

2. Heat a large Dutch oven over medium-high heat and add the olive oil. When hot, season the brisket with salt, pepper, and coriander and add to the pan. Sear on both sides until brown, about 3 minutes per side. Remove the brisket to a large plate and add the bacon to the pan. Cook the bacon until crispy, about 5 minutes. Once cooked, remove from pan and set aside.

3. Add the onion, garlic, carrots, and jalapeño pepper to the pan, and sauté until tender, about 3 more minutes. Season with salt and pepper. Stir in beer, water, and the apple cider. Add the brisket and the bacon back to the pan. Bring to a boil, cover, and place into the oven. Cook the brisket for 2–2½ hours at 325 °F, until tender.

4. For the salad, place the carrots, mint, and scallions in a large bowl with the vinegar. Season with salt and pepper and toss to coat. Drizzle in the olive oil and toss.

5. Slice the brisket and serve with the carrot salad. Use any leftover brisket to make Bahn Mi (see page 153).

BAHN MI

SERVES 4 TO 6, depending on the amount of leftovers	Skill Level: EASY	Cook Time: 20 mins.

Prep Time: 20 mins. | COST: $

Whenever you make a brisket or a pot roast, you are pretty much guaranteed that there will be leftovers. If you want something more exciting than reheating in the microwave, these sliders make for a completely new and delicious use of yesterday's beef.

Leftover pot roast from Pot Roast with Shaved Carrot Salad (see page 152)

FOR THE PICKLES:

1 cup rice wine vinegar

2 tablespoons sugar

1 bunch radishes, thinly sliced

2 carrots, julienned

FOR THE CHILI MAYO:

½ cup mayonnaise

1 tablespoon Sriracha

8–16 soft slider buns, to serve

1 English cucumber, thinly sliced, to serve

1 bunch cilantro leaves, to serve

1 bunch mint leaves, to garnish

2 scallions, sliced on the bias, to garnish

1. Place the leftover brisket and all of its juices into a baking dish and back into the oven at 350 °F until warmed through, about 20 minutes.

2. For the pickles, heat the vinegar and sugar together until the sugar is dissolved, and pour over the radishes and carrots. Set aside to cool. Meanwhile, combine the mayonnaise and Sriracha and set aside.

3. To serve, place some of the shredded brisket on the bottom half of a bun, and top with pickles, cucumber, and cilantro. Spread some of the mayo on the other half of the bun and top. Garnish with the mint and scallions.

Get down with brown

A lot of people think that when you brown the outside of a piece of meat, you are "sealing in the juices," but scientists tell us that you are not really sealing in anything. What you are doing, though, is one of the most wonderful things in cuisine. They call it the Maillard Reaction, and it's responsible for that brown crust full of beautiful flavors that you get when you take the time to get the meat good and brown over high heat. Don't be shy here. We're talking brown, not a light tan.

SPRING

153

RED VELVET CAKE

SERVES 12 | Skill Level: EASY | Cook Time: 1½ hrs. | Prep Time: 20 mins. | Cost: $

Who doesn't like winning an election? I sure was happy when viewers were asked to vote for a favorite recipe, because my Red Velvet Cake came in first! That's saying something when you consider the runners-up were hush puppies and waffles, which are two of my favorites. Hey, I'm a southern girl, and the southern part will always love her hush puppies, while the girl in me remembers waffles so fondly. People say this is a sexy cake (Clinton does, but he says that about everything except maybe boiled turnips). The color red no doubt has a lot to do with its sexy reputation: think Valentine's Day. This is a fun cake to make with kids, and I guarantee that after eating this cake, most kids will be happy to have learned that beets aren't yucky!

FOR THE CAKE:

Butter, for the cake pans

2½ cups all-purpose flour, plus more for the cake pans

1½ cups sugar

1 teaspoon baking soda

1 teaspoon salt

2 tablespoons cocoa powder

½ cup vegetable oil

¾ cup buttermilk

½ cup roasted beet puree (recipe follows)

2 eggs at room temperature

2 tablespoons red food coloring

1 teaspoon white vinegar

1 teaspoon vanilla extract

FOR THE FROSTING:

16 ounces cream cheese at room temperature

1 stick butter at room temperature

2 cups white chocolate chips, melted

1 teaspoon vanilla

2 cups powdered sugar

1. Place 2 large red beets in a piece of foil and season with salt. Top with olive oil and a splash of water and roast in the oven until a knife or skewer comes out with ease when inserted into the beet. This should take around 25–30 minutes. Remove the beets and set aside to cool just enough to handle. Peel the beets and place into a blender with any remaining juices and puree.

2. Preheat oven to 350 °F. Butter and flour two 9-inch round cake pans. Line with parchment. In the bowl of a standing mixer, combine the dry ingredients. Mix for 30 seconds with a paddle attachment.

3. In a separate bowl, combine the wet ingredients. In two parts, pour the wet ingredients into the mixer. Mix on medium speed until combined. Do not overmix. Pour the batter into the prepared pans. Bake on the center rack for 35 minutes or until a toothpick inserted in the center comes out clean. Cool for 10 minutes, then turn out on a wire rack. Cool cakes completely.

4. Meanwhile, beat the cream cheese and butter in a large bowl with an electric mixer until combined. Add the melted chocolate and vanilla, and then continue to mix until incorporated. Next, slowly add the sugar, beating until the frosting is light and fluffy.

FOR THE ROASTED BEET PUREE:

2 large beets

¼ teaspoon salt

1 tablespoon olive oil

splash of water

5. Cut each cake in half horizontally to make four layers. Frost the top of each layer, then sides, finishing with the top.

SEBADAS

| SERVES 8 | Skill Level: MODERATE | Cook Time: 15 mins. | Prep Time: 30 mins. | Cost: $ |

Inactive Prep Time: 1 hr.

Sebadas are fried raviolis with a sweet stuffing: just imagining that combo makes you want to pick up your fork. I make sebadas on the sweet side as a dessert, but in Sardinia, where the sebada originated, it was originally served as a savory course. Depending on how much honey you use, you can go either way, but I love them best as a dessert fritter. Chestnut honey, if you can find it, has a nutty, floral perfume that pairs up magically with fresh ricotta and yogurt. If you have a farmers' market nearby, pick up some fresh goat's milk yogurt.

Turn the page and see Daphne's healthier version. At least she says it's healthier. I think it's just the difference between her Turkish ancestors and my Italian peeps.

2 cups sheep's milk ricotta

Zest of 2 lemons

1 egg

1 cup yogurt

¼ cup sugar

1 cup all-purpose flour

½ cup bench flour

1 cup superfine semolina

½ cup warm milk

4 ounces butter, softened

2 cups olive oil

Powdered sugar, to garnish

1 cup chestnut honey, to serve

1. In a mixing bowl, stir together the ricotta, lemon zest, egg, yogurt, and sugar until well blended.

2. In another mixing bowl, place both flours and the semolina in a well.

3. In a small saucepan, stir together the milk and butter until butter is melted. Pour into the well of flour and incorporate wet into dry to form a dough. Knead the dough for 1 minute, form a ball, then wrap and refrigerate for 1 hour.

4. In a 12- to 14-inch frying pan, heat the oil to 375 °F.

5. With a pasta roller, roll out the pastry to ¼ inch thick. Cut 20 3½-inch rounds out of the pastry. Place 2 tablespoons cheese mixture on 10 rounds, and cover each like a sandwich. Press the edges together to seal, and fry in the oil until golden brown, about 1 minute. Remove and drain on paper towels.

6. Sprinkle with powdered sugar and serve with warm honey.

SWEET PHYLLO PACKETS

SERVES 8 | Skill Level: EASY | Cook Time: 15 mins. | Prep Time: 15 mins. | Cost: $

All of us on The Chew—*and that includes the crew and the audience—really love Mario's Sebadas. Here's a version with less calories from fat, white flour, and sugar. I realize that you're not going to make a pastry with no fat, no flour, and no sweetener: Why bother? The big difference here is Mario's recipe has a rich filling in a heavy dough, while I make a slightly less sweetened ricotta filling inside of wafer-thin phyllo dough, and then I bake instead of frying. You're always cutting down on calories from fat when you bake instead of fry. If you count calories, mine have 600 calories less. If you can get true dessert satisfaction with fewer calories, it's definitely worth thinking about.*

2 cups sheep's milk ricotta

1 egg

2 tablespoons honey

1 teaspoon vanilla

Pinch of salt

1 package phyllo dough, thawed

4 ounces butter, melted

1. Preheat the oven to 350 °F.

2. In a mixing bowl, stir together the ricotta, egg, honey, vanilla, and salt until well blended.

3. Lay out the phyllo sheets, two at a time, with the shortest side closest to you, and brush with butter. Cut the phyllo vertically into three equal pieces. Place 2 tablespoons of the mixture at the end closest to you, and fold the corner upward to make a triangle. Continue folding all the way up (you should have a triangular packet).

4. Place the packet on a sheet pan and brush with a little more butter. Once all of the packets are made, place the sheet pan into the oven and cook until golden brown, about 15 minutes. Remove from the oven and transfer to a platter. Drizzle a little extra honey over the packets.

Agave—sweeter than sugar

If honey isn't your cup of tea, try some agave sugar: nectar is made from the heart of the agave cactus, which is the same plant that provides the raw material for tequila. Ounce for ounce, it is sweeter than table sugar and vegans often use it as a substitute for honey. I like it because it's all natural. If you keep track of such things, it has a lower glycemic index than many sweeteners, so it spikes your blood sugar less than refined sugar. Still, even without resorting to a long chart, you want to be mindful of how much sugar of any kind you consume.

COCONUT PECAN POUND CAKE

SERVES 8 to 10 | **Skill Level: EASY** | **Cook Time: 1 hr. 10 mins.** | **Prep Time: 10 mins.** | **Cost: $**

For pure knockout flavor, nothing on this whole planet gets my vote like this cake. My grandmother made it every year at Christmas. I do the same. It is worth every calorie—and there are plenty of them, so don't make it every day as my Chew *family took great delight in pointing out:*

Clinton said, "When you give this as a gift, you're basically saying, 'Here's 5 pounds right on the belly.'"

And Michael chimed in, "You may think you're giving the gift of love, but what you are really giving is a gym membership."

Oh, well, I guess it was National Pile on the Health Guru Day. I don't mind. If you can't tease your family, then who can you tease? I look at this cake as a gift of love. How many gifts do you give that end up cluttering the closet a year later? This one gets eaten in a day. It rings all the bells: it's appreciated, it brings back warm memories of childhood, and—here's the kicker—it's eighty-five cents a serving.

FOR THE CAKE:

2 cups sugar

1 cup unsalted butter

4 eggs

3 cups flour

½ teaspoon baking powder

½ teaspoon salt

1 cup buttermilk

1 cup unsweetened flaked coconut

1 cup pecans, chopped

FOR THE GLAZE:

½ cup water

2 tablespoons salted butter

1 cup sugar

Powdered sugar, for dusting

TO MAKE THE CAKE:

1. Preheat the oven to 350 °F.

2. In a large bowl, combine the sugar and butter and beat with an electric mixer until light and fluffy, approximately 3 minutes. Add in the eggs one at a time, until combined.

3. Combine the flour, baking powder, and salt in a separate bowl.

4. Add the dry ingredients, alternating with the buttermilk, in three parts to the batter and mix gently, until just moistened. Stir in the coconut and pecans. Pour the batter into a pound cake mold. Bake for 60 minutes, or until a knife inserted in the center comes out clean.

TO MAKE THE GLAZE:

5. Five minutes before the cake is finished baking, make the glaze. Combine the water, butter, and sugar in a saucepan, and bring to a boil. Reduce heat and cook for 5 minutes.

6. Slowly pour half the syrup over the cake, invert the cake onto a serving plate, and pour the remaining syrup over the top. Dust with powdered sugar. Let sit for 10 minutes, and eat warm!

BANANA PUDDIN

| SERVES 6 | Skill Level: EASY | Cook Time: 10 mins. | Prep Time: 10 mins. | Cost: $ |

Inactive Cook Time: 2 hrs.

If you're from the South and you've been to a church supper, or a barbecue, or a tailgate, then you have had banana puddin. That's not a spelling error. I was almost a grown woman before I realized there is a g at the end of pudding. That's the way we talk where I come from. No recipe could be easier or creamier . . . or yummier. The classic calls for vanilla wafers, but I often use shortbread, which is even richer. I also like to give mine a little kick with some rum.

1 cup sugar

⅛ teaspoon salt

⅓ cup all-purpose flour

2 cups milk (low fat or whole)

2 eggs, separated

2 bananas, very ripe and mashed, plus 2 bananas, ripe but firm, sliced

2 tablespoons butter, softened

1½ teaspoons vanilla

About 44 small vanilla shortbread cookies

2 cups whipped cream

1 teaspoon rum

Zest of 1 lemon

1. Combine ¾ cup granulated sugar, salt, and flour in a medium bowl. Slowly stir milk into dry mixture.

2. Put the mixture on top of a double boiler over simmering water, and cook until the mixture begins to thicken, about 5 minutes.

3. Beat the egg yolks and mashed bananas in a small bowl, then briskly stir a small amount of the hot milk mixture (about ½ cup).

4. Add the egg-milk mixture into the hot mixture on top of the double boiler, and stir in the butter and vanilla. Cook until mixture thickens again, about 5 more minutes.

5. Place a layer of vanilla shortbread cookies in an 11-by-7-inch baking dish (or any other shape 2-quart shallow baking dish). Add a layer of sliced bananas. Continue layering until all the cookies and banana slices are used. Pour the pudding mixture over top, and place in the refrigerator to cool (at least 2 hours, and up to overnight).

6. When cooled completely and ready to serve, in a bowl, whip the remaining ¼ cup sugar into the heavy cream. Mix in the rum and lemon zest, and whip until soft peaks form. Top the pudding with whipped cream.

Temper, temper

It is so important that you temper the eggs when you add in the hot flour, sugar, and milk mixture. Think about getting into a hot tub. You'd never jump right in. You'd dip your toe and then slowly work your way in. It's the same idea when you temper ingredients. Take your time. With Banana Puddin, this means that you gradually warm the eggs so that they don't scramble and separate from the other ingredients. An easy way to do this is to slowly add the hot milk mixture to the eggs and bananas. When the bowl starts to feel warm, the eggs are tempered and you can go ahead and combine the rest of the hot milk mixture with the rest of the ingredients.

MINT JULEP

SERVES 1 | Skill Level: EASY | Cook Time: 10 mins. | Prep Time: 5 mins. | Cost: $

This is the traditional cocktail that they serve at the Kentucky Derby. It's a great drink to usher in spring and summer: a beautiful horse race, people in their warm weather finery, and a cold, delicious glassful of good cheer. If you can't make it to the Derby, it's perfect at a slightly fancy backyard party. Most of the time when people come over for a barbecue, they're wearing their plaid shorts and a wifebeater. Sometimes it's just nice to say on an invitation: "A slightly fancy barbecue."

Crushed ice

2 ounces bourbon

1 ounce simple syrup (recipe follows)

1 slice sugar cane (optional)

2–3 sprigs mint, to garnish

1. Place the ice in a glass and top with the bourbon and the simple syrup. Stir with the sugar cane and garnish with mint.

MINT SIMPLE SYRUP

1 cup water

1 cup sugar

½ bunch mint (leaves only)

2. Heat the water and sugar in a small saucepan over medium heat until the sugar dissolves, about 10 minutes. Remove from the heat and add the mint leaves. Steep for 3-4 minutes, and then strain and refrigerate.

STRAWBERRY WHITE WINE COOLER PUNCH

SERVES 6 | **Skill Level: EASY** | **Prep time: 15 mins.** | **Cost: $**

The 1980s brought many memorable things: the "Thriller" video, Miami Vice, and, of course, Big Hair, but nothing better than wine coolers. The ones that came in a box were a nice way to charge five bucks for fifty cents' worth of ingredients. I find you can do a whole lot better cost-wise and flavor-wise if you make your own. When she tried this, even Miss I'm-Not-Into-Alcohol Carla said, "Oh, I love it!"

2 cups strawberries, plus extra for garnish

⅓ cup sugar

1 bottle of dry white wine

Crushed ice

Ginger ale

1. In a bowl, combine the strawberries and sugar and let sit for 10 minutes. In a blender, puree the strawberry mixture with wine until smooth and pour through a fine sieve into a pitcher.

2. Wine cooler may be made 4 hours ahead and refrigerated. Serve chilled over ice, and top with ginger ale and strawberries.

Luke Mangan joins the crew in some Easter Funday laughs.

SPRING

RHUBARB PUNCH

SERVES 10 | Skill Level: EASY | Cook Time: 10 mins. | Prep time: 10 mins. | Cost: $

One of my favorite times of the year is late spring when the roses are in bloom, the strawberries are dark red, and pucker-your-mouth rhubarb is in season. I don't know where rhubarb would find a place in life if it didn't go so well with strawberries. It just goes to show you that it's important to have a good side-kick—in life and in your glass. So fire up the grill for the first barbecue of the year, and while you're waiting for the coals to reach perfection, kick back with this tangy, fizzy drink. This recipe doesn't call for any alcohol. I suppose you could add some gin, or vodka, or tequila, but it's nice to have a special, fun drink for the teetotalers in the crowd (like me).

8 cups fresh rhubarb, chopped

2½ cups sugar

2 cups pineapple juice

¼ cup lime juice

1 pint strawberries, hulled and chilled

6 cups ginger ale

1. In a Dutch oven, bring the rhubarb and 2 quarts water to a boil. Reduce heat and simmer, uncovered, for 10 minutes. Strain, reserving liquid.

2. In a large bowl, dissolve the sugar in 2 cups boiling water. Stir in the pineapple and lime juices. Stir in the reserved rhubarb liquid and refrigerate until chilled.

3. Just before serving, pour into a punch bowl, add the strawberries, and stir in the ginger ale.

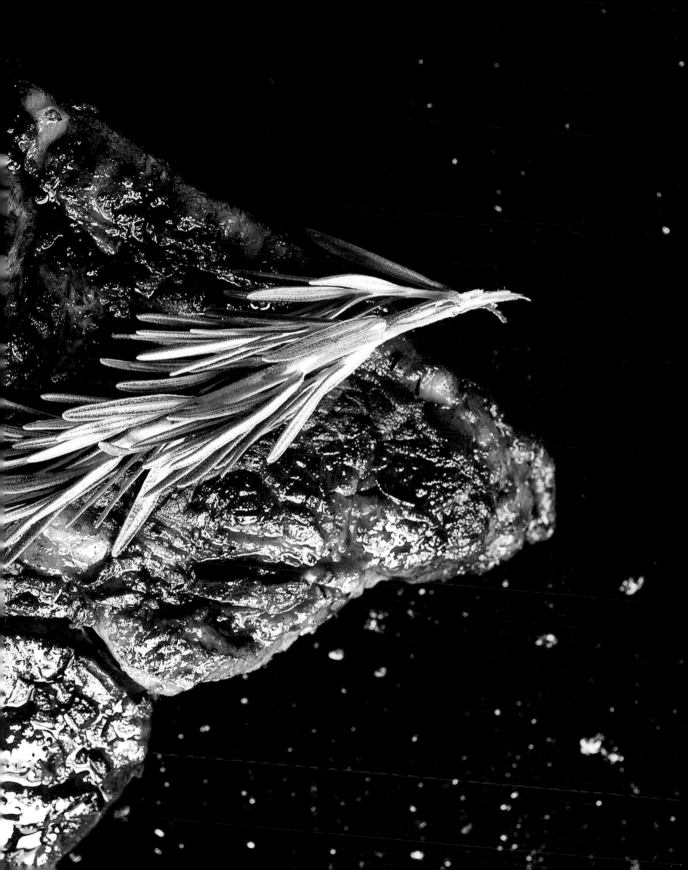

SUMMER

A gluten-free pork dish satisfies both Michael and Elisabeth Hasselbeck.

Michael

Q: What makes cooking on *The Chew* special for you?

Michael: I love a live audience, I love to watch it, I love to do it, because you can see the mistakes. Take it from someone who's worked and run restaurants for over 25 years, mistakes happen . . . in my restaurant and in my home. It's your ability to be able to fix them that makes you a good cook. And I think that's what someone like Julia Child used to bring to us. She'd make a mistake, she'd do something to fix the mistake, and it was okay. After Julia, what happened with cooking on television is what I call the Martha effect; everything got so perfect but wasn't necessarily real or attainable. If a viewer made something that didn't look exactly like it did on the cooking show, they thought that they were a bad cook, got discouraged. And in reality, that's life in a nutshell: sometimes the dish doesn't look perfect, but it doesn't mean it's any less delicious. That's what people learn when they see a show like this.

Q: **Does that mean cooking on *The Chew* is oversimplified or dumbed down?**

Michael: No way. The cool thing about *The Chew* is it's not dumbed down at all. Most of the stuff is made on the show without dump and stir. One of the things that makes it approachable is the comradeship among the five of us. I loved doing *Iron Chef* and I'm proud that I could do that show very well. But is that how I cook at home, for friends and family? Absolutely not! Food should bring people together. It should be delicious. It should be nourishing. And it should make people happy.

Q: **When you guys came on the show, you fit certain roles. How did you see yours?**

Michael: Heartland food is what I like talking about because that's how I was raised. No matter how much you evolve as a TV host or chef or whatever, there's always going to be a pocket for you that's most comfortable. And the heartland has always been my pocket.

Q: **Clinton was hired for his hosting chops and his Mister Mingle personality, but he's a pretty good cook, isn't he?**

Michael: I knew instantly when I met him how much he loved food. But there's a lot of people in the world that can cook, and there are a lot of people that can host. There are very few people who can cook *and* host. He does both very, very well. He's very comfortable in the kitchen. He thinks about the dishes and he's a great entertainer.

Q: **Are there any mistakes that have happened on the show that are really memorable?**

Michael: Oh, yeah, I mean the one that's most memorable and obvious for me is I worked with a woman in the audience who wanted to learn how to make a perfect omelet. I've made thousands of omelets; it's the test I give my cooks when they apply for a job. This particular omelet didn't work at all. It stuck to the pan, but it was still fine. When we got done with the show, they asked, "Did I want to reshoot it?" I said absolutely not. I want people to see that even with someone who is a professional, these things could happen and there's no reason to get frustrated, it's still delicious. Maybe I wouldn't serve it in my restaurant, but it's fantastic at home.

Q: **You have so many guest stars on the show. Who stands out in your mind as being especially memorable or fun or revealing?**

Michael: The ones that stick out for me are the ones that are actually good cooks. Every star that comes on the show *says* they can cook. You quickly see which ones can or can't. Hugh Jackman came and was very comfortable in the kitchen. He was comfortable in the process. Elisabeth Hasselbeck was very comfortable cooking. Gwyneth Paltrow—super comfortable. You could tell this woman spends a lot of time in the kitchen and has no problem cooking.

WATERMELON GAZPACHO

SERVES 4 | **Skill Level: EASY** | **Prep Time: 15 mins.** | **Cost: $**

I think if Dr. Seuss had ever written a cookbook, he might have come up with the word gazpacho *if it didn't exist already. It's fun to say. Classic gazpacho combines the freshest, ripest summer vegetables in a cooling, thirst-quenching recipe. When I think of summer, I also picture juicy, sweet watermelon, so the thought occurred to me: Why not make my own gazpacho with watermelon? Add some yogurt or sour cream, and it becomes silky smooth. If you want an extra little kick for a summer brunch, skip the Bloody Marys and add some tequila to this recipe.*

6 ripe tomatoes, chopped

2 cups fresh watermelon, chopped, plus more to garnish

2 medium seedless or English cucumbers, peeled and chopped

¾ cup sweet onion, chopped

½ jalapeño pepper, minced (optional)

1 clove garlic, minced

¼ cup flat-leaf parsley, chopped

¼ cup fresh mint, chopped

¼ cup red wine vinegar

¼ cup lime juice

1 cup tomato juice, for consistency

¼ cup feta cheese, crumbled, to garnish

Tabasco, to serve

Worcestershire, to serve

1. Process all the ingredients in a food processor or blender until smooth. Refrigerate until cold, but overnight is better. Pour into a serving bowl and garnish with the crumbled feta and some chopped watermelon. Serve with Tabasco sauce and Worcestershire sauce on the side.

WHITE GAZPACHO WITH FROZEN GRAPES

SERVES 4 | Skill Level: EASY | Cook Time: 10 mins. | Prep Time: 10 mins. | Cost: $

This is inspired by the Spanish favorite known as sopa de ajo, *which translates as garlic soup. I didn't think that would sound so appealing in English, so I changed it to White Gazpacho. It reminds me of the way one of the legends of the New York restaurant world, Sirio Maccioni, decided to serve cured lard in his very fancy place. He called it white prosciutto, and it became a favorite of the forerunners of the* Sex and the City *girls, Manhattan's "ladies who lunch." Frozen grapes make for a surprising and flavorful treat in your soupspoon.*

1 cup whole almonds, blanched

2 cloves garlic, minced

½ cup sherry vinegar

4 ice cubes

1 cup extra virgin olive oil

Sea salt

1 bunch seedless grapes, halved and frozen

Grated zest of 2 lemons

1. Put the almonds in a small saucepan, cover with cold water, and bring to a boil. Turn off the heat and let stand for 10 minutes, to soften slightly.

2. Drain the almonds, transfer to a blender, and add the garlic, vinegar, and 4 cups cold water. Blend until smooth, about 1 minute. With the motor running, add the ice cubes, then add the olive oil in a slow, steady stream, blending until thoroughly combined. Season with salt, and refrigerate until chilled.

3. Divide the grapes and zest between four small bowls, pour the soup over, and serve.

GRILLED VEGETABLE AND PEACH SUMMER SALAD

| SERVES 4 | Skill Level: EASY | Cook Time: 15 mins. | Prep Time: 15 mins. | Cost: $ |

I grew up in New Jersey. They don't call it the Garden State for nothing. It has the most delicious vegetables: sweet corn, beautiful tomatoes, endless zucchini. And in August, when the peaches ripen, I'm in heaven. This recipe was born out of my love for these hallmarks of summer in New Jersey. Or maybe I should say reborn, because it started with some leftover vegetables that we had made the night before. Then some grilled peaches and a fresh dressing. It's the whole flavor profile of summer. Serve it with grilled chicken or sliced steak, and it's a perfect summer supper.

FOR THE SALAD:

2 ears sweet corn

2 medium zucchini, sliced lengthwise

1 bunch asparagus, tough ends removed

2 yellow peaches, pitted and cut into quarters

2 heads romaine, finely chopped

3 Persian cucumbers, sliced into thin rounds

2 avocados, diced

2 cups cherry tomatoes, halved

12 leaves fresh basil, shredded

FOR THE DRESSING:

8 tablespoons extra virgin olive oil

4 tablespoons red wine vinegar

2 tablespoons shallots, minced

2 teaspoons Dijon mustard

2 teaspoons honey or maple syrup

1 tablespoon fresh lemon juice, plus lemon wedges for garnish

½ teaspoon fresh ground coriander

Salt, to taste

Pepper, to taste

1. Shuck the corn and grill on a hot grill or cast-iron griddle until kernels are golden brown and some have slightly charred, rotating to cook all kernels evenly. Remove from the grill to cool. Once cool, remove the corn from the cob and set aside. Grill the zucchini and asparagus until tender, about 2–3 minutes. Grill the peaches flesh side down just until heated through, about 1 minute. Remove the vegetables and peaches from the grill and chop. Add the grilled vegetables and peaches to a large bowl, and add the rest of the salad ingredients. Blend all the dressing ingredients until emulsified in a blender. Toss the salad with the vinaigrette and serve with fresh lemon wedges.

SWEET CORN WITH ONIONS AND BASIL

SERVES 10 | Skill Level: EASY | Cook Time: 50 mins. | Prep Time: 15 mins. | Cost: $

Sweet corn, sweet basil, and sweet Vidalia onions—that's my idea of a sweet and savory summer dish. It's not much more difficult to make than corn on the cob, and when these vegetables are at their peak it is a divine combination. As for jalapeños . . . why not? Corn and hot peppers are two of the great gifts of the Americas to the world. They make great dance partners.

2 Vidalia onions, sliced into ½-inch slices

¼ cup extra virgin olive oil

Salt, to taste

10 ears fresh corn, shucked

1 cup basil leaves

4 Fresno or jalapeño peppers, seeded and thinly sliced

Juice and zest of 2 lemons

1½ teaspoons sugar (optional)

Pepper, to taste

1. Preheat the oven to 400 °F.

2. Toss the onions in 3 tablespoons olive oil, and season with salt. Spread out on a large baking dish and roast until tender, about 20 minutes. Transfer to a large bowl and set aside.

3. Place the corn on the same baking sheet and drizzle with the remaining olive oil and roast, tossing every few minutes, for 15 minutes. Add to the bowl with the onion, along with the remaining ingredients, and toss to combine. Serve warm or at room temperature.

SUMMER SCAFATA

SERVES 6 | Skill Level: EASY | Cook Time: 20–25 mins. | Prep Time: 20 mins. | Cost: $

The French, with their ratatouille, may think they've cornered the market on fun words for a vegetable stew, but all that means is they have never heard of the dish called scafata. It's a traditional Friulian dish that the great Lidia Bastianich first made for me. Ah, Lidia! She is such a gentle critic. She will say ten nice things about you before she mentions that you burned the chicken to a crisp! Her scafata is a stew of spring vegetables. I liked it so well, I figured I'd try it with summer vegetables, and the following recipe was my reward.

¼ cup extra virgin olive oil

½ Spanish onion, thinly sliced

1 teaspoon hot red chili flakes

1 large bulb fennel, diced

2 pounds zucchini, cut into ½-inch-thick chunks

2 pounds ripe tomatoes, cut into chunks

1 tablespoon freshly ground black pepper

Kosher salt

¼ cup basil leaves

Drizzle of good balsamic, optional

1. Heat the olive oil in a 12-inch sauté pan or Dutch oven. Add the onion, red pepper flakes, and fennel, and cook until the fennel is tender, about 8 minutes. Add the zucchini, tomatoes, and pepper, and cook over medium-low heat until the zucchini and tomatoes have broken down a bit, about 10–15 minutes. Season with salt.

2. Tear the basil leaves into pieces, sprinkle over the scafata, and serve. This dish is also good at room temperature, or served over grilled or toasted bread with a drizzle of good balsamic.

GRILLED EGGPLANT WITH GREEK YOGURT

SERVES 6 TO 8 | Skill Level: **EASY** | Cook Time: **12–15 mins.** | Prep Time: **15 mins.** | Cost: **$**

Once again, my Mediterranean background—specifically Turkish—comes into play. Eggplant was one of the most common ingredients in our family's cooking when I grew up, but it's often a vegetable that many Americans are afraid of cooking. I think that's because we don't know how to make it except for eggplant parm, or frying it in buckets of oil. Nothing could be easier than this recipe. You wash the eggplant, grill it, and top it with a savory and creamy yogurt sauce, and you're good to go.

4 Japanese eggplants

¼ cup plus 1½ tablespoons extra virgin olive oil

Salt, to taste

Pepper, to taste

2 teaspoons fresh thyme (leaves only)

2 teaspoons fresh oregano (leaves only)

1 cup Greek yogurt

2 cloves garlic, minced

1 teaspoon cayenne pepper

1 tablespoon honey, plus more for garnish

1 tablespoon red wine vinegar

2 tablespoons mint leaves, finely chopped, for garnish

1 cup walnuts, roughly chopped, for garnish

1. Cut the eggplants in half lengthwise, and score the flesh without piercing the skin in a crisscross pattern. Toss the eggplant with ¼ cup of the olive oil, salt, pepper, and the thyme and oregano leaves. Set aside to marinate for up to 20 minutes.

2. Preheat the grill or grill pan to medium-high heat.

3. Place the eggplant on a hot part of the grill and cook until slightly charred, about 3 minutes per side. Transfer to a cooler part of the grill or grill pan, and cook through, until soft when pierced with a knife, about 8 more minutes. Remove to a platter and set aside.

4. Meanwhile, make the sauce by whisking together the yogurt, minced garlic, remaining olive oil, cayenne pepper, honey, and red wine vinegar. Season with salt and pepper

5. To serve, top the eggplant with a generous portion of sauce and garnish with mint, chopped walnuts, and another drizzle of honey.

Eggplants are easy... really!

Eggplant plus heat source pretty much tells the story. Basically, you roast an eggplant the way you would roast a pepper, turning it as each side shrivels and chars. The skin will shrink as the water pushes out, leaving you with a sad-looking, shriveled eggplant. Don't worry, that's how you want it, because when you cut it in half the insides are creamy soft and easy to scoop out.

SUMMER

DAPHNE'S SUPERFOODS SMOOTHIE

SERVES 1 | **Skill Level: EASY** | **Prep Time: 5 mins.** | **Cost: $**

When I was little, my parents had their hands full trying to get me to eat a healthy breakfast. I guess that means I was a pretty normal child. The world knows my dad as the super health expert Dr. Oz, but to me he's just Daddy, and when your daddy is a nutrition expert, he will do whatever he can to make sure his daughter eats right. His solution was a delicious smoothie, chock-full of fresh fruit and yogurt. He called it the "Magic Drink." Now that I am no longer a little girl, I have learned to add some more good-for-you ingredients to my magic drink. The Chew gang had a lot of fun teasing me when I told them my superfoods smoothie gets a boost from psyllium husks. Psyllium is just extra fiber. This is a good thing. Fiber leaves you satisfyingly full and aids in good digestion. I have yet to meet somebody who has tried this smoothie who doesn't like it.

½ **cup yogurt (plain or flavored, but avoid artificial sweeteners)**

1 **cup fresh fruit of your choosing**

1 **teaspoon honey (optional)**

½ **banana (optional)**

1 **tablespoon psyllium husks**

3 **500-milligram ester-c capsules (about 1 tablespoon)**

1 **cup ice (or frozen fruit and skip ice)**

Water, to blend for consistency

Juice, to blend for consistency

1. Combine the ingredients in a blender and blend until smooth and creamy. If you have trouble blending, try adding a little water or juice to thin the smoothie. Make sure to have at least two 8-ounce glasses of water with each serving of smoothie to help the psyllium husks expand so they digest properly.

Daphne gets a surprise visit from her dad, Dr. Oz.

MUSSELS ALLA PIASTRA

SERVES 6 | **Skill Level: EASY** | **Cook Time: 15 mins.** | **Prep time: 10 mins.** | **Cost: $$**

If you are ever on the coast of Emilia-Romagna, south of Venice and north of Ancona, chances are you will eat some seafood made on a griddle—that's piastra *in Italian. And when you return to the States, chances are even greater you are going to want to eat more seafood made this way. It's actually quite simple: some seafood, some lemon, some bread crumbs, and that about tells the tale. Don't let me forget prosciutto! In Emilia-Romagna, even if you order a vegetarian dish, they're probably going to sneak some prosciutto in there. They don't think of it as meat. It's a seasoning. I agree. There's very little in cooking that can't be improved with a little prosciutto.*

3 dozen small mussels, scrubbed and debearded

Extra virgin olive oil

Salt

Pepper

1 cup bread crumbs

4 tablespoons prosciutto, coarsely chopped

1 bunch lemon thyme (leaves only)

Grated zest and juice of 1 orange

Grated zest and juice of 1 lemon

1 jalapeño, thinly sliced

½ bunch chives, thinly sliced

2 tablespoons white wine

1. Preheat a griddle or piastra over medium-high heat.

2. Put the mussels in a large metal bowl. Drizzle with some olive oil and season with salt and pepper.

3. Place the bread crumbs, prosciutto, lemon thyme, orange and lemon zest and juice, jalapeño, and chives in a food processor, and pulse until well mixed, 6 or 7 pulses.

4. Add the bread crumb mixture to the mussels, and toss to combine.

5. Pour 2 tablespoons olive oil onto the griddle. Working quickly, dump the mussels (with everything else in the bowl) onto the griddle. Add a splash of white wine, and cover with the inverted bowl. You may have to cook the mussels in batches if your griddle isn't large enough. Remove the bowl after 2 minutes, and gently stir the mussels around. Continue cooking, uncovered, for about 3 minutes longer, until they all open (discard any that do not open); transfer the mussels to a platter. Scrape up any bread crumb mixture remaining on the griddle, and scatter it over the mussels. Squeeze a little extra lemon juice on top and serve immediately.

The iron age

In Italy, they call it a *piastra*. In Spain, it's a *plancha*. In America, it's a cast-iron griddle. For most of us, we use it to make pancakes and that's about it, but it's really a wonderful tool for making fish, steaks, chops, vegetables, flatbreads, and even desserts outside on a grill. If even heat is what you are looking for, think *grrr . . .* as in *Griddles Are Great*!

SUMMER

181

FRIED CLAM SANDWICH

SERVES 4 | **Skill Level: EASY** | **Cook Time: 4 mins.** | **Prep Time: 15 mins.** | **Cost: $**

My wife, Lizzie, lived in Boston before we met, and, on a later visit there, she took me for my first really great fried clams. We ate our way through piles of clam sandwiches, steamed lobsters, the whole thing. I wondered: How did they get such perfection? Try as I might, I couldn't figure it out. Instead of overthinking it, which we chefs sometimes to, I went in the kitchen and asked them how they did it. Some chefs treat these things as The Secret of the Ages. Not these guys. They told me right off the bat: evaporated milk and corn flour, and fry them in lard, that's it. Moral of the story: quite often the greatest things in life are the simplest.

Canola oil, for frying

¼ cup all-purpose flour

Salt

Pepper

1 egg, lightly beaten

1 12-ounce can evaporated milk

½ cup panko bread crumbs

2 dozen Littleneck clams, shucked

¼ cup tartar sauce (recipe follows)

4 potato hot dog buns

Lemon wedges, for garnish

1. Preheat the oil to 375 °F.

2. Create a dredging station by placing three baking dishes side by side. The first dish will be the flour, seasoned generously with salt and pepper. The second dish will be the egg and evaporated milk, beaten together. The third baking dish will be the panko bread crumbs.

3. Dredge the clams first into the flour, then the egg mixture, then the panko, and drop them into the hot oil. Fry until golden brown, about 3-4 minutes.

4. Spread a generous amount of tartar sauce on each of the buns, and divide the clams evenly among the four buns. Serve with lemon wedges.

TARTAR SAUCE

1 cup mayonnaise

½ cup sour cream

2 tablespoons capers

2 tablespoons pickles

1 tablespoon parsley, chopped

1 tablespoon horseradish

Juice of ½ a lemon

Salt, to taste

Pepper, to taste

1. Mix all ingredients until combined. Refrigerate until ready to serve.

Mind your buns

I'm not a fan of tarting up this kind of sandwich with gourmet bread. When I eat a humble sandwich—a hamburger, a fish sandwich, a lobster roll—I like a soft, squishy roll, and I think a potato roll is perfect for that.

Michael I like fried chicken so much that when I make it I fry it twice. Once to cook it, seal in flavor, and begin to crisp it, and then a second time to add even more flavor and crunchiness. As far as I am concerned, you can't get too much crispness or too much flavor. I like to mix my seasonings and then coat the chicken parts with it and leave them overnight. All of that flavor mingles and mixes and creeps up into the chicken. Then, the next day I dredge the chicken pieces in flour, and for the moment of truth—actually, about 22 minutes of truth—I fry the chicken. What kind of oil do I use, you ask? No kind of oil. I'm a good old-fashioned lard guy.

So first I fry it in hot oil with some garlic for extra nutty flavor, and then I finish with a second frying with rosemary and sage for even more extra flavor.

MICHAEL SYMON'S TWICE-FRIED CHICKEN

SERVES 6 | **Skill Level: EASY** | **Cook Time: 30 mins.** | **Prep Time: 15 mins.** | **COST: $$**

2 tablespoons seafood seasoning

1 tablespoon coriander seeds, toasted and cracked

1 teaspoon chipotle powder

1 teaspoon smoked paprika

Kosher salt

1 4- to 5-pound chicken, cut into 12 pieces

1½ cups instant flour (such as Wondra)

3 tablespoons honey (optional), plus more for garnish

Sriracha (optional)

Vegetable oil or lard, for frying

6 cloves garlic, skin on

2 strips bacon

4 sprigs rosemary

4 leaves sage

Freshly grated Parmesan, for garnish

1. In a small bowl, combine the seafood seasoning, coriander seeds, chipotle powder, paprika, and a generous pinch of salt, and mix well. Coat the chicken pieces with the spice mixture, and place in a bag to refrigerate overnight.

2. If you decide to make this a spicy dish, in a small bowl, combine the honey and Sriracha. Stir well and refrigerate until ready to fry the chicken.

3. Remove the chicken pieces from the refrigerator and dredge in flour.

4. In a large Dutch oven, put in enough lard to come 4 inches up the side of the pot. Heat the lard to 300–325 °F.

5. Add garlic and bacon to the hot oil and fry for a couple of minutes.

6. Beginning with the thighs, add the chicken to the pot, making sure not to crowd. (This may take several batches.) Cook until golden and cooked 80 percent through, 8–10 minutes. Remove the chicken to a wire cooling rack, and repeat with the remaining chicken, if necessary.

7. Once all the chicken is done, raise the heat of the lard to 365 °F. Add rosemary and sage to fry and season the oil, fry 2–3 minutes then remove to a paper towel. Add the chicken in the same batches, and cook until dark golden and crispy, 2–3 minutes. Remove onto paper towels and serve immediately, topped with a drizzle of honey, a pinch of salt, and some freshly grated Parmesan.

Bacon's good too

Sometimes it's hard to find lard in the market. Or maybe you prefer to cook with oil. Either way, for yet another flavor booster, I toss a couple of slices of bacon in the hot oil. Daphne says basically my method is to cook fat in fat. I say, anything that adds flavor can't be bad.

GRANDMA THELMA'S FRIED CHICKEN

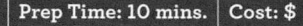

| SERVES 6 | Skill Level: EASY | Cook Time: 8–10 mins. | Prep Time: 10 mins. | Cost: $ |

Inactive Prep Time: 12 hrs.

FOR THE DRY RUB:

1 tablespoon salt

1 tablespoon black pepper

1 tablespoon garlic powder

1 tablespoon onion powder

1 tablespoon cayenne pepper

1 small organic chicken, broken down into 10 pieces

Peanut oil, for frying

FOR THE BATTER:

3 eggs

1 cup buttermilk

¼ cup water

2–3 cups flour, to dredge

2 tablespoons cornstarch

Salt

Pepper

1. In a mixing bowl, combine the salt, pepper, garlic powder, onion powder, and cayenne pepper. Combine the spice mixture and chicken pieces in a plastic zip bag, and toss to coat. Refrigerate overnight.

2. Preheat ½ inch of peanut oil in a cast-iron skillet to 360 °F.

3. Lightly beat the eggs, and combine with the buttermilk and water in a shallow dish. In another shallow dish, add the flour and cornstarch, and then season with salt and pepper. Dip each chicken piece into the buttermilk mixture and then coat in flour mixture. Fry the pieces until golden brown on all sides, about 3–4 minutes per side.

4. Remove to a wire rack to drain excess oil, then serve.

Carla My fried chicken isn't really *my* fried chicken. Like a lot of good things in my cooking, it comes from my Grandma Thelma. She wasn't on *Top Chef* like me, but if *Top Chef* had the guts to have some grandmas on, Thelma would've knocked Tom Colicchio's socks off. Like Michael, I season my chicken the night before to give the flavors a chance to make their presence known. Next day, I dip the chicken parts in an egg-buttermilk batter and then dredge in some flour. It adds up to one heck of a crispy crust. Michael may need to fry his twice, but Grandma Thelma's is such a flavor powerhouse that once is plenty—make that plenty good!

FETTUCCINE WITH LOBSTER, TOMATOES, AND SAFFRON

SERVES 6 | **Skill Level: EASY** | **Cook Time: 20–25 mins.** | **Prep Time: 20 mins.** | **Cost: $-$$-$$$**

Three recipes in one: first I do it simple, then I throw in another ingredient that makes it special, then I add still another and it's spectacular. Actually, with the right ingredients and a good cook, they're all spectacular. So first we have pasta with onion, celery, garlic, and potatoes. Real simple and real good.

Then I add in a little saffron, which ups the price about a buck a serving but gives the dish a special something.

Then I dice up some lobster meat, which adds a good ten to twelve dollars, but, hey, it's still a darn sight cheaper than lobster in a restaurant. Make sure you chop your lobster into bite-sized pieces so that you can use your fork to pick up both pasta and a lobster chunk for a bite-sized mouthful.

Salt

4 2½-pound lobsters, steamed 10 minutes and cooled

4 tablespoons extra virgin olive oil

1 medium red onion, cut into ⅛-inch julienne

2 stalks celery, cut into ¼-inch dice

2 medium waxy potatoes, cut into ⅛-inch dice

4 cloves garlic, thinly sliced

½ pound overripe tomatoes, cut into ½-inch dice with juices, or 1 can whole peeled San Marzano

¼ cup dry white wine

Pinch of saffron

1½ pounds fettuccine

½ cup chopped fresh chives

1. Bring 8 quarts water to a boil in a large spaghetti pot and add 2 tablespoons salt.

2. Remove the lobster meat from the shells and cut into ¼-inch pieces.

3. In a 14-inch sauté pan, heat the olive oil until smoking. Add the onion, celery, potatoes, and garlic, and sauté until golden brown, 6–7 minutes.

4. Add the tomatoes, wine, and saffron, and bring to a boil. Lower the heat and simmer for 3 minutes.

5. Drop the fettuccine into the boiling water and cook to 1 minute less than the package instructions. Just before it is done, carefully ladle ½ cup of the fettuccine water into the pan with the sauce.

6. Add the lobster to the tomato sauce in the pan and toss through. Drain the pasta in a colander and dump into the pan with the sauce, add the chives, and toss over medium heat, about 30 seconds, until nicely coated.

7. Pour into a bowl and serve.

Tomato tip

In season, you can't beat fresh tomatoes, but during the rest of the year, you'll do much better with a great canned tomato, like the ones they harvest in San Marzano.

SUMMER

187

CORN DOGGIN'

SERVES 6 | Skill Level: EASY | Cook Time: 10 mins. | Prep Time: 15 mins. | Cost: $$

If you grew up in the Midwest, you know what I am talking about when I mention corn dogs: hot dogs fried in a sweet and savory corn batter and topped with whatever struck your fancy, and since those were the days before fancy food, that meant mustard, mayo, or ketchup. I made my rep in the 1990s taking comfort food like this and upscaling it a little bit. Those were great days. All I did was work, party, and sleep. To tell you the truth, it was so much fun I don't remember a lot of it. One day I said to myself, "What if I corn dogged some lobster, shrimp, sausage, or zucchini?" I did, and they all were great. So were all the endless toppings and dips you can come up with.

Vegetable oil, for frying

12 colossal shrimp, shelled and deveined with tails only, or hot dogs, or zucchini spears

FOR THE BATTER:

1 cup flour

1 cup corn meal

2 tablespoons sugar

1 egg, lightly beaten

½ teaspoon baking powder

1 cup milk

Kosher salt

FOR THE CHIPOTLE MAYO:

1 cup mayonnaise

Juice and zest of ½ lime

3 tablespoons pureed chipotle in adobo

2 tablespoons chives, finely chopped

SPECIAL EQUIPMENT:

Skewers

TO MAKE THE CORN DOG:

1. Preheat the oil to 365 °F.

2. Thread a skewer through each of the shrimp, from head to tail.

3. In a shallow baking dish, mix together the batter ingredients until a smooth batter is formed. Batter each of the shrimp.

4. Fry each of the shrimp in the oil until crispy and golden brown, about 2 minutes. Do this in batches, if necessary. Transfer to drain on a paper towel–lined plate.

TO MAKE THE CHIPOTLE MAYO:

5. In a small bowl, whisk together the mayonnaise, lime juice, and chipotle until it is consistently incorporated. Fold in the chives.

6. Serve the chipotle mayo alongside the shrimp.

Better batter

You can buy store-bought batter mix, but it often has a ton of sugar. As with most things in cooking, you are always better off making your own from scratch. As Carla pointed out to me when I started lecturing on the fine points of batter making to fill time on the show, "Hey, it's cornbread with more milk in it." Leave it to Carla to bring it back to basics.

BIG MIKE BURGER

| SERVES 4 | Skill Level: EASY | Cook Time: 10 mins. | Prep Time: 20 mins. | Cost: $ |

We all know the Big Mac. This is the Big Mike. I know I'm tootin' my own horn a little, but my burgers have taken the top prize at the South Beach Wine and Food Festival three years in a row, so I hope that gives me the right to a few extra words on America's—and maybe the world's—favorite food, the burger.

You could make this with regular supermarket burger meat, but I find a custom mix, made from scratch, is what separates great burgers from regular old burgers. My preferred mix is about 75 percent meat and 25 percent fat.

There are two kinds of burgers. One I call the diner burger and the other is the bar burger. A diner burger is thin. When you grill it, you get a crunchy, crusty, salty texture on the outside and the meat is medium to medium-well all the way through. A bar burger is thicker and takes longer to cook and develop a crust, but you can pick the amount of doneness. The Big Mike is a double-patty diner burger.

These burgers are designed for a griddle. Griddling is the best way I know to get all those beautiful crunchies. Don't forget you can always put a griddle outside on the barbecue.

Then you've got your sauce. Get inventive. This one has a garlic aioli—a kind of tangy mayonnaise—with some hot sauce and, to finish it off, my secret ingredient: a little pickle juice.

And you must toast the bun. Serving a burger on an untoasted bun is a sin. You put it all together—maybe with some pickles, lettuce, tomatoes, and on-ions—smoosh it down a bit, and take a nice big bite. Don't worry if you get some juice running down your arm. That's Nature's way of telling you that you made a great burger.

Melted cheese is a must

If you are going to put cheese on your burger, then make sure it's melted. There's a neat trick to this. Lay a slice of cheese on the patty, then spritz a little water on the griddle next to the burger and immediately cover the burger with anything dome-shaped that won't melt on the griddle. The super-hot steam melts the cheese and saturates the burger with juiciness.

SUMMER

2 pounds ground beef
(75-25 blend)

Salt

Pepper

4 slices aged Cheddar cheese

2 tablespoons butter

4 brioche rolls, cut into
thirds, like a Big Mac

FOR THE SPECIAL SAUCE:

¼ cup garlic aioli

¼ cup brown mustard

¼ cup ketchup

Hot sauce, to taste

Pickle juice, to taste

Sweet Hot Pickles and
Peppers, to serve

Pickled red onions, to serve
(recipe follows)

1 cup romaine lettuce,
shredded, to serve

1. Preheat a griddle over medium heat.

2. Make eight equal-sized patties from the ground beef, about ½ inch bigger than the bun you want to serve it on. Season with salt and pepper.

3. Cook the patties on the griddle, about 3 minutes per side. Top four of the patties with slices of cheese when cooking the second side. Set aside.

4. Butter the brioche and toast on the griddle until golden brown.

5. Make the special sauce by whisking together the garlic aioli, mustard, and ketchup. Add a couple dashes of hot sauce and a splash of pickle juice.

6. Assemble with the cheesed patty on the bottom, topped with pickles and onions. Add the middle bun, then the second patty. Top with special sauce, shredded romaine, and the top bun.

PICKLED RED ONIONS

2 pounds red onions, sliced

3–3 ½ cups white wine
vinegar

2 tablespoons sugar

2 tablespoons kosher salt

2 teaspoons mustard seeds

1 tablespoon crushed red
pepper flakes

2 tablespoons coriander
seeds

2 tablespoons black
peppercorns

4 garlic cloves

2 bay leaves

1. Pack the onions into two 1-quart jars and cover with water to come within ½ inch of the rim. Pour the water out into a measuring cup. Note the volume, pour off half the water, and replace with vinegar. Add 2 tablespoons sugar and 2 tablespoons salt for every 3 cups of liquid.

2. Pour the vinegar mixture into a nonreactive saucepan, add the mustard seeds, red pepper flakes, coriander seeds, black peppercorns, garlic, and bay leaves, and bring to a boil over high heat. Allow the liquid to boil for 2 minutes, and then remove it from the heat.

3. Pour hot liquid into the jars to cover the onions and screw on the lids. Refrigerate for up to 1 month.

Food, Fire, and Family: Memories of the Grill

Michael

My dad felt he was the master of fire, and we let him think that because he was pretty good, but the truth is everybody worked the grill, including my mom. We did lots of lamb and a ton of spit roasting. A couple of times throughout the year, we made lamb or goat on a spit just brushed with olive oil and oregano and a little bit of red wine and vinegar. We always used hardwood charcoal. It makes the best heat and has the best flavor. My favorite grill meal these days: rib-eye with tomato salad. Perfection!!

Mario

In my family, everything went on the fire. The division of labor was pretty old-fashioned: the boys got the fire and the ladies got the kitchen, but everyone cooked—grandmas, grandpas, uncles, aunts, cousins.

All of my cousins, particularly on my mom's side, were big fishermen: they owned, like, half the state records for steelhead and salmon. There were also lots of hunters in the family, so after every fishing or hunting trip, they would bring back their edible trophies and grill them, smoke them, cure them, hang them.

We always did hot smoked salmon and planked salmon on cedar. That burned flavor was so delicious and unforgettable. Not only salmon. We grilled, smoked, and roasted duck every way you could dream of.

We had a spit roaster, and we did everything from chickens to legs of lamb all over open wood fire or lump charcoal. We even had the Green Egg back in its prototype days in the late 1970s. For us, the idea of using fire for food was one of the basics of life.

Carla

My go-to barbecue meal is pulled pork shoulder like they used to make at Mary's down on Jefferson Street, in Nashville, Tennessee. It was the greatest. Of course, people in the other part of town, East Nashville, had their own favorite, and they would swear by it just as religiously. All over town, you'd see those big oil drums that they'd use to smoke pork, and every smoker had its true believers. Bottom line, I want pulled pork on a soft bun with pickles and coleslaw.

And then it's all about the sides too. You have to have potato salad. Also grilled corn. I like corn, but I *love* grilled corn, especially with butter and something tangy like lemon and lime. Delish! And you absolutely need some coleslaw. I used to want it very mayonnaise-y, but just like with the grilled

corn, I now look for a good bit of tang, so I pickle my cabbage in vinegar and then add a little mayonnaise.

The great thing about a barbecue is you can feed so many people. I like to keep mine to twenty, but somehow they often end up being thirty or forty and somehow there's always enough.

Clinton

I grew up on Long Island, and we grilled as much as possible. My dad would be in the backyard grilling in the middle of winter, if possible. In my adult life, it's very rare that I cook indoors on a hot day in the middle of the summer, so I'm a big fan of chicken thighs on the grill. It's one of those things that you can be three sheets to the wind and still destroy on the grill. This isn't a recommendation for grilling while incredibly intoxicated, but you can talk and grill chicken thighs and not feel like you have to be spending all your time staring at them,

wondering if they're done or not. I'm big on steaks too. For sides, I love grilled asparagus—that's my favorite. I need to get Mario to show me how to plank a salmon. I so want to do that.

Daphne

One of my favorite memories was going to visit my grandparents and having my grandpa throw a whole fish on the grill. It was the simplest preparation: fresh-caught fish, a little bit of fresh olive oil and lemon. I don't know why more people don't try it. A whole fish is hard to mess up and sooo delicious.

Grilling is one of the best ways to bring a family together, because everyone can do something. I'm one of four children. My mom was one of six. So when our family gets together for a barbecue, it can be a lot of people—like thirty-five! Grilling is the easiest way I know to feed a big group. My fave specialty is grilled corn, Mexican-style. I think Carla would second that emotion.

Amani Toomer officiates a grill-off in the rain.

CHEESE-STUFFED MORTADELLA ON BRUSCHETTA

SERVES 6–8 | **Skill Level: EASY** | **Cook Time: 6–8 mins.** | **Prep Time: 20 mins.** | **Cost: $**

Great Italian appetizers are less about technique and more about buying the right stuff. That's actually true of all cuisine. Mortadella, also called baloney because it comes from Bologna, is a wonderful cold cut, so smooth as it slides over your tongue when you have it sliced super thin. Sometimes it has pistachios in it. Robiola cheese is, to my way of thinking, the sexiest cream cheese of all time. It's from Piemonte. When he saw me putting this together, Michael couldn't resist chiming in with, "I love this, Batali is making baloney and cream cheese sandwiches." He had a point; you could use regular old baloney instead of mortadella, and cream cheese works too. You roll 'em up with a basil leaf, cook 'em up on a grill pan. Finito!

12–14 thin slices mortadella, without pistachios

12–14 ounces fresh Robiola

12–14 fresh basil leaves

Olive oil

½ baguette, sliced

3 cups baby arugula

1 tablespoon red wine vinegar

Coarse sea salt

Black pepper

SPECIAL EQUIPMENT:

Toothpicks

1. Preheat a gas grill or prepare a fire in a charcoal grill.

2. Lay the mortadella out on a work surface. Place 2 tablespoons of the cheese in the very center of each slice. Place a basil leaf on top of each mound of cheese. Fold the bottom of each slice over the cheese, then fold over the sides and roll the cheese up in the mortadella. Secure each with a toothpick.

3. Place the mortadella packets seam side up on the hottest part of the grill and cook until lightly charred on the bottom, about 2 minutes. Turn over and repeat on the second side, about 2 minutes longer. Transfer to a platter, and remove the toothpicks from each packet.

4. Brush the slices of bread with a little olive oil and grill, about 30 seconds per side. Place a mortadella packet on each piece of bread.

5. In a medium bowl, toss the arugula with 3 tablespoons olive oil and then the vinegar. Season with coarse sea salt and black pepper, and pile the greens over the hot and delightful mortadella packets.

SUMMER

195

TURKEY SLIDERS

SERVES 4 | Skill Level: EASY | Cook Time: 8–10 mins. | Prep Time: 20 mins. | Cost: $

I basically live on these in the summer, and people say that I make the world's best turkey sliders. People aren't just saying that to be nice. You can always tell the sincere complimenters from the people pretending they like something by who goes back for seconds . . . and thirds. When we made this on The Chew, *I seasoned it, but Mario walked over and picked up the pepper grinder to give it another two million turns. That's the difference between a restaurant chef and a home cook. The resto guys ain't shy about seasoning.*

1 pound ground turkey

1 onion, grated

2 tablespoons Dijon mustard

1 egg

½ cup panko bread crumbs

1 teaspoon cumin

Salt, to taste

Pepper, to taste

1 package of 8 mini potato buns

FOR THE TOPPINGS:

Ketchup

Dijon mustard

Mayonnaise

Tomato

Lettuce

1. Preheat a grill pan over medium-high heat. In a large bowl, mix the turkey, grated onion, Dijon mustard, egg, panko, cumin, salt, and pepper until combined. Mold the mixture into small patties. Grill the patties for 3–4 minutes per side or until cooked completely through. Remove from grill, and build the sliders on potato buns.

Shapely is good

When I have combined all the main ingredients, if it's too mushy, I add Japanese panko bread crumbs (they really hold their crunch) until the patty will stay together.

Done plus one

Turkey must be cooked all the way through. When you think that they're done, cook them another minute. I have never overcooked a burger using this method.

Always add a whole grated onion to the recipe. Because turkey has to cook all the way through, it can dry out. Onions add moistness and sweet flavor.

197

DAPHNE'S BEST BURGER

SERVES 4 | Skill Level: EASY | Cook Time: 25 mins. | Prep Time: 20 mins. | Cost: $

Calling all meat eaters! This tempura mushroom burger is guaranteed to make the most committed carnivore swoon. There are tons of veggie burgers out there—cashew curry burgers, grain-based burgers, tofu burgers—but if I had to pick one, this gets my vote. The secret is portabella mushroom and crunchy tempura. When you put it in a burger with all the toppings and condiments, it nearly fools your palate into thinking that it's meat. Deep-thinking chefs say that's because it has that mysterious flavor called umami. *If you're not familiar with* umami, *it's the Japanese word for "yummy." Finally, topping with a roasted garlic and tarragon aioli puts my burger's flavor off the charts.*

8 portabella mushroom caps, plus 2 cups portabella stems, minced

1 tablespoon olive oil

2 shallots, minced

FOR THE TEMPURA BATTER:

1 cup all-purpose flour

2 tablespoons cornstarch

½ teaspoon salt

3 egg whites, stiffly beaten

1 cup seltzer

Vegetable oil, for frying

4 onion brioche buns

Garlic Tarragon Aioli (recipe follows)

SPECIAL EQUIPMENT:

16 toothpicks

FOR THE TOPPINGS:

Lettuce

Tomato

1. Preheat the oven to 350 °F.

2. Place the mushroom caps on a baking sheet and put in the oven for 12–15 minutes, until soft. This helps take moisture out of the mushroom for a better fry. Remove the mushrooms from the oven and pat dry excess moisture.

3. In a medium sauté pan, heat 1 tablespoon olive oil. Add the portabella stems and shallots. Sauté for 2–3 minutes. Cool mixture and set aside.

4. To make the tempura batter, combine the dry ingredients. Fold in the stiff egg whites and then seltzer.

5. Fill each portabella mushroom cap with the mushroom-shallot mixture. Make a sandwich with another cap, and secure with toothpicks. Dip in the tempura batter, and fry in oil at about 360 °F.

6. Place the fried mushroom caps on a toasted onion bun with aioli and eat 'em up!

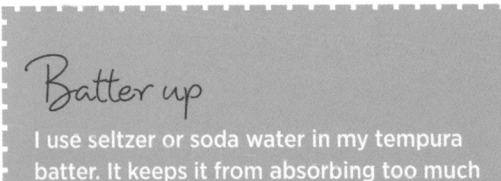

Batter up

I use seltzer or soda water in my tempura batter. It keeps it from absorbing too much fat, and the bubbles help keep the batter crispy and light.

GARLIC TARRAGON AIOLI

1 head garlic

Salt

Pepper

2 tablespoons olive oil

1 cup mayo

2 tablespoons fresh tarragon, chopped

1. Cut a head of garlic in half along the equator and place on a piece of foil. Season with salt and pepper and drizzle with olive oil, then fold the foil over garlic to form a pouch. Roast until tender, about 15–20 minutes. Remove from the oven and set aside to cool. Remove the pulp of the garlic from the head, and place in a blender or food processor. Add the mayo and the tarragon, and puree until smooth.

Emeril and Carla demonstrate some classic Southern cooking.

Twice-cooked mushrooms

Portabellas give up a ton of water, so you need to roast them before you batter and fry them. Otherwise you will have a soggy tempura burger, and no one ever used the word *soggy* to describe something delicious.

DRY RUB BABY BACK RIBS WITH SCALLOPED POTATOES

| SERVES 6 | Skill Level: EASY | Cook Time: 2 hrs. | Prep Time: 30 mins. | Cost: $ |

Whenever we visit my husband's family in Chicago, my mother-in-law makes these ribs for us. Like all rib makers, she has always kept it a secret, but I am happy to tell you she has given me permission to share it with all Chewsters. It starts, as all great ribs do, with a spice rub. Mario offered to rub my ribs, and it was clear that he didn't mean the spareribs. Naughty boy!

My mother-in-law makes her barbecue sauce from scratch, and I recommend you do the same. Once you taste her ribs, you are going to wish you had my mother-in-law, but too late. I already have dibs on her and the husband to prove it.

FOR THE DRY RUB:

2 tablespoons paprika

2 tablespoons cayenne pepper

1 tablespoon freshly ground black pepper

2 tablespoons garlic powder

2 tablespoons onion powder

2 tablespoons kosher salt

1 tablespoon dried oregano

1 tablespoon dried thyme

2½ pounds baby back ribs

FOR THE BARBECUE SAUCE:

5 tablespoons butter

½ yellow onion, chopped

3 cloves garlic, minced

2 cups tomato sauce

½ cup apple cider vinegar

½ cup light brown sugar

3 tablespoons paprika

1 tablespoon chili powder

TO MAKE THE RIBS:

1. In a medium bowl, combine all the dry rub ingredients and mix thoroughly. Rub the ribs all over with the dry rub, and allow to marinate for at least 1 hour.

2. Meanwhile, in a medium saucepan over medium heat, add the butter. Once it has foamed and subsided, add the onion and cook until softened, about 5 minutes. Add the garlic and cook an additional minute. Add the remaining sauce ingredients and stir until thoroughly mixed. Reduce heat and simmer sauce for 2 hours.

3. Preheat the oven to 350 °F. Place the ribs in a baking dish and cover halfway up with the barbecue sauce, then cook in the oven for at least 2 hours, until meat is tender. Serve with extra barbecue sauce on the side and the scalloped potatoes.

It pays to ask questions

In shopping for ribs, look for lots of marbling and a light pink color, and make sure they haven't been frozen. Even if you shop in a supermarket with aisles a half mile long, remember there is a real live butcher in the meat department. He or she will be able to advise you, and most of them enjoy the chance to go beyond the shrink-wrap and talk to an actual human customer.

FOR THE SCALLOPED POTATOES:

3 tablespoons extra virgin olive oil

3 yellow onions, cut into ¼-inch-thick slices

Pinch of kosher salt

Pinch of freshly ground black pepper

¼ teaspoon sugar

6 tablespoons butter, melted

2½ pounds russet potatoes, peeled and cut into ¼-inch slices

¼ cup flour

3 cups milk

¼ cup Parmesan cheese, grated

¼ cup parsley

TO MAKE THE SCALLOPED POTATOES:

4. Preheat the oven to 350 °F. In a pan over medium heat, add the olive oil. Add the onions and season with a pinch of salt and ground pepper, and the sugar. Cook the onions in an even layer until caramelized, about 30 minutes. In a 9-by-13-inch casserole dish, grease lightly with butter, and add a layer of the potatoes. Alternate layers of potatoes and caramelized onions sprinkled with a large pinch of flour and drizzled with butter. Continue until almost full, then add milk to cover. Top with grated cheese. Bake until bubbling and golden brown, about 1½ hours. Top with parsley to serve.

The Chew crew discovers their inner burlesque babe with the Pussycat Dolls.

T-BONE FIORENTINA

SERVES 6 | Skill Level: EASY | Cook Time: 40–45 mins. | Prep Time: 15 mins. | COST: $$

We Americans think of ourselves as steak eaters. The Tuscans think of us more as steak nibblers when they compare an American steak to a classic fiorentina. It's big and it comes from big steers, the giant breed known as Chianina. Rubbed with salt and olive oil and rosemary, the meat develops a great charred, salty, crispy crust and the rosemary puts in mind the scent of a pine forest when the wind blows through it. And that, of course, makes me think of opening great wine. Don't ask me why. All I know is there are a lot of things in this world that make me think of opening a delicious red wine. You can make this on the grill or pan roast.

2 tablespoons rosemary, chopped

1 tablespoon sage, chopped

1 tablespoon thyme, chopped

2 tablespoons kosher salt

2 tablespoons freshly ground pepper

1 3-pound T-bone steak, about 3 inches thick

2 tablespoons extra virgin olive oil

Juice of ½ a lemon

1. Preheat the oven to 350 °F and preheat a grill or grill pan. In a small bowl, combine the rosemary, sage, thyme, salt, and pepper. Rub the steak with 2 tablespoons of the oil, and then rub with the herb mixture. Grill the steak over medium-high heat until lightly charred all over, about 10 minutes, halfway through. Transfer to a small roasting pan and roast for about 30 minutes, or until an instant-read thermometer inserted into the thickest spot registers 120 °F. Let rest for 10 minutes before slicing. Squeeze a little lemon over the top of the steak.

BLUEBERRY HAND PIES

SERVES 10 | Skill Level: **EASY** | Cook Time: **20 mins.** | Prep Time: **45 mins** | Cost: **$**

Call it a turnover, or maybe a blueberry empanada, or a baked fruit ravioli, or a dessert taco, or anything you want. I call them Blueberry Hand Pies. These are easier to make than a full-on blueberry pie, and the neat thing is each little hand pie is a single serving of pie. No runny fruit filling puddling in your pie dish. And you can eat a whole piece with your hands without getting your fingers messy, at least in theory. On the other hand, you might want to use a fork if you top it with whipped cream or your favorite flavor ice cream. Fran Drescher helped me make these, and she really liked that it is a dessert but not overly sweet. Daphne gave me extra health points because we made the crust with whole grains: that means added fiber even without her magic psyllium husks (sorry, Daph, couldn't resist).

FOR THE DOUGH:

12 tablespoons unsalted butter, cold

1 cup whole wheat flour

1 cup spelt flour

¼ teaspoon salt

¼ teaspoon baking powder

1½ 3-ounce packages cream cheese, cold, cut into fourths

2 tablespoons ice water

1 tablespoon apple cider vinegar

FOR THE FILLING:

¼ cup sugar

Zest and juice of 1 lemon

3 cups fresh or frozen blueberries

3 tablespoons cornstarch

1 teaspoon salt

TO FINISH:

1 egg

1 tablespoon water

Granulated sugar

TO MAKE THE DOUGH:

1. Cut the butter into small ¾-inch cubes. Wrap in plastic and freeze until frozen solid, about 30 minutes.

2. Place the flours, salt, and baking powder in a gallon-sized plastic freezer bag, and freeze for at least 30 minutes. Place the flour mixture in a food processor with the metal blade attachment, and process for a few seconds to fully combine all the ingredients.

3. Add the cream cheese and pulse until it has achieved a coarse meal texture. Add the frozen butter and continue to pulse until the butter is the size of peas. Next, add the water and vinegar. Continue to pulse until the butter is the size of small peas.

4. At this point, the mixture is not going to hold together. Transfer it back to the plastic freezer bag. Fold the ends of the zipper with your fingers, and knead the mixture with the heels of your hands until the dough holds together in one piece and stretches when pulled. Split the dough into two pieces. Wrap them in plastic, flatten them into discs, and then transfer to the refrigerator for at least 45 minutes, though preferably overnight.

TO MAKE THE FILLING:

5. Combine the sugar, zest, blueberries, and salt. Allow the mixture to sit for 30 minutes, and then strain any excess liquid. Mix in the cornstarch and set aside.

TO MAKE THE PIES:

6. Combine the egg and water in a small bowl.

7. Roll out the dough on a lightly floured work surface to ¼ inch thick. Using the largest ring mold, cut out discs. Spoon 1½ tablespoons of the blueberry filling onto the circle, fold over, and pinch close. Cut a small slit on the hand pie, and brush lightly with the egg mixture and sprinkle with sugar. Repeat with remaining dough.

8. Bake at 360 °F for 15–20 minutes.

Carla pauses in her pie-making for a hug from Paula Abdul.

PEACH COBBLER

| SERVES 8 | Skill Level: MODERATE | Cook Time: 45 mins. | Prep Time: 20 mins. | Cost: $ |

I couldn't love anything more than a ripe peach, the kind that is so juicy you need to eat it standing over the sink. My Grandma Thelma's peach cobblers were the dessert highlight of the summer. She would make it with a crust on the bottom that was crumbly and flaky on the outside, and soft, smooth, and juicy on the inside, like a dumpling. My version backs off a bit from Grandma's use of sugar, but I do that with a lot of desserts. You need to remember to balance with salt. That makes all the flavors bloom.

FOR THE FILLING:

2 tablespoons butter

4 cups peaches, peeled and sliced

½ cup sugar, plus more to sprinkle

½ cup brown sugar

½ teaspoon cinnamon

¼ teaspoon nutmeg

¼ cup water

¼ cup amaretto

FOR THE CRUST:

2 cups all-purpose flour

½ cup sugar

4 teaspoons baking powder

1 teaspoon salt

2 tablespoons shortening

4 tablespoons butter, divided

½ cup yogurt

⅓ cup milk, plus more to brush

1 tablespoon water

1. Preheat the oven to 350 °F.

2. Heat the butter in a large cast-iron skillet over medium-high heat until it foams and subsides. Add the peaches, sugars, cinnamon, nutmeg, water, and amaretto. Cook until broken down slightly, about 10–15 minutes.

3. In a bowl or food processor, combine the flour, sugar, baking powder, and salt. Cut in the shortening with your fingertips or in the food processor (using quick pulses), then cut the butter into the dry mixture using the same method.

4. Combine the yogurt, milk, and water. Make a well in the dry ingredients, and pour the wet mixture in. Using a wooden spoon or rubber spatula, stir until just combined and pour into a 9 x 9 baking dish.

5. Drop tablespoonfuls on top of the peach mixture. Brush the exposed dough with milk, and then sprinkle sugar over the whole thing. Transfer to the oven and bake for 20–30 minutes, until the crust is golden brown.

ZOMBIE

SERVES 1 | **Skill Level: EASY** | **Prep Time: 10 mins.** | **Cost: $**

What party would be complete without a rum cocktail? Not one that Clinton Kelly would throw. And, if television and the movies are to be believed, there are sure to be a few vampires and zombies whenever people gather these days, and you want to stay on their good side. So here is the Zombie cocktail. Daphne asked me, "Is the point of this to kill the zombie or wake it back up?" That depends on how healthy your zombie friends are. They go down easy, so be careful or you will wake up feeling like a zombie the next morning.

1 teaspoon Falernum

1 ounce lime juice

1 ounce orange juice

1 ounce pineapple juice

1 ounce orange curaçao

1 ounce dark rum

2 ounces gold rum

Ice

1 slice orange

1 wedge pineapple

1 Maraschino cherry

1 sprig mint

1. Put the Falernum, lime juice, orange juice, pineapple juice, curaçao, dark rum, and gold rum into a mixing glass over several ice cubes and stir well. Pour over cracked ice in a 14-ounce Collins glass.

2. Garnish with a slice of orange, a wedge of pineapple, a cherry, and a sprig of mint.

The word is falernum

Falernum sounds like the name of a villain who has a walk-on part on *Game of Thrones*, but actually it's a delicious mix of almond, ginger, clove, lime, and vanilla. It is absolutely wonderful in cocktails. I suspect it also wouldn't be too bad in gingerbread batter, or a fish stew. If serving to a vampire, beware: it may put them in a romantic mood, and that can sting.

WHITE SANGRIA

SERVES 6 | **Skill Level: EASY** | **Cook Time: 5 mins.** | **Prep Time: 15 mins.** | **Cost: $**
Inactive Prep Time: 12 hrs.

Our White Sangria is a great summer drink because it allows you to feel lighter than a big, chewy red wine sangria … or, in a word, more summery. It pairs really easily with a lot of summer foods. If you're barbecuing chicken, White Sangria goes really nice. Imagine getting some fresh fish that you just caught and putting them on the grill, then washing it down with this sangria. It's summer in a glass. Heaven!

1 cup water
1 cup sugar
2 bottles crisp white wine
2 apricots, sliced
2 white peaches, sliced
1 lemon, sliced
1 quart sparkling water
½ cup mint leaves
1 cup frozen white grapes

1. To make a simple syrup, combine the water and sugar in a saucepan, and heat just until the sugar has dissolved, about 5 minutes, then set aside to cool.

2. Place the wine in a large pitcher or punch bowl, and add the apricots, peaches, lemon, and ½–1 cup of the simple syrup, depending on how sweet you like it. Refrigerate overnight.

3. Remove from the fridge and top with the sparkling water, and stir in the mint and frozen grapes.

FROZEN FRUIT SORBET

SERVES 6 | Skill Level: EASY | Prep Time: 5 mins. | Inactive Prep time: 2 hrs. | Cost. ¢

One of the joys of summer is sweet, juicy ripe fruit. I agree with Carla, who said you can't do better than peaches, picked at the peak of flavor and tossed in the blender. Canned fruit, packed in sugary syrup, just doesn't cut it, health-wise or taste-wise. This is a dessert that's sweet but won't make your fillings vibrate. You simply put all the ingredients in a blender, freeze, and serve. If Michael doesn't mind my poaching on his turf, I'd like to add this to our 5-in-5 recipes. Actually, it's 3 ingredients in about 3 minutes!

3 cups frozen peaches

1⅓ cups coconut milk or almond milk, plus more if needed

2 tablespoons honey

1. Using a blender, combine all ingredients until smooth. Pour into freezer-safe container. Freeze for 2 hours, scoop, and serve.

Q&A WITH Carla

Q. **You didn't start out as a cook. You were a model. What got you into cooking?**

Carla: Before I became a chef, I worked as a fashion model in France and I never cooked. I wasn't interested in what happens between the grocery store and food getting to the table. My girlfriends would always be in the kitchen, cooking and talking about how their mothers would make things. I had nothing to contribute. But I grew interested. That sort of comes with the territory when you live in France, so I started buying cookbooks and I was fascinated by them.

Q: **What kind of cookbooks?**

Carla: When I lived in France and then London, I would look for books on a subject instead of a particular author or chef. It would be about bread or it would be on breakfast (because my friends and I were doing lots of brunches then).

Carla and Paula Deen—two smiling Southern gals!

Q: **You have little folk sayings and made-up words. What's with that?**

Carla: I do ticky-boo, doink, slap my momma, and, of course, hootie-hoo, which just came out one day when I was on *Top Chef*. I don't know where these things come from, because I don't think about them until I'm saying them. They just occur to me when I am cooking and talking to people, especially when I am teaching. They are made-up words that people somehow connect with. They add some emotion to what could be a rote cooking lesson.

Q: **How do you like being the go-go dancer on the show? How did that happen?**

Carla: Kind of a fluke. One day, I was watching Mario and Michael and marveled at how they could cook, and talk, and look at the camera all at the same time and make it look so easy. Things didn't come that naturally to me. I felt like I wasn't really focusing on my food the way I wanted. And when you don't focus, you can't communicate. So one day they were playing some really good music when we went to a break, and I just went

up and I started dancing. The audience really liked it, and it made me feel free in spirit. When we came back from break, I was more relaxed. Everyone complimented me on that particular segment, and I said, "Oh, that's because I went and burned my energy on the music." So Gordon Elliott (our executive producer) looked at me for a second and said, "Carla, from now on you will have music every time you do a segment. Give us your playlist." Now I get to go up to dance with every chance. It really connects me to the audience and to my cooking.

Q: **It's spontaneous, like your cooking. People like the spontaneity of the show.**

Carla: I'm a performer—I consider myself a MacGyver in the kitchen, so if something goes wrong, it's all about the recovery. That's the way it was for me in real life before TV. For many years, it was just me and my catering business. I didn't have money to trash something and then get more ingredients, so I had to make it work. It's the same on the show. It's real. Things don't always come out perfectly. One time we had a cheesecake that had a big crack in it, and we tried to cover it over with some chocolate we were working with. We added some oil to the chocolate in an attempt to get it all melted and smooth again, but that didn't work. Something just kicked in and told me to try rolling the chocolate between plastic wrap and then spread it all over the cake. It worked! I sometimes tell people if you're on a desert island or if you're having an emergency, you want me on your team, because I'm the person who can probably get out of it. I'm not going to panic. I'm all about "We can do this."

Q: **In one sentence, what is your philosophy on cooking?**

Carla: It sounds kind of mystical, but I think what this does is give power back to people to learn and then to trust their own cooking instincts. You have to start with a sense that it's an honor to cook for people, you need to take it very seriously. Have fun, but take it seriously.

Q: **That's three sentences.**

Carla: I don't always have to follow the recipe.

What Not to Bring to a Party

You FINALLY SCORE THAT INVITATION to the best dinner party in town and you're wondering what kind of gift you should bring. Well, I'll tell you what not to bring so that you are the season's most requested guest. Oh, somebody's at the door! Let's see who it is!

Daphne: Hi, Clinton!

Clinton: Hi, Daphne!

Daphne: I brought you some flowers!

Clinton: Oh, thanks.

Clinton I cannot believe Daphne bought me these tacky flowers. Now I have to trim the stems and find a vase and put them in water.

Now here's the deal about bringing flowers to somebody who's hosting a party. It's really inconvenient for a host to cut the stems, get rid of the paper, find a vase, and put 'em in water. So don't do it. Okay? What you can do is the day before somebody's having a party, have flowers delivered to them. And that way, they can incorporate them into their design scheme. Or, even better, to thank them for spending their whole day entertaining you, you can send flowers the next day, so that they can enjoy them in the privacy of their own home.

Clinton: Somebody else is here! I feel like Pee-wee Herman a little bit. Okay. Who is it? Oh! It's Carla!

Carla: Clinton, I brought you a seven-layer dip. Let me just tell you. It's Michael Symon's sister's recipe!

Clinton: Great!

Clinton Hellooo. I made my world-famous six-layer dip. Is Carla trying to show me up with seven layers? Don't bring unwanted food. That can really throw off a host's game. If they ask for it, then that's great—bring it. But if they didn't ask for it, don't bring food. What you can do is bring a box of chocolates and tell the host that they are to enjoy a little bit later on or maybe even for dessert. Another nice thing to do is to bring a plate of scones that the host can eat the next morning, because he or she will have been spending the whole day cooking and will appreciate a homemade gift for breakfast

Clinton: More people! Love it! It's Michael Symon!

Michael: Clinton! As a good Greek boy, I bring you a sculpture for your table! It was either that or plastic for furniture. I stole it from my mom.

Clinton Gee whiz! I thought Michael and I were friends. Does he really think I have no taste? Do not bring a decorative object to somebody's house. And especially do not expect them to display it. Okay? But what you can do is bring a nice seasonal plate or platter, or, if it's a holiday party, a holiday decoration is a nice option because your host can display it during the holidays and then put it in a closet for eleven months of the year.

Mario: Ciao, Clinton!

Clinton: Oh, Mario!

Mario: I brought you a killer bottle of Barolo. Let's crack it open right now.

Clinton But I already picked out the perfect sauvignon blanc and Pinot Noir. This Barolo does no-go-lo.

Here's the thing about bringing wine. Wine is a wonderful gift. However, you should not expect it to be drunk that day or at that event, because your host probably spent time picking out wine already. So when you present it to your host, you can suggest that it is not for the party but to enjoy later in the evening or for their wine cellar.

Mario: Oh, I also forgot to tell you, my cousin Quintillio just got out of Rahway Prison!

Clinton Please say you're kidding!

Never bring an uninvited guest! Really bad form, plus if it's his first meal since getting out of prison, he may eat everything in sight.

Follow these tips and you'll be the perfect guest for your next party.

Carla and RuPaul bust a move!

Our Last Supper

IT'S A TIME-HONORED FANTASY GAME: If you had to pick one last meal, what would it be? You kind of wish it were a Top Ten list, but they asked for just one.

Michael: BEET AND GOAT CHEESE RAVIOLI WITH BUTTER AND FRESH TARRAGON

I would have Bobby Flay make me a burger—because if I'm going out, I'm going out big. Paul Kahan would roast me an entire suckling pig—he owns a great restaurant called Blackbird in Chicago—and I would have a little bit of Marc Vetri's raviolis and a perfectly roasted chicken from Jonathan Waxman from Barbuto. Lizzie, in front of the fireplace at home.

SOUNDTRACK: Led Zeppelin, Van Halen, Stevie Ray Vaughan—let it rip!

Carla: ### HAMBURGER AND ONION RINGS AND GINGER LEMONADE

My grandfather, George Hall Sr., had a five-and-dime store, where he ran numbers in the back. Up front we had nickel candy, big burgers, and the world's best onion rings. I think onion rings are really special—more special than French fries. And to drink, I just want to say that my ginger lemonade is the nectar of the gods.

SOUNDTRACK: Anything I can really dance to.

Clinton: ### LOBSTER THERMIDOR

The main event would be lobster thermidor. I first tasted it when I was thirteen at the Clam Box in Carmel, California, and I was like, "This is the food of the gods." Ever since, I have it about once a year on a special occasion. It's a little on the expensive side . . . but it's your last meal, so charge it—you're never going to get the bill.

SOUNDTRACK: Sondheim all the way, probably the soundtrack to *Company*.

Daphne: ### CHICKPEA AND DUMPLING STEW

I'm sitting in a French bistro, there are candles around me. I've already finished a bottle of Verdejo, and I am now sitting down to my green salad . . . then a huge, perfect baguette slathered with salted honey butter . . . then I'm going to eat my vegetarian version of chicken and dumplings that I make with chickpea soup. When I discovered matzo ball soup, I wanted to be Jewish; when I discovered chicken and dumplings, I wanted to be from the South. Today, I just want to be me.

SOUNDTRACK: I've got Christmas carols going all the dinner, then David Guetta when I open that second bottle of Super Tuscan.

Mario: ### TRUFFLE OMELET

Piedmont, in truffle season, surrounded by the great vines of Barolo and Nebbiolo—delicious, evocative, powerful, and simple. The egg is perhaps the single most perfect food, as it encapsulates both our wonder with which came first and the idea of creation. It's amazing what an egg represents! Food is a little bit about philosophy, a little bit about technique, a lot about lighting. I'm making a simple omelet. The truffles are expensive, about $3,500, and put it on Clinton's credit card.

SOUNDTRACK: R.E.M., U2, and Jimi Hendrix.

Acknowledgments

Mark Schneider, who makes sure that every step this show takes is perfectly planned and executed. Without his meticulous eye for detail, the show would have no lights, no cameras, and no ovens.

Aimee Rosen Householder, our midwife/producer with extraordinary creative instincts, who cheerily provides midnight rewrites and big, bold ideas. Without you nothing would be in the ovens.

Pat De Fazio, you cut and pasted the emerging face of the show, frame by frame, and set us on a glide path to Victual Valhalla. You have the skill and speed of a caffeinated ninja.

Paul Starke, you were born to produce this show (or be the world's leading sit-down comic). You show us every day how far you can push a plate of pasta into an hour of broadcasting fun.

Randy Barone, you're a gift from ABC to the show, a vice president who "got it" from the start and a full creative partner in birthing the biggest TV food program in the world. It's a kick to do it with you every day.

Brian Frons, we owe you a huge personal debt. You believed in us personally and professionally from day one. It was your wise, experienced voice that steadied our rudder during those early days of confusion.

Anne Sweeney. Because every project needs someone with the courage to throw the big switch. No one had ever done this kind of show, but you understood it immediately. Without your support and belief, there would never have been a *Chew*. It was your vision of bringing people back to the family table that made this show a reality.

Sophie Elliott, who has listened lovingly to hundreds of hours of bad ideas over the years and provided insight and support to create the good ones—like *The Chew*. X.

The Chew list of recipes

Index